Back from the Land

ELEANOR AGNEW

Back from the Land

HOW YOUNG AMERICANS WENT TO
NATURE IN THE 1970S, AND
WHY THEY CAME BACK

Ivan R. Dee

Chicago 2004

The paperback edition of this book carries the ISBN 1-56663-664-7.

Library of Congress Cataloging-in-Publication Data:
Agnew, Eleanor.
    Back from the land : how young Americans went to nature in the 1970s, and why they came back / Eleanor Agnew.
        p. cm.
    Includes bibliographical references and index.
    ISBN 1-56663-580-2 (alk. paper)
        1. Farm life—United States. 2. Urban-rural migration—United States. 3. United States—Social conditions—1960–1980. 4. Rural-urban migration—United States. I. Title.

HT421.A42 2004
307.2—dc22

                                                            2004045582

For Derek, Shawn, and Kent, who lived it;

Paul, Erin, Liberto, and Lorren, who have heard about it;

and grandson Nicholas Sikes Thurston, who will someday read about it

Contents

Preface

MY FRIEND Cynthia Frost, whose story appears in this book, is a librarian at my university. When she told her library colleagues that she'd been interviewed for this book because she had been a '70s hippie who had gone to the land, one colleague replied, "*You?* But you're a conservative *librarian*, aren't you?" Appearances can be deceiving.

Most of us who participated in the 1970s back-to-the-land movement have left the remote log cabins or farmhouses, returned to cities and suburbs, and blended into the mainstream, where we walk around undetected. We tried to live self-sufficiently on the land, growing much of our food, heating with wood, hauling water, and avoiding nine-to-five jobs. We wanted to live close to nature and free from the larger capitalistic system around us. Eventually we came back from the land. Either we came back literally, by leaving the farm and moving to an urban area, or we came back figuratively, by staying on the land but slowly taking on a way of life befitting middle-class people who just happen to live in a rural area.

As a former back-to-the-land person myself, I have loved hearing others' stories over the years about their back-to-the-land experiences, especially the years afterward. In most cases the 1970s back-to-the-land story can be told collectively—a person goes to the land to be self-sufficient and free, the freedom loses its luster when the poverty grinds, the person and his or her spouse divorce, and the person slides back into the mainstream, gets a professional job or entrepreneurial gig, and remarries. But there's so much more to it than that. I wanted to hear all the juicy details. How did the back-to-the-land people get from the days of hauling water to the library reference desk?

I originally envisioned this book as an anthology, but the format changed. Some (not all) of the writers who sent me stories have allowed me to use their stories anyway, weaving them into the narrative. Special heartfelt thanks to the following people for use of their unpublished essays: John Armstrong, Cyndy Irvine, Patricia Manuele, Keddy Ann Outlaw, Bill Pearlman, Sandy Sanchez, June Spencer, and Kathie Weir, who are all outstanding writers.

Then I began interviewing people. Each person I interviewed seemed to know someone else, who knew someone else, and on it went.

Special thanks to friend and colleague David Starnes, who was the first person to be interviewed for the book and who offered encouragement, as did Peter Christopher and others.

It was a special treat to reunite with old friend John Verlenden through this project. Our lives intersected once during the '80s, after both of us had come back from the land. We had ended up in the same city, and our sons became best friends. We used to share funny and heartbreaking stories about our days on the land, but then our paths diverged again as we went on to our careers. Thanks to John for spending six hours with me in Baltimore during the 2003 convention of the Association of Writers and Writing Programs, and giving me a fabulous, thoughtful interview. It was great to meet again.

This project also reunited me with fellow Middle Earth homesteader Bruce Lemire, who lived on the same homestead with me in Maine and whom I hadn't seen or heard from in twenty-five years. Special thanks to Bruce for spending all that time on the phone for an interview and also for spending the time in noninterview conversation catching up again.

Thanks to Cynthia Frost for all her hard work getting me those hundreds of interlibrary loan books for this project.

Many thanks also to Christina Adams, Gail Adams, Kathy Barrows, "Linda Clarke," "Jim Carlson," Tomas Diaz, Michael Doyle,

Stacia Dunnam, Steven Engelhart, Jane Fishman, Chris Fichtner, Patricia Foley, Pam Read Hanna, Vicky Hayes, Marlene Heck, June Holley, Geraldine Jones, Thomas Kidder, Gordy "Stewart," Copthorne Macdonald, David Manning, John Matz, Timothy Miller, Jodi Mitchell, Phil Morningstar, Rob "Morningstar," "Lucy Joseph," David Paige, Carlyle Poteat, Ellen Rocco, Miriam Ross, Sandra Sleight-Brannen, Allan Sirotkin, Valerie Summer, Kent Thurston, Shawn Thurston, Janice Walker, and Don Wirtshafter for their contributions.

And thanks to all the people I talked to and corresponded with but didn't formally interview, whose informal stories became part of my general knowledge base.

There are so many more unrecognized people that I can't list here who are part of this project, the people I knew and potlucked with during the homesteading days in Maine, and others who've informally told me their back-to-the-land stories over the years. You know who you are. Thanks.

E. A.

Savannah, Georgia
April 2004

Back from the Land

CHAPTER ONE

The Lure of Back to the Land

"I felt the simple life calling me. The compulsion was strong and unquestioned."—Keddy Ann Outlaw

"One night in New York City, I dreamed of such peace that I couldn't bear to wake up in the real world. My dream was of a girl dancing in a wheat field. It was a picture of the country."
—Sandy Sanchez

🌿 *In August 1975 my husband, Kent, quit his radio career in Massachusetts, packed his camping gear into the van, placed his Leilah-blasting headphones over his ears, and took off up Route 95 to move permanently onto our newly purchased sixty-two acres of land in Maine. While the children and I stayed in the city waiting for our house to sell, Kent arrived in Troy, pitched a tent among the tall pines, donned his bandana, and revved up his chainsaw. It roared through the silent woods, spewing oil-smoke. One by one, cedar trees creaked and smashed onto the forest floor with a boom. As the maples, oaks, and elms turned orange and red, Kent spent his days shaving the bark off of logs. He built a foundation for a log cabin and arranged the horizontal beams. As autumn passed and the trees shed their leaves, he stacked twenty-foot cedar logs horizontally into the wall frames and cemented and spiked them in place.*

By the time the first snowflakes spit through the grey air, he had just finished hammering the last nails into the roof. That same month we finally got an offer for our house in the city at a break-even price. I resigned from my job. We held a yard sale and jettisoned our major appliances and other vestiges of middle-class waste. At last we packed up the kids and the dog and, giddy with anticipation, headed for the country—along with millions of other young adults across the nation.

❧ When Kent and I moved to Maine in 1975, the back-to-the-land movement had already attracted untold numbers of converts who had grown increasingly estranged from mainstream American society. By the millions, visionaries much like us were moving into woods, mountains, orchards, and farmlands in order to disconnect from the deleterious influences of modern life. We moved into log cabins, A-frames, geodesic domes, underground homes, tents, old schoolhouses, and rundown farmhouses, and we grew our own organic crops, hauled clean water from wells, avoided doctors and pharmaceutical giants in favor of natural cures, and renounced energy-guzzling appliances. We yearned for psychic rewards and spiritual wealth, not money, so we planned to generate mere trickles of cash flow from our cottage industries, manual labors, and crops. The payoff was to be freedom.

Free spirits that we were, we sometimes appeared unorthodox to onlookers as we sped along the highways and roads in our overstuffed vans, school buses, or trucks, but our mission couldn't have been more serious. Linda Clarke remembers her journey to the country. She drove the pickup with the camper top, and her husband went in the U-Haul, as they proceeded north out of Maryland to their new farm in upstate New York. Their convoy was a sight. The VW beetle rested on a tow bar behind Linda's truck. All her houseplants had been secured to the top of the camper's roof. Inside the back of the truck, five cats yowled in their crates, along with "what I was hoping was going to be a commercial, viable goat herd for our farm—which included a giant buck with a full set of curved horns," says Linda. "We had him chained in because he was a mean, horrible animal, and we had four other goats in there." Late that night, the procession crossed the New York state line. Unsure of their location, Linda and her husband pulled over to reassess their route and began arguing about which direction to take. Finally Linda's husband sulked back to the U-Haul, gunned the engine, and drove straight ahead onto what turned out to be the wrong road, with Linda reluctantly following. But they became separated, and in the dark Linda became confused. The next thing she knew, blue lights were flashing. A police officer had noticed that her towbar had no lights. He pulled her over.

"The cop starts looking over this load," remembers Linda. "I've got a crying kid in the front seat beside me, the other kids are screaming in the back of the car on the tow bar, and then he starts to look in the back of the truck with his flashlight. That's when this big buck goat with the big horns *lunges* at him. The cop jumps back. Finally he just shakes his head and tells me to go on."

All across the country, similar caravans of earnest people were driving out of the cities toward the land.

We constituted "a major sector of the population," according to the historian Eric Foner. The author and researcher Timothy Miller placed the number of commune dwellers of the 70s at somewhere between 750,000 and 1,000,000, an estimate that did not even include the independent homesteaders and farmsteaders who did not live communally. Jeffrey Jacob reported in *New Pioneers* that "by the end of the 1970's, at the height of the urban-to-rural migration flows, there were over one million back-to-the-landers in rural North America, almost all on small acreages rather than living in communes or on large farms." A study by the Stanford Research Institute estimated that "from four to five million adults were wholeheartedly committed to leading a simple life and that double that number 'adhere[d] to and act[ed] on some but not all' of its basic tenets."

America, with its assurance of the Dream fulfilled, has always been particularly fertile ground for experimental, independent societies, notes Elizabeth Gilbert. "America has always lent herself generously— lent both her body and her capacious character—to the visions of utopians." Many back-to-the-land movements, seeking utopia, have cycled in and out over history, but the 1970s version, populated by post-war baby boomers who had come of age during one of the periods of greatest economic prosperity, represented one of the largest.

Typically we were young, white, middle class, and educated. The irony was apparently lost on us that "the world created by [our] elders," which we were rejecting, had allowed us the luxury of experimenting with alternative ways of living, as the writer David Shi points out.

John Verlenden, now a college professor, recalls an awkward moment at "this little rural bank in some town in West Virginia" where he and a small group of friends had assembled to inquire about applying for a mortgage to buy a farm. The loan officer naturally asked what their assets were, and the group fell silent. That was one detail they had not thought much about.

Laughing deeply, John recalls, "These people had traveled hundreds and hundreds of miles to be there. And it was a great moment of realization of what it really meant to buy property. You couldn't just talk about it, you couldn't just want it. It's obvious to me that all of us had eschewed all the practical realms of life. I think the reasons are well documented in the lifestyles we were obtaining after World War II. We were privileged." John and his friends returned to their home state to work for another year, save money, and pool it for the down payment.

Why Go to the Land?

A spiritual malaise had settled upon many of us. One back-to-the-land memoir offers a ubiquitous profile: "[Brad] gradually realized that something was vaguely, yet definitely, wrong with his life. . . . More and more, [his friends] seemed to be following a meaningless existence, content with frivolity and mediocrity, consumed by a nervous tension which he no longer found bearable."

We often attributed this inner discontent to the state of the world at the time. By the mid-seventies, inflation had reached 14.1 percent and the average cost of a new home $42, 600, while the median salary was only about $11,800. The price of gasoline and oil had risen sharply. Creating self-sufficient, closed-off societies made good sense in light of the precarious economy. For most back-to-the-land people, dogma played an even stronger role, as our disaffection from American culture and Western ways peaked in response to the confluence of environmental, economic, and social woes of the seventies.

Michael Doyle, a back-to-the-lander who is now a college professor, recalls, "We had the oil embargo in '73 and the whole crisis that went along with that. A lot of us came to the conclusion that our capitalist economy was on the verge of collapse and that going to the land was tied to survival—though not survivalism in the way the term connotes these anti-government types today that are off the grid and armed and paranoid. We back-to-the-land people really conceived of ourselves as about to win. Our analysis of American society, we thought, was about to be proved accurate. America had vast idealistic promise but was rotten to the core, largely because everyone was given over to the rat race and materialistic pursuits. What we wanted to do was eventually carve out niches, which were convivial for people, of an alternative lifestyle that we were convinced would serve as laboratories of the next civilization that would supplant the existing discredited American civilization."

As David Frum notes, "The crucial decade for . . . the institutionalization of scare-mongering, the willingness of the mass media and government to lend plausibility to wild surmises about the future . . . was the 1970s. . . . The media displayed a limitless appetite for this malarkey." A 1973 study traced the number of times the media reported certain events between 1960 and 1970 and concluded that public opinion was influenced more by how often a subject was covered by the media than by the reality of an event. For example, between 1964 and 1970, "environment and pollution . . . showed no obvious trend one way or the other . . . there is no statistical evidence that the actual conditions underlying this issue got either better or worse over the course of the decade." Admittedly, though the problems of the time were to a certain degree legitimate, most of us did not investigate the issues as carefully as we might have by researching a variety of credible sources, as I would tell my students to do today. We crafted our doomsday-leaning canon without much critical scrutiny.

With this in mind, consider the state of the world in the 1970s:

One of the great national malfunctions was the unchecked pollution, a by-product of progress, that was inflicting irreversible damage upon natural resources. Factories from coast to coast were dumping toxic waste into the rivers and emitting poisonous fumes into the air. Industries were paving over the world's woodlands, parks, and jungles, destroying animal and bird habitats, ruining the aesthetic quality of our countryside, and throwing off the earth's delicate ecological balance. The razing of the forests was reducing the earth's remaining oxygen supply. As though air and water pollution were not enough, the farming industry, now a big business, routinely sprayed massive doses of pesticides onto growing crops and fed synthetic hormones to steers. Processing factories later injected these foods and meats with preservatives to extend the shelf life of the products (as well as the profit margin). "Before World War II," reflects Frum, "bread would begin to spoil within hours of purchase, even in the tightest breadbox. Alas, the preservatives that triumphed over mold and other contaminants had their dangers too— and because these dangers issued from the hand of man, they carried a sharp sting of betrayal."

While business and industry were busy poisoning natural resources, the average consumer was busy wasting them by driving gas-guzzling cars that emitted toxic fumes, buying fast food housed in Styrofoam containers, and using frivolous spray products.

Each flush of a toilet squandered dozens of gallons of water, and millions more swirled down the drains of dishwashers, washing machines, and bathtubs. People turned their thermostats too high, burned every light in the house, trashed perfectly good items the second they grew tired of them, and frittered away money on replacements. America had turned into a sedentary, unhealthy nation of people who were unwilling to walk a block to the grocery store. They led spurious lives for spurious returns, selling their souls to their workplaces and living out their careers trapped in unfulfilling jobs so that they could purchase ostentatious houses with colossal cars in the driveway. Though cruising for early heart attacks, they were too afraid to quit and do something worthwhile. In contrast, writes Amy Saltzman, the baby-boom generation, unscathed by memories of the depression, wanted meaningful jobs and "believed they were entitled to far more than what they perceived as the complacent, emotionally stultifying existences of their parents. They looked at the 'organization men' of the 1950's and vowed to be different."

"Back in my college days," recalls David Manning, who graduated from college in 1968, "there were a lot of bitterly satiric lyrics about that sort of thing; people ticking away their lives in blind service to meaningless functions. We were going to be different, devote ourselves to life itself, work with purpose."

Modern American life had become dangerous as well as decadent. The population was multiplying too fast, crime was increasing, houses were crammed together, traffic was jammed. Former homesteader Sandy Sanchez and her husband were living in New York City in 1972. After her husband came out of a meeting and discovered his car had been stolen, "he was susceptible to my suggestion that we chuck it all and go find ourselves some wildnerness retreat away from nasty civilization," recalls Sandy. Soon they moved to West Virginia.

The land, notes Robert Houriet in *Getting Back Together*, was "the primal source of consciousness, the true basis of culture" where young Americans would "[keep] to the main road and to the central spirit and consciousness which modern man had lost along the way."

The universal mystique of the country, shared by city and suburban idealists, only added magic to the escalating back-to-the-land movement. Our culture's glorification of the pastoral, through song, poetry, literature, and myth, fed our growing desire for the land. The term "country" conjured up appealing images of ripe corn swaying in an autumn breeze, fireflies glowing at dusk, the smell of maple logs burning in the wood stove, the raging snowstorm pounding the side of a cozy house. We believers, of course, had never in our lives cleaned out a barn or spent long hours weeding under the broiling sun.

Veneration of pioneers, explorers, and early frontiersmen, another enduring thread of our cultural heritage, added a delightful spirit of heroism to our mission. Simon Shaw, series producer of the popular documentary *Frontier House*, confesses that in his childhood he was "spellbound by the lure of a life where men and women pitched themselves against a world full of rugged challenges. For years, every movie, television show, comic, and book detailing heroic endeavors in cow towns and across prairies was a favorite escape from my real life. . . ."

In the 1970s, before the advent of cell phones, faxes, the internet, and other technologies, going to the country demanded a more serious disconnection from the advantages of civilization than it does today, and a greater exposure to the "wild frontier." Our vision of moving to the land shimmered with the same visceral excitement. David Starnes, now a college instructor, feels that this sense of adventure may have been his primary reason for moving in 1972 to an abandoned old farmhouse in northern Colorado, which had been used by migrant workers. He had just dropped out of college again and was working in the city library in Port Angeles, Washington, "But something was missing, I guess," he admits. "I was working my way up, young man about town." When a college friend, Thomas Kidder, invited him to move to Colorado and work on the farmhouse, David agreed. "I don't know why. I could have just stayed where I was and become a pillar of the community. I think it was just . . . the sense of adventure. Maybe nothing was missing in my life in Port Angeles; maybe I was dissatisfied—just out of habit."

David's friend Tom had grown up in Montana with his grandfather, a very strong father figure in his life, who had been a real homesteader in the state. When Tom decided to co-rent the farmhouse with David in Colorado, he excitedly told his grandfather about the outhouse, the hand water pump, and the wood heat they would be using on the farm.

His grandfather said, "Why do you want to do all that when we've got all these modern conveniences?"

Tom said, "Well, Grandpa, *you* lived like that. And you home-steaded in Montana."

"Yeah, but we had to."

"Well, *I* never had a chance," responded Tom.

Influences in the Popular Culture

By the early '70s the back-to-the-land mythology had become firmly en-trenched in the popular culture. A tidal wave of songs, books, and arti-cles spurred us on, providing encouragement for rustic lifestyles. Three Dog Night's 1970 "Out in the Country" intoned,

> Whenever I feel them closing in on me
> Or need a bit of room to move
> When life becomes too fast, I find relief at last
> Out in the country.

By 1971 John Denver's request for country roads to take him home—to the place he *belonged*—was piping out of millions of radios across the nation. As the decade unfolded, other songs by Denver and popular rock artists literally sang the praises of the pastoral life as a cure for "the future killing me." Billy Joel's "Movin' Out" promoted a similar theme, that moving to the country was preferable since "workin' too hard can give you a heart attack . . . is that all you get for your money?"

The books flew off the presses. Maurice Grenville Kains's *Five Acres and Independence*, a 1930s survival guide for the depression, underwent a revival in the 1970s. Kain observed that middle-class people "are eking out a narrowing, uneducative, imitative, more or less selfish and purpose-less existence; and that their 'expectation of life' is shortened by tainted air, restricted sunshine, and lack of exercise, to say nothing of exposure to disease," a message that resonated with would-be homesteaders. Self-sufficient living in the country, he suggested, gave one pride, a restored sense of dignity, and "true success—development and revelation of char-acter and citizenship in himself, his wife, sons, and daughters."

A number of books made alternative lifestyles sound workable and desirable. Another popular one, Carolyn and Ed Robinson's *Have-More Plan*, published in 1970, described the Robinsons' exodus from the city in 1942 and shared their plan for living affordably in the country with "health, happiness, and security"—and a minimum cash flow. John and Sally Seymour's *Farming for Self-Sufficiency: Independence on a 5-Acre Farm*, took off in the United States three years after its 1973 publication in England. The authors and their four children had thrived on five acres of land for eighteen years; others could therefore do the same. They noted that people who stayed in the city and specialized in one occupation became bored, so "a surprising number of the more intelligent people who have passed through the big-city-industrial stage are reacting against it; they *want* to advance to a more interesting and self-sufficient life."

Living the Good Life, by Helen and Scott Nearing, reigned as the bible of the back-to-the-land movement. First published in 1954 and then reprinted in 1970, the book was a huge hit among the counter-culture people, and as Paul Goodman stated in the Introduction, "Today very many young people across the country have decided to try subsistence farming and natural foods for nearly the same reasons as the Nearings told themselves forty years ago."

Considered the father and mother of the homesteading movement, the Nearings had homesteaded in Vermont from 1932 to 1952, then moved to Harborside, Maine, where they established a second successful homestead. The Nearings provided unshakable proof that self-sufficient living could work.

Magazines and newspapers whet our appetites for going to the land. Upbeat stories appeared frequently in the popular press profiling hippies who were living communally on a farm in Colorado or homesteading in New Mexico. The subjects of the story would be quoted as saying how awesome it was to bake their own bread from scratch with organically grown oats, and to milk their own goats instead of buying quarts of pesticide-filled milk at the supermarket. A *Glamour* magazine article from 1971 featured just such a couple, Jim and Alexandra

Eldridge, who had moved to the country outside of Athens, Ohio. "Once upon a time there lived two young people who wanted no part of this cruel world," the article began. "So they and some friends made a world of their own in the hills of Appalachia."

Jim had bought 25 acres of land with a 145-year-old cabin on it for $2,500.

"There is electricity, but Jim stopped at plumbing," the article read. "The small conical outhouse of brick which he built is reached by a series of whimsical steps from the kitchen door. Jim and Alex take their showers at the University and get drinking and dishwashing water from a well."

Because of their cheap back-to-the-country lifestyle, Jim and Alex were free to pursue their arts. "The world outside [the cabin] doesn't really exist for Jim and Alex or for many of their friends. For them the real world is in the productions of their inner lives—writing or painting or sculpting," noted the article.

How romantic and appealing this must have sounded to any readers who hungered to connect with their own inner lives—which must have been most of them. Who *wouldn't* want the time and serenity for introspection?

Mother Earth News

Another influential publication of the seventies was *Mother Earth News,* a bimonthly magazine extremely popular among would-be homesteaders. She (as we called *Mother Earth*) provided instructional articles with technical illustrations on everything from how to breed goats to how to cure maladies with herbs.

Most issues also featured at least one article profiling a couple, worn out by the strife of the city, who had resigned from their high-tension jobs, bought a run-down farm in upstate New York, and were making modest ends meet by selling crafts or crops, or trading bushels of vegetables or hay with neighbors.

Mother influenced John Armstrong to go homesteading in Michigan. He remembers borrowing an issue from one of his homesteading friends and becoming captivated by the articles, which were written by and about people he could relate to. "They were people who had a desire to live their lives independent of work schedules, processed food, and the rat race in general," recalls John. "I subscribed and eagerly consumed each issue two or three times before the next one arrived. Then I bought John Vivian's book, *The Manual of Practical Homesteading*, and virtually inhaled it. I got so caught up in the idea of homesteading that I began to consider the possibility for myself."

The idea of going to the land spread rapidly through word of mouth as well as through the media. Everyone knew someone else who was doing it.

Cyndy Irvine, who was living in Austin, Texas, in 1973, documents her experience in her unpublished essay "Remembering New Mexico." She notes, "I recall very specifically my friend Caroline telling me that her brother and his wife had moved 'to the country' and were growing their own vegetables and canning their own peaches. 'How do they know how to live that way?' I thought. I wasn't naive to camping or roughing it; I had experienced summer camp and family camping trips. I had experience with roughing it in the outdoors, but not with permanently bringing it into the indoors.

"How do they wash their face and hands?" Cyndy asked Caroline.

"Well, they have a table with a pitcher and a bowl, and a towel hanging nearby," Caroline replied.

"How simple," Cyndy remembers thinking. "Like living in summer camp."

Soon after, Caroline told Cyndy about visiting a commune in the East where the members lived in tents and log cabins, without plumbing or electricity. Modern ways did not intrude upon their peaceful, natural environment. In addition to growing their food and sewing their clothes, they gave birth to their babies at home, without anesthesia, attended by midwives.

"They played flutes and guitars, worked cooperatively at the communal tasks, and didn't have to leave for days on end," says Cyndy.

"'Work' was at home in your jeans, with your music, outside under the sun, with your friends. We began to realize that this life sounded like what we were yearning for, full of enjoyment and satisfaction as well as friends and dogs and nature. How enticingly easy it sounded. . . ."

Finding Land with Little Cash

Cyndy found her land in a serendipitous manner. After hearing the above story from Caroline, she, her boyfriend, and another couple bought a used orange van from the Austin, Texas, Highway Department. After sewing flowery curtains for the van's windows, they crammed the vehicle with their sleeping bags, backpacks, two dogs, a portable tape deck, books, and two crates of peaches, and drove west with no destination in mind.

They had driven as far as Santa Fe, New Mexico, when they spotted an ad in the local newspaper offering "free rent" in exchange for caretaking and repairing an adobe country house. After talking to the owner, they decided that his little homestead sounded perfect.

"No rent, no deposit, also no furniture, no electricity or plumbing," remembers Cyndy, who is now a nurse in Wisconsin. "We would need to dig a new hole for the outhouse, replace some windows, and also replace most of one side of the house." That sounded acceptable to the group, so they followed their new landlord in his old Ford pickup, driving fifteen miles down a dusty gravel road and passing through two small villages that "resembled scenes from old Mexico, with dusty streets, adobe houses, and chickens scratching the dry ground. Past the second village, the road became even less maintained and certainly not suited for most automobiles, as it wound toward the national wilderness area and the nearby mountains."

They arrived on the scenic, mountainous land. Disembarking from the crowded van, they walked with the landlord toward the small, run-down house, which had one door and three windows. Cyndy remembers feeling "a fleeting moment of awkward forlornness." She thought, "This is going to be our home? Not a camping trip here, not summer camp, but actually home." But the feeling quickly dissipated, replaced by "a sort of joyous disbelief."

Allan Sirotkin, now the owner and CEO of Green River Chocolates in Hinesville, Vermont, found land in northern New York through an aunt. He drove over from Michigan to take a look. He remembers viewing the snow-covered spread and saying, "'OH YEAH SURE THIS LOOKS GREAT!', having not a clue what we were looking at. It was late February, northern New York, so we didn't know what was what."

Land was relatively cheap, but the number of buyers was high. Patricia Foley arrived in Alexander, Maine, with the early-1970s wave of back-to-the-land people and has stayed long enough to learn some town history:

"During the back-to-the-land revolution," she explains, "a couple old Mainers in our area decided the quickest way for them to get rich would be to subdivide the old family farm. They divided it into 50-, 75-, 100-acre parts, and sold it off to the back-to-the-land types. And became tycoons. One guy became the richest man in town, cruising around in a pale blue Cadillac. I remember coming across a picture of these guys taken in the early '50s. The two of them are there in old flannel shirts and long underwear shirts, looking kind of seedy and miserable. They turned into the town's two millionaires."

Although many back-to-the-land people wanted to own their own land for the sake of self-sufficiency, ownership was not essential. Many rental or caretaking situations were available as well as opportunities to move into established communes, where the question of ownership or individual territory rarely ruffled the harmony, at first anyway. Communes usually welcomed everyone who came walking up the path. Phil Morningstar joined Morningstar Commune in this way, while Tomas Diaz was welcomed onto Tolstoy Farm after alighting from the bus.

🌿 Kent and I had planned our homesteading project for over a year. He had been feeling trapped in his job as a radio "personality" and operations manager. He spent four hours of his eight-hour workday in a soundproof glass booth, bubbling into a microphone, "And THAT was Elton

JOHN, with Bennie and the JETS and THIS is WXXX in Pittsfield, at 10:52, with a temperature of SIXTY-FIVE—wow, what a beautiful day." His voice would smile, but his face wouldn't. Queuing up another record, he would start the music and, with a definitive click, shut off the mike, remove the clunky headset with a sigh, and write another entry into the station's tedious log. He had exactly two minutes and fifteen seconds until the song ended. Outside, the autumn foliage might be at its peak, with colorful shades of fuchsia, russet, and gold splashed across the Berkshire Hills under an azure sky, but he couldn't see any of it. The soundproof studio had no windows. Balding, with a bushy beard, Kent was of middle height, handsome, with astute blue eyes behind his wire-framed glasses. At twenty-nine, he felt the heaviness of responsibility deflating his vitality. He could foresee many years of the same daily imprisonment stretching painfully ahead. How he longed to escape. Restlessly, with one eye on the second hand of the large institutional black-and-white clock on the wall in front of him, he would reach down to his briefcase and pull out the new issue of *Mother Earth News*, folded open to an article like "How to Make a Profit Raising Poults."

For the next two minutes and fifteen seconds he would read voraciously.

Meanwhile, across town, in the newspaper building, I would sit at my typewriter, pounding out another feature for the Sunday supplement. As I wrote, I would intermittently gulp coffee from the paper cup on my messy desk and replay voices from the interview on my tape recorder. Writing gave me a rush, but the constant pressure to churn out the same cute stories week after week was burning me out. I was twenty-six, with a serious face encircled by long blond hair parted down the middle. I too felt trapped in my job. Unlike my husband, who could expunge all thoughts of work from his mind the second he arrived home, as he lost himself in *Living the Good Life* or *Diet for a Small Planet* or *Mother Earth News*, I could never leave work mentally. As soon as one story was en route to the press room, I was already pouncing on the next one, grinding them out fast enough to keep the Sunday supplement filled with human interest. I interviewed artists, politicians, travelers, oddballs, authors, inventors, people with causes, people with theories, people with historically relevant experiences, and people with newsworthy disabilities or diseases. I interviewed on weekdays, weeknights, and weekends, driving to interviewee's homes or businesses at their convenience, setting up my tape recorder on the table, and asking thought-provoking questions designed to evoke effective quotes. Fearful of getting fired (yet perversely delighted at the prospect), I nevertheless plodded ahead, day after day, feeling torn between my hunger for fun and freedom, and my sense of responsibility. We had two young children, a dog, two cars, a mortgaged house, and credit-card bills.

Kent had been campaigning for us to go homesteading, to sell our shoebox of a house, quit our boring jobs, leave the crowded city, and buy a few acres of land in an isolated location, say, Maine. We could build a simple house, nothing fancy, grow our own food, heat with wood, and draw or pump water from our own brook or river. The boys would thrive in the country. We'd be healthier with all the heart-building exercise we'd get working the land.

"It makes sense," he kept saying. He would then pull out a paper and pencil once again to demonstrate in cold, hard figures how little money we'd need if we only weren't paying Pittsfield Gas and Oil a fortune to heat our house or paying Banker's First a ransom to let us live in it in the first place. If we owned land, we wouldn't need to relinquish half our salaries to Shop 'N Save for food; we could grow our own food. With land we could raise chickens for eggs and goats for milk; we wouldn't have to work long hours to pay some corporation, already rich, for food and commodities that we could harvest directly. And if we didn't work at jobs, we wouldn't need to pay a baby-sitter to care for the boys. We could improve our quality of life. We wouldn't be wasting water and fuel, like the rest of the world. And on and on.

Before I knew it, we had placed an ad in the Positions and Situations (P&S) section of *Mother Earth News*. "Kent, 29, Ellie, 26, Derek, almost 3, and Shawn, 1, looking for compatible partners to buy land to create self-sufficient homestead. . . ."

Mother's P&S section at the back of each issue bulged with classified ads from individuals, couples, or groups seeking other individuals, couples, or groups with whom to buy land. *Mother* offered countless opportunities to find Paradise with minimal cash. A typical ad might read "Sam, 26, Sarah, 25, and kids Freedom, 6, and Peace, 4, wish to buy 30 acres with a brook in Montana, with compatible people. . . ."

Finding Partners

Over the next seven months we traveled across New England on weekends to meet potential land partners and to observe homesteads in progress. We met Roger and Mary, a soft-spoken, religious couple who prayed before their dinners of eggplant and wheat bread. Roger, a young man with a long beard who wore overalls, worked out as a carpenter, while Mary, a short woman with a crocheted shawl wrapped around her shoulders, tended the homestead. She was supremely, enviably calm, her voice quiet and steady. Her canned preserves and vegetables neatly lined her shelves. Bright flowers stood at attention in beds of pine straw that bordered the path to their front door, and orderly rows of green shoots filled the garden, not a seed out of place. When Mary wasn't outside gardening, milking the goat, or splitting logs, she sewed contentedly by the wood stove. Apparently she handled it all unflappably.

She had nearly bled to death once. Roger related this story because Mary had no memory of it. They'd been logging. One of Roger's trees toppled the wrong way and struck Mary, slashing her head open. She blacked out, the blood gushing profusely. Terrified, Roger knew he'd never be able to carry her unconscious body all the way to his pickup truck at the far end of the property, nor would an ambulance ever be able to get in to their isolated tract—even if he'd had a phone to call one, which he didn't. Suppressing his panic, he dragged and hoisted Mary through the woods, back to their log cabin. He swiftly shaved her head and applied herbs and pressure to the cut. When he got the bleeding under control, he sealed her scalp securely with butterfly Band-Aids. As Roger finished this story, Mary smiled serenely.

I blurted out, "Doesn't it scare you a little to live this way?"

"Oh, no," she shrugged.

I was very impressed. Maybe a life in the woods would make me tranquil too.

We met Rob and Jaki, who were assembling a group to buy land on Murtagh Hill in upstate New York. A delightful couple, they had already built their first house and planned to build an underground home next. We visited Matt and Betsy, who hadn't quite sealed off the drafts in their frigid A-frame in western Massachusetts; a northern Maine couple, Neal and Linda, who lived in a one-story log cabin with unusually low ceilings and raised livestock in the pungent little barn attached to their house; and many others, including Ken and Wendy, who lived in New Jersey but wanted badly to escape.

Buying Land

In April 1975 we pooled $500 with Ken and Wendy's $500, and purchased outright 62 acres of woods in Troy, Maine, a small town midway between Belfast, Bangor, Waterville, and Augusta. Although Troy ("population 335") was little more than a strip of two-lane road with the Troy General Store, a church, and Phil Shible's car repair shop, dozens of other homesteading hippies were concealed in the surrounding woods. Little did I imagine on the day we signed the papers that Troy, Maine, of all places, would turn out to be a surprisingly active mecca for counterculture people.

As soon as the land was ours, Ken and Wendy quit their jobs in New Jersey, hurried to the land, pitched their tent, and began constructing their log cabin. But Kent and I, still encumbered by a mortgage and other obligations, had to return to Massachusetts to sell our house, which we'd purchased for less money than the average car today. The profit from the sale was earmarked to finance our relocation and transition into self-sufficiency. That summer expanded into a long, slow torture as we struggled through each muggy day dreaming of the sanctuary

Kent spent the fall of 1975 building our log cabin from trees on our land.

that awaited us in the Maine woods. Thoughts of green pines, blue sky, chirping birds, wild flowers, and meadow grass tormented us daily as we juggled jobs, kids, and the annoying visits of prospective buyers who were led from room to room by the realtor. The oppressiveness of the city bore down on us more than ever before. The new world lay at our feet—if only we could get there. But no one was buying.

Kent quit his job in August and moved onto the land to begin building our log cabin. If he didn't complete it before winter, he explained to me, we'd have to wait another eight months before the climate was once again amenable to construction. Yes, he'd better move now before it was too late. How I envied him, off in the woods, free at last, living the dream while I remained in the city, working full-time, mothering two hyperactive boys, and scrubbing the house constantly for each new futile real estate visit. The pressure mounted. But in late November, just about the time Kent finished the log cabin, we received a lowball but firm offer, which we accepted, too tired to hold out for a higher amount. It was time to get on with our mission, even without enough funds.

We would face that problem later.

❦ *On December 14, 1975, Kent and I made the final move from Massachusetts to our land in Maine. Snow was falling lightly as our VW bumped down the rutted road to the clearing in the woods. When I saw our log cabin for the first time, nestled in the tall pines, smoke puffing out the chimney, my heart soared. Ken and Wendy, who had kept the fire going in the woodstove, had also strung a white banner across two fir trees near the front door which read in big handwritten letters "WELCOME HOMESTEADERS!" This was it! Let the fresh start on the land begin!*

As we stepped out of the VW into the soft snow, the freezing air assaulted my nostrils as it burned its way into my lungs. I covered my face with one gloved hand. Although I was wearing heavy socks under my L. L. Bean insulated boots, long johns under my jeans, a turtleneck and sweater under my parka, and a ski hat and gloves, the power of the winter was a force to be reckoned with. I lifted Shawn, heavy and slippery in his red snowsuit, out of his car seat while four-year-old Derek climbed out and sank to his waist. He screamed as he struggled to lift his legs above the ice-cold snow. Kent swept him up, and the four of us trudged through the snow to the front steps with Zeke the dog following curiously.

December was the worst possible time to move into an uninsulated cabin with bone-chilling drafts, no electricity, and no running water. But we had no choice, having finally sold the house in Massachusetts. Where else could we live? The bridge to the past had been burned.

CHAPTER TWO

Early Days in a Technology-free Zone

"I was always aware of the phases of the moon, due to the evening walks and trips to the outhouse."—Cyndy Irvine

"Primitive became chic and living without plumbing a sign of heightened spiritual consciousness."—Alston Chase, former homesteader and author of *Harvard and the Unabomber: The Education of an American Terrorist*

"[They had] . . . this dream of starting over, of building something from the ground up like the pioneers they all secretly believed they were, and so what if they suffered? So what if it was cold? Did Roger Williams worry about physical discomfort when he went off to found Rhode Island? Or Captain John Smith when he set sail for the swamps of Virginia?"—T. C. Boyle, *Drop City*

❧ *Kent beamed a flashlight into the darkness of the 34-by-24-foot log cabin. The light illuminated a chaotic jumble of cardboard boxes, tools, furniture, and unmounted insulation. The floor was littered with piles of sawdust, nails, bolts, wood chips, and debris from five months of construction. A Jotul woodstove hissed softly, struggling to generate enough heat, but a woodstove can take forty-eight hours or more to heat a frozen house, and the temperature had fallen to zero during our two-day trip from the city. Icicles hung from the outer rafters, and our breaths hovered in white clouds. The cabin was clearly too bitter to be habitable, so for our first night as homesteaders we swallowed our pride and slept on the floor of Ken and Wendy's log cabin, next to their humming woodstove.*

For the next ten days the children and I stayed at Ken and Wendy's house while Kent hurriedly worked on our log cabin. He stapled insulation onto the inside walls, fed the woodstove, and monitored the room temperature. After five days he realized that the Jotul woodstove alone would not heat the house, so we drove into Waterville and bought a second woodstove, an Ashley, the first of many unexpected expenses we could not afford and had not planned for. But it did the trick. The temperature began to rise. Late one afternoon, as the sky was already darkening, Kent pushed open the door at Ken and Wendy's house, his hair and beard white with snow. Shaking flakes off his beat-up parka and stamping his wet L. L. Bean boots on the mat, he removed his steamed-up glasses and said, "I've got the temperature up to sixty degrees in the upstairs loft. We can move in tonight." Dressing the boys in their snowsuits and boots and gathering up our sleeping bags, we said goodbye to Ken and Wendy, stepped out into the frosty twilight and crunched down the slope to our cabin five hundred feet away, shining the flashlight through the dark woods. That night we slept fully dressed in the upstairs loft, shivering in our sleeping bags. Even with both woodstoves cranking, we could still see faint clouds of our breaths the next morning and in the days that followed, as we unpacked boxes and organized clutter. The cabin was on a slope and partially above ground on beams, so the winter breezes blew up through the floorboards. The bare wood floor was freezing. When the dog had an accident on the floor, it froze. I had to use a pick ax to dislodge it. We had no refrigerator and kept perishables in a cardboard box on the floor next to the north wall. We hauled our water from a hand-dug well, heated it on the woodstove, and took baths in the kitchen. The sheer excitement of living like pioneers kept my blood pumping against the cold.

❦ Like pioneers of old, the millions of us who moved into woods, farmlands, or mountains during the 1970s were strong, independent

Kent built the cabin on beams to allow room for a root cellar where we would later store the vegetables we grew.

souls who refused to put up with all the nonsense going on in the mainstream. We intended to strike out on our own, with few possessions and little cash, and rebuild our lives on our own quixotic terms, away from the crowds, the pollutants, and the politics, free from dependence on the grid, on grocery stores, on banal careers, and on cultural expectations. Our goal was self-sufficiency. Our "pioneer willingness" to live with "pioneer self-reliance and diversification of skills" in alternative rural lifestyles, has been documented. We back-to-the-landers clearly identified with the ethos of the Old West, whose mythology has left an indelible imprint on American culture and which invokes images of an "agrarian utopia, [a] landscape of the future, [and a] realm of hope and regeneration." We envisioned "the frontier past as a golden age of grand events, yet-undiminished landscapes and epic men and women."

Because most of the continent was still wilderness when the United States was founded, the Western mythology lives on in our national literature, lexicon, and legends. To pioneers, explorers, cowboys, and homesteaders, we attribute admirable qualities: individualism, strength, health, common sense, and ingenuity. We romanticize their adventures, challenges, and accomplishments. Tacit endorsement of our back-to-the-land mission was built right into the culture.

The dawn of television in the 1950s rekindled America's love for the Western tradition. The Western has been a focal point of television programming since its inception, and from the 1950s through the late 1960s popular shows included *The Gene Autry Show, Death Valley Days, The Lone Ranger, Hopalong Cassidy, The Roy Rogers Show, Bonanza, The Rifleman, Rawhide, Wild Wild West, Gunsmoke,* and *The Big Valley.* "It was in the Western landscapes that the mythic spirit of the country was founded and forged," says John A. Murray, author of *Mythmakers of the West*, "and television Westerns will always provide Americans with a visual recollection of their legendary past." The baby-boom population, to which the back-to-the-land contingent largely belongs, was the first generation to grow up with television. Our increased exposure to Hollywood versions of heroic cowboys, Marlboro men, westward wagon trains, and Davy Crockett taming the wilderness may have pumped us up with expectations that fresh beginnings and better opportunities always awaited us just across the next mountain or plain, and that the outcome would always be good. The Joads' westward trip in *Grapes of Wrath* did not come to mind in the 1970s when we set out by the millions for rural destinations across the United States. Instead we had more in mind an adaptation of *Wagon Train.*

While simplicity models varied across the country, most homesteads, farms, or communes relied on wood for heat; wells and streams for water; lanterns and candles for lighting; latrines, self-contained toilets, or chamber pots as substitutes for flush toilets; wringer washers, scrub boards, or tin tubs for clothes washing; and portable tubs or imaginative home-rigged shower systems for bathing. Somewhere down the line, many of us hoped to graduate to gravity-based plumbing, solar power, compost toilets, and other more sophisticated but environmentally friendly arrangements. But in the early stages of launching self-sufficiency, most of us were as broke as we were high on saving the earth's resources.

Freed from the complications of modern technology, many of us bathed in portable tubs, using hauled water that had to be heated on the woodstove.

It felt exhilarating.

Like the pioneers of old, we saw industry and progress as the enemy of the natural world. Humans and progress have a long history of conflict, and since the Industrial Revolution, movements such as ours had rallied against the inroads made by new technologies. The spread of business and industry across the pristine landscape of the young United States not only eradicated the wilderness but corrupted the national mind-set: progress spawned a need for consumerism. As machines pounded out new products by the trainload, it was necessary to create larger markets for them. Hence by the nineteenth century, the advertising industry, aided by a proliferation of newspapers, magazines, and catalogues, was already in full gear trying to entice Americans to *want* products they didn't know they wanted, nourishing what the environmental historian Richard Tucker refers to as "the hegemony of consumerism in the United States" and "the national culture of material craving and with it an insatiable appetite for goods from around the world." When we rejected modern machinery and technology, we were also snubbing what these things represented: American slothfulness and acquisitiveness, a tragic by-product of industrial progress.

In addition, American culture's persistent strain of Puritanism, which associates self-denial and moderation with virtue, may have fortified our back-to-the-land allegiance to bare-bones surroundings. Historically, in a nation abundant with freedom, wealth, and, often, bad choices, our country's original Puritanical attitudes calling for *restraint* on a wide range of vices never entirely disappeared from our social heritage. Calls for simple living and the abandonment of materialism have resounded through the centuries in response to the country's increasing appetite for spending. Americans have a "long history of tension between the pursuit of material pleasure and the quest for simplicity," observes Gary Cross, author of *An All-Consuming Century*. Those who *simplified* were exercising self-restraint, a value Americans have always admired even while they contradict it in practice. We back-to-the-land people, by renouncing the material objects and technologies desired by the rest of our weak and gluttonous society, demonstrated our superior integrity. *We* had control over the irrepressible cupidity that debased the rest of the American population and would reap mystical rewards by participating in the manual processes long ago taken over by machines. Bread pounded and shaped from homemade dough and cooked in a woodstove heated by the wood of our own sun-splashed forest produced a food item that was morally as well as chemically superior to an anonymous loaf of bread from the store because it had been fashioned by our own hands, with detail and love. Clear, cold water drawn directly from our own wells and carried into our kitchens in our own buckets meant more to us than the gallons that had flowed recklessly through our faucets in our previous homes. "The gospel of the simple life proclaimed that pleasure and meaning could be found in quiet, repeated, and simple experiences and in work with ordinary objects . . .," explains Cross.

Happily, then, we junked our modern machines, gadgets, and conveniences. By jettisoning these accoutrements of the Industrial Age, we had stripped down to a state of purity.

Freedom from Modern Technology

"All of those chores that our parents, and more so our grandparents and their parents, had been burdened with and finally escaped from, we embraced with newfound enthusiasm," remarks former homesteader Cyndy Irvine, well aware of the irony. "We rejoiced in chopping wood, baking bread, making our own candles, and creating herbal concoctions." Certainly novelty played a role as we leaped enthusiastically into a primitive environment that poor people have worked all their lives to escape. In her book *Where We Stand: Class Matters*, bell hooks speaks bitterly about the lack of modern conveniences in her childhood home: "It lacked too much. There was no bathtub. Water had to be heated, carried, and poured into huge tin tubs. Bathing took place in the kitchen to make this ritual of boiling and pouring and washing take less time. There was no such thing as privacy." But, like Henry David Thoreau, we wanted to "suck all the marrow out of life" by "reduc[ing] it to its lowest terms."

We were a very inventive group of people, figuring out ways to accomplish our goals with the minimum of machinery and money. One former homesteader described how he put the old Chevy pickup truck to work. "I'd take the back fender off, put a belt around the wheel, and run the other end of the belt around the mandrel for a buzz saw. We'd run the buzz saw and saw up all our wood. That was fun."

A Homestead in New Mexico

"The silence on our land was initially so . . . silent," observes Cyndy Irvine. "If we were quiet, absolutely no sound. No hum of the refrigerator, no dishwasher or washing machine, much less telephone or television or stereo." In the evenings the calming sounds of their voices filled the kitchen. They read aloud to each other while washing the dishes by the light of kerosene lanterns.

She continues, "The lack of bright lights was a severance from previous dependence on electric utility companies and also kept us more in touch with the changes in weather and darkness around us. I was always aware of the phases of the moon, due to the evening walks and trips to the outhouse."

When Cyndy and her friends agreed to caretake and repair an adobe country house in exchange for living rent-free, two villagers offered to help. These local people "were mostly poor, drawing their water from the same village well as we did, some of them living without electricity (although probably not out of choice as we were), some hardly speaking English, a few probably illegally in this country. They were curious as to why we chose to live like them," Cyndy remembers.

The neighbors taught the novices how to make new bricks from a sand-colored mixture and how to stack them to form new walls. "It was great fun for us and personally satisfying too. I think, just as important, to the local people it was a source of genuine pride for them to be teachers to us, especially involving a skill so intrinsic to their heritage. When had any white people asked them about anything, especially living at their level and respecting their expertise? So I think that adobe instruction sessions benefited all of us in many ways and eased the development of some of our friendships with local people."

Far from feeling deprived, the group of homesteaders enjoyed living without electricity, telephone, and plumbing, for the absence of these utilities freed them from dependence on the grid. "We learned how basic a home can actually be—prepare your food, seek shelter from the cold, and sleep in your warm bed. Those are the necessities. Other functions may be convenient, even desirable, but are actually superfluous."

The kitchen of the old house contained a potbelly heating stove and an old cookstove. Cooking with wood was a real art. If the wood did not generate heat evenly within the stove's belly, the food would cook unevenly too, half burned, half raw. Cyndy recalls, "We became adept at cooking chapatis on the range top, baking breads in the oven, learning where the hot spots were, adjusting the dampers as needed to regulate the temperature."

She adds, "I wondered why in Hollywood movies they don't show black smudges on the pioneers' faces as they labor in their log cabins. We always had smudges on our wrists and foreheads from stoking the firebox and then wiping our foreheads."

Best of all was the social life. Unannounced visits from friends and neighbors brought spontaneity to their lives. Without a phone, they never knew when people might appear at the door.

"We always appreciated our visitors for the news and fresh conversation they would bring to us," she recalls. "It was easy to see how in more primitive times storytelling was an appreciated art. Most traveling hippies carried an instrument, usually the proverbial guitar, but sometimes a fiddle, a flute, or a dulcimer. There was always someone playing an instrument if there were several people gathered together. Music was one of our common bonds, both listening to it and creating it. Many present-day musicians evolved from those evening jam sessions in those cozy homesteads all across the country."

A Homestead in Michigan

John Armstrong had grown up in a middle-class family in Michigan and was expected to carry on the family tradition of becoming a dentist. He started a premed program in college but "quickly discovered that medicine wasn't my bag, which shouldn't be misconstrued to mean that I had the slightest clue as to what my bag might be." For a while he played in a string band at local bars and restaurants, then worked as an orthopedic technician in a hospital.

"The idea of dropping out first came to me when I was working at the hospital," John says. "I was on the evening shift, which was often slow, and for nearly a week I'd been immersed in an issue of the *Mother Earth News* I'd borrowed from a friend. The economy was crashing, and I was getting damn nervous."

John was dating Darma, who was raised on a farm, and when he told her about his homesteading idea, she agreed to try it. They married, and then they moved to Michigan's upper peninsula where they spent the summer and part of the fall searching for a suitable piece of property. Finally they found it.

In his own words, John, now an architect and author of *The Way We Played the Game*, describes the land in his essay "The Hard Return":

"The place we finally settled on was an abandoned, twenty-four-acre Finnish homestead in shambles, and we got it for a pittance, which was fine because that was all we could afford. . . . There were a few farms scattered about, but most of the area was forest. Our rolling acreage had a small, tumbling white-water stream with a waterfall that flowed into a deep pool before eventually finding its way to Lake Superior. The two-track to the house passed over the stream by means of a crude, handmade concrete bridge with weathered cedar posts and railings, and then it wound its way through thickets of tag alder, rowan, and serviceberry trees. The house was situated on a small knoll. Behind the house, the yard sloped downward until it disappeared into a dark ravine where another stream found its way into the hardwood forest beyond.

"The property included a small clapboard house and four ancient, cedar-sided outbuildings in various stages of disrepair—two barns, a sauna, and a generator house. The windmill was gone as was the generator except for some bits and pieces of rusty hardware. We had electricity and running water, but the water came from a stone-lined well below the hill that was protected by a tarpaper-covered plank hatch. Heat was supplied by an antique octopus coal furnace—extremely inefficient—and I immediately sold it to a family of Apostolics and bought a Scandinavian airtight woodstove and installed it in the kitchen."

Because the homestead was in such a ruinous state, John and Darma worked tirelessly that entire fall preparing for winter.

"We cleared away the fallen trees and branches that littered the house and driveway, and then we mowed the grass. That took a week," John continues. "Next, I scraped and painted the house and repaired windows, many having no glass at all, while Darma picked apples and gathered sugar plums from along the forest edges. I hunted grouse and rabbits for meat."

Getting fuel for the woodstove was essential for survival. Every spare moment was spent cutting and splitting firewood, then stacking it in the basement. By November one complete side of the basement was filled to a height of six feet.

Then winter struck with a vengeance.

"Winter in the Keweenaw was a beast that one had to see to believe," John writes. "Once the snow began to fly, it didn't stop for six months." Like many homesteaders in northern climates, John and Darma were forced to leave their vehicle at the end of the drive and walk to the house, a distance of four hundred feet, hauling their groceries and other supplies on a toboggan. Snow shovels were nearly useless. John discovered the locals used scoops to clear snow, so he got one. "They had to be pushed along the ground with both hands," he explains.

Although the winter seemed eternal, it finally loosened its grip in April. The snow on the ground softened and dissolved, mud took its place, and then buds began to appear on the trees. John and Darma resumed outdoor work, planting fruit and nut trees, clearing more brush, repairing the barn, building a chicken coop and rabbit pen. They bought Leghorns for eggs and White Rocks as a source of meat. In the summer they started a garden. John was content. The work was hard but rewarding, and he loved the north country. He felt good about his new way of life and looked forward to many years of homesteading in a place that allowed close interaction with nature.

After nearly a year of isolation on the homestead, John made the ten-hour drive downstate to visit his family, and while there he spent an afternoon with his sister eating lunch and shopping. He needed new clothes, and one of the places they stopped was a mall.

"It was the first time in nearly two years I'd been in a mall," he says, "and the plastic and chrome and the odor of the carpet and furniture glue was overwhelming—I was accustomed to living with the smell of mulch, pine sap, and pollinated air. Wood smoke had become a part of me. I would've preferred the musty odor our malamute gave off when she was wet, or the chicken shit in our coop, compared to that mall," he smiles.

Middle Earth Homestead in Maine

When we set up Middle Earth Homestead in Troy that winter of 1975–1976, our cabin consisted of one dark freezing room without electricity or indoor plumbing. Our water source was a twenty-five-foot hand-dug well, located three hundred feet uphill from the cabin. To transport water to the house, I tied two camping sinks to the toboggan and pulled them to the well. Removing the well's protective boards, I lowered the rope and bucket into the shiny circle of water below. I could feel the wooden bucket growing heavy as it sank slowly below water level. When I felt the familiar heavy tug of a full bucket, I pulled the rope, hand over hand, leaning almost backward, as the bucket thudded upward, bouncing off the sides of the well. Raising the bucket over the edge, I poured the icy water into the camping sinks, tied them onto the toboggan, and towed them home. Back inside the house, if I was doing laundry that day, I would pour the entire ten gallons from the two camping sinks into the metal container we kept on the woodstove for heating water. Or one water-filled camping sink could be placed on the table in lieu of a real sink, to be used for face-washing or teeth-brushing. You had to pump the creaky plastic "taps" vigorously in order to coax pressureless little spurts of water from their spouts. A plastic plug at the bottom of the sink bowl contained the water until you had accumulated enough to splash on your face or wash your hands. You became adept at holding a toothbrush in one hand and pumping fresh spurts of rinse water with the other. When you finished, you popped the plastic drain plug out, and the wastewater trickled *very* slowly down the drain and out the bottom of the sink, where it ran into a bucket. When the bucket was full, you carried it to the door and tossed the grey water into the yard. Needless to say, you now conserved water jealously. Anyone would who had to hike to a well in the freezing cold, tug the water up from a hole by the bucketful, and haul it home. Besides, how much could you really waste when it squirted out half an ounce at a time?

We bathed in a portable tub. The icy well water had to be heated on the woodstove for several hours before it was warm enough to pour into the tub. I'm not sure which was more difficult, disrobing in that frosty house before stepping into the tub of bathwater, or emerging from

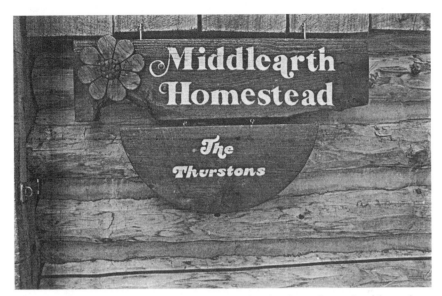

An artistic friend made a wooden hanging for the front door of our log cabin. Although we spelled Middle Earth as two words, his one-word spelling made the words line up evenly.

the hot water into the cold room temperature. Of course, the used water from bathing or dishwashing, just like the used sink water, had to be carried outside and poured onto the ground.

Because most household uses called for warm to hot water, we kept the woodstove's fire crackling. We needed at least lukewarm water for washing dishes and cleaning wooden countertops, and slightly warmer water for shampooing hair, which was done the old-fashioned way, leaning over a bowl, pouring a pitcher of water onto the head, sudsing up, then rinsing with a second or third pitcher of water. You can imagine how much water ended up on the floor, soon to become frozen tributaries in the crevices between the floorboards.

Soon after we moved to Troy, Kent bought a wringer washing machine for me. In time I grew to hate that white porcelain cylinder with the tight beige wringers. The children, who were always hovering underfoot, seemed to have a penchant for sticking their fingers in them.

Washing clothes took hours. First, of course, I had to retrieve water from the well. Back at the house I hoisted the filled camping sinks up to woodstove level and poured the water into the metal container on the stove, splashing much of it onto the floor. An hour later, when the fire's heat had taken the edge off the water's chill, I groaned as I lifted the heavy container off the stovetop, carried it with potholders across the room, and poured the water into the washer with a tidal wave of a splash. As the water agitated, I added a cup of nonpolluting biodegradable Ivory Flakes (great for that homestead mud and chicken manure!) and then the reeking clothes. After fifteen minutes of swishing they were "clean," by homestead standards anyway, but then I had to feed them through the wringers. When they emerged, squeezed dry, they fell limply into a basket below. The dirty, soapy water had to be drained through a long hose at the bottom of the machine which snaked out the door and into the gravel septic field. Then another container full of fresh rinse water had to be hoisted into the machine for the rinse cycle; the clothes were replaced in the washer, agitated in clear water, and fed through the wringer once more.

Wringer washing machines were hell on buttons. When the clothes were squeezing their way through the wringer, you couldn't leave buttons exposed. You had to halt the process and turn the drenched item inside out or fold it sideways; otherwise, after draining the water out, you'd find a pile of them, threads dangling, at the bottom of the machine alongside the pebbles, twigs, piles of hardened chicken poop, and other surprises from the pockets of little boys' blue jeans.

I also learned after a few cold dousings that you had to feed pillowcases through the wringer seamside first. A pillowcase traveling through backward would quickly swell up like a sail on a boat, sending a shower of water onto the unfortunate washer of the clothes.

Down the slope from the cabin, a clothesline swung between two pine trees. Tramping through the snow, I would carry, push, and slide the wicker basket of wet clothes to the line and hang them with wooden clothespins. They froze. Later, looking out the window, an observer would see humanlike forms—trunks, torsos, feet, hands—standing stiffly in the woods beneath the clothesline. The next day I'd return to the line, stack the clothes into a rigid pile on the snow, and, cradling

An electric clothes dryer was unthinkable for environmentally conscious people like Kent and me. When our clothes froze on the outside line, I'd have to hang them from hooks around the woodstove to thaw them.

them like babies, carry them awkwardly back inside, where I'd hang most of the freeze-dried shirts, underwear, socks, and jeans from hooks above the woodstove and stand others up against beams. Slowly the standing ones would relax their unbending shapes and slump onto the floor, still damp. Sometimes clothes would not dry thoroughly for days.

Attempting to wash a stinking quilt that Derek had thrown up on, whose fumes saturated the house, I learned my lesson about the washer's capacity for bulky material. Although the quilt somehow fit into the washer cylinder, it jammed in the wringers as I desperately tried to feed it through. Putting the wringer into reverse, I pulled it back out. Perhaps six inches had been squeezed dry, the rest remained a monstrosity of waterlogged fabric, swollen tight within the machine. I had no choice but to wrestle the dead weight of quilt out of the machine and drag it across the floor—leaving a river of grey water on the floorboards—and out the front door. Tugging and pulling it, I maneuvered the quilt down the snow-covered slope to the clothesline and, panting heavily, threw one end over the line and pulled the rest over. The clothesline sank to the ground. By evening the quilt had frozen into the snow, brightening the white landscape with its ice-glazed colors.

Capped with an ice-cold seat, the "hopper," as we called the indoor commode, was a trial for any human being, especially in the winter. A heart-stopping, ice-cold draft blew up from its underside, which was open to the outside. Many back-to-the-land people preferred outhouses because they were economical, easy to construct, and environmentally conscientious. One homesteader built a pyramid-shaped outhouse, in which positive energy fields whirled like eddies. "At the time, Pyramid Power was the big thing," he explains. "They had experiments where you take a pyramid, built the same way as the great pyramids, same dimensions but on a small scale, and you could actually put a piece of meat in a certain place within that pyramid, and it wouldn't rot. You could supposedly store your razor blades at that point, and they'd never go dull. So I built my pyramid-outhouse and put the throne right at that place. So I figured, while I'm sitting there, I might as well preserve myself." He also installed the windshield from an old Gremlin, so the outhouse, which sat on a ledge facing a wood-filled valley, had a lovely picture window, creating a room with a view.

"It was pretty nice," he admits. "A good view out into the woods."

Another person with an outhouse recalled how another member of the household "was reading a novel in the outhouse. Every time he'd go out there, he'd read a chapter.

"We had this visitor friend of mine who was kind of an alcoholic, but we kept him around for a while. Eventually we sent him on his way, but my friend went to the outhouse to finish the book, and the last couple of pages had been torn out. I think you can figure out why. He never did figure out how that book ended."

Most back-to-the-land people, such as the friend of a friend pictured above, preferred outhouses as the commode-of-choice because they were cheap, easy to construct, and environmentally sound.

A Toolshed Home in Maine

In the summer of 1972, Patricia Foley and her husband did not plan to spend the following winter in the six-by-ten-foot toolshed. In fact they meant to return to New Jersey in the fall and work for another year. They had purchased their fifteen acres in Alexander for $3,000 and had only $300 left. But somehow they never left Maine. As winter closed in, the prospect of living in a small toolshed seemed far less painful than the thought of returning to New Jersey. The preceding year Patricia and her husband, then graduate students at Rutgers University, had married and traveled to Maine for their honeymoon. They found the Maine landscape delightful, and for the next year their minds wouldn't let go.

"You can imagine if the last sight you saw before you hit New Brunswick, New Jersey, was the Maine seacoast. The image would linger," Patricia explains. "After the honeymoon we spent a year in the yellow skies of New Jersey. You could smell the reeking Raritan River into which the Union Carbide plant had plenty of time to pump anti-freeze, so the Raritan had one of the odd distinctions of being one of those slow, sluggish streams that never freezes in winter, even when it gets cold enough. In addition, it's very boring to live in an apartment in New Jersey. You're stuffed in an apartment with noisy small children with plastic tricycles roaring around, and doped-up graduate students in the parking lot getting into big fights, both high as kites, at two o'clock in the morning. So we decided the hell with it, and in the summer of '72, we headed north."

As the winter of '72 swept in, they were still in Maine.

The toolshed had a low ceiling. "You couldn't stand up straight," remembers Patricia. "We kept bashing our heads in the back. We had a little woodstove that I'm sure the Sears, Roebuck or Montgomery Ward catalogue used to sell for people to plant geraniums in. I can't believe that anyone ever used them for actual woodstoves. But we bought one of these little turkeys, which would hold only one piece of wood one foot long. It was the damn coldest winter of my life."

She continues, "We were keeping a temperature chart just to see what the scope of our suffering was. Were we really at the Homeric level yet or what? I remember the average temperature in January 1973 was thirteen degrees, which I thought was pretty bad for a daytime room temperature. The average temperature in February was twelve degrees. So that was even worse. There was a stretch of days where the daytime high was five below zero. I thought we were getting to the epic level then. Not good."

They hauled water that winter and for years after.

"We used to joke that we didn't have running water, we had walking water," says Patricia. "I walked down to the spring with two six-gallon buckets. The worst was in the winter. That was a hideous time. You had to break out a square of ice just big enough to put the bucket in and pull it out. The snow was so deep that you would invariably slosh half the water all over yourself tripping through the snow, and it would freeze before you got it back to the woodshed where we kept it. You'd get in there, and you'd have dungarees that were ice-sodden, heavy thick things, and you'd have to do the whole trip to the spring again because of course you'd only brought back half as much as you'd planned because so much spilled."

Patricia boiled all their drinking water too. And she laundered clothes by hand with a washboard.

"That was awful. Just as bad in summer as in winter. You're mixing cement to build a house, so clothes get really, *really* grubby, with cement all over and through them. When I wasn't washing clothes after mixing cement, I was actually mixing cement, and cement is really abrasive, so my fingers were always abraded from its caustic quality. I still remember the raw state of my palms as I scrubbed those clothes. Washing took *all day*.

"I would do it one day a week while my husband did the building. I deeply resented that one day. I'd be up there in the shed from eight in the morning till three in the afternoon, scrubbing clothes on a washboard and fetching more water, bringing it up, heating it up—you can't wash filthy dirty clothes with cold water—and then rinsing them in cold water, which, coming from a spring, was very cold water indeed. My hands would just ache! Laundry day was never a good day. It was the day when anybody with any common sense would not speak to me. I thought while I was doing laundry with a scrub board that I had definitely wasted my parents' tuition money."

They bought a wringer washer in 1978 after they finally had running water.

An Apple Orchard in Northern California

"I remember one year we caught five hundred trout," says Stacia Dunnam, who was taken back to the land by her parents in 1974. "We'd sit at this huge table, assembly-line fashion, cleaning and gutting fish. We had two freezers for storing them, so we ate fish for the next year. I couldn't eat trout for a long time after that."

Before moving to the land, Stacia and her family lived in a populated area of southern California. Her father decided the city was detrimental to the family, sold his jewelry business, and bought a beautiful mountainside apple orchard in northern California. "It was really pretty," she remembers. "We used to come down in our backyard and eat the apples all the time."

The old house had been built around the turn of the century when the region had been a mining area. Stacia shared a bedroom with five sisters. Her father custom-built plywood and two-by-four bunk beds that rose from floor to ceiling, three bunks with a ladder going up the side.

A pump sent ice-cold creek water up the hill into a holding tank, from which it descended to the house through gravity-fed pipes. Two wood-burning stoves and an ineffective fireplace provided heat. They raised chickens, pigs, and a cow. They attempted geese, but the birds kept flying back to their original owners. The goats became pets for Stacia and her siblings.

"We had seventeen goats," says Stacia. "I really liked having them. The billy goat was nasty, but the female goats were really nice, and their milk tasted good. Before we got our own goats, my father used to buy goat's milk because it was better for us. But it tasted horrible! We learned that the taste depended on what you fed your goats. We got used to the awful taste by mixing it half and half with cow's milk or powdered milk, which is also horrible. When we finally got our own goats, we fed them right, so their milk tasted good."

The large apple orchard offered much for the children to do. Stacia and her brothers and sisters would choose a location on the property, pitch a tent, and camp out for a couple of days. They felt completely safe. They also fished—many lakes in the area were stocked regularly by the state. A river flowed five miles from the house, so they also swam and kayaked.

One day Stacia saved her brother from a near drowning. "We used to dive into the river from a high rock called White Rock. The river had a really strong undercurrent. One day we were all down there, us kids along with these three hippie 'ranch hands,' though I think all they ever did was get stoned—which was interesting, because it kept me away from that. Anyway, my younger brother dove into the water. I stood on top of the rock because I was going to dive next. Then I noticed that he was caught in the undertow. I'm a very tiny woman; I'm five-foot-one now, and at the time I was even tinier. My nickname was Peanut. Even though these big guys, the 'ranch hands' were there, they weren't near enough to see what was going on. I yelled, 'Oh, my God, he's drowning!' and I dove into the water. I still remember fighting against the undertow, pulling him up, and starting to slip to the side when one of the bigger guys caught on to what was going on and helped both of us out."

Blackberry brambles grew prolifically on the land. "We used to have to go out and pick them and pick them and pick them! One time my younger brother and sister and I spent an entire Saturday picking ten quarts of blackberries. My mom never got around to canning them, and they rotted. I don't think we ever forgave her for that."

Stacia learned to hunt, helping to skin the bagged deer. She also panned for gold in the creeks. "We'd actually find little nuggets sometimes," she says. "My father had been a jeweler, so he would take them and sell them to his friends."

During the winter holiday season the family would hike into the woods and select a Christmas tree. "That was neat," says Stacia, who now lives in southern California and runs an antiques studio specializing in vintage art deco clothing and home accessories. As an adult she continues to have a strong appreciation for nature and for books. She read avidly during her years at the orchard, because, of course, they had no television.

A Homestead in West Virginia

Sandy Sanchez loved the baths. While the freezing water heated on the woodstove most of the day, she would walk into the woods and gather hemlock branches to make an oily liquid to pour into the warm bathwater. That night, climbing in, she would relax in the tub with a cup of hot spiced cider and watch the snow fall outside the mint-framed window.

When she, her husband, and young daughter moved to their land in West Virginia, they occupied the shack ("textbook depression-era Appalachian structure," she notes) that stood on the property. In her unpublished essay, "Remembering West Virginia," Sandy describes the house as somewhat lopsided: "Every door, every window hung at a different angle." The kitchen, separated from the other rooms by a quilted yellow curtain, contained a decrepit woodstove, an old gas range, and the big bathtub with claw feet.

Sandy enjoyed walking the land, which she did frequently. "I walked for miles up the road watching the trees and streams move past me as though I stood on a conveyor belt that carried me past one perfect scene after another. When it rained ever so lightly at night, I could watch the mist rising and falling, stretching and spiraling. I loved to see the lights of my house filtered through the colored windows through the night mist. I could not bear to go inside where it was too warm and still, the sounds dulled yet not soft. The autumn chill set in late in August, and the apples came ready and some leaves turned.

"Apples and leaves and the feathers of molting birds and berries all mingled underfoot in the cool dry earth of early autumn," she continues. "With sap-stained hands smelling of pine, I picked berries. Tiny insects crawled from leaf to hand to leaf again, unaware of me, my hand fluid with the leaves. Green and gold beetles coupled among the leaves; the berries crashed through the leaves in wounded fall.

"It was a frightening world beneath the low-slung berry bushes, full of violence and delicacy. Life passed meteorically and died and lived again with the slow rhythm of a rising winter sun. The light was most electric at five o'clock and then earlier and earlier until soon there was no light, only the dullness of grey winter days except when it snowed and then the world was bright and golden and blue and magical all encased in ice and turned silver and white as a tapestry."

Sandy filled the kitchen shelves with her canned fruits and vegetables. From the ceiling rafters hung ropes of her comfrey, mint, red peppers, garlic, and onions. She baked bread. She repaired the old hen-house, bought two hundred chicks, and raised them in a child's plastic swimming pool. Soon they had eggs.

"I remember sending my daughter out to gather them, and she came back terrified of the rooster that was pawing the ground and getting ready to charge her, a real danger given that his beak was at her eye level," remembers Sandy. "I had to use a two-by-four to bat him off like an oversized baseball, and he survived to bother us again. We also found lots of eggs in trees, in the hayloft, and even in the cows' feed bins."

Their homestead abounded with fruit trees. "It would have been wasteful not to keep bees, so we did that too and had honey for baking, for sale, for gifts, and just for eating."

Because sassafras grew prolifically, she dug up the roots to make root beer. Sandy, now a former homesteader turned lawyer turned author, lives in Denver but has fond memories of her life on the homestead.

Life at Tolstoy Farm

At Tolstoy Farm near Seattle, Tomas Diaz chopped the wood each morning, then carried two five-gallon square cans to the creek and filled them with the chilly water. He loved being outside in the bracing morning air. Back in the house, he hefted the tanks of water onto the large woodstove to heat. Another person would start the fire while Tomas got the red wheat, placed it in the mill, and ground it. After he had sifted the wheat, the women at the farm would cook a breakfast of pancakes or mush. Tomas's next chore of the morning was to churn the butter. He walked to the creek to retrieve the big glass jar of milk that had been left there from the previous evening's milking. Since they had no refrigeration at Tolstoy Farm, the cold creek served the purpose. He poured the top layer of cream into the three-sided jar with paddles. Now was the best part: Tomas sat contentedly on the front porch of the house churning butter.

"When that paddle would go around, the cream would hit the sides of the jar, separate, and become butter. It's a no-brainer. Sometimes you can look up at the sky and know exactly what time it is? That's the way it was with the butter. After a while you just looked at the butter and you could tell it was ready. A pound of butter would rise to the top as a big clump; the rest would be skim milk, and the women would use that to make cheese."

After lunch the group of Tolstoy residents would work outside in the garden, talking and joking as they moved down the rows. In the evenings they would attend meetings—one social, where members could discuss personal differences, and the other financial. Everyone was expected to contribute cash or time to the farm.

"I absolutely loved this period of my life," notes Tomas in his website memoir. "One evening at dinner, we were all sitting at the very long (chow-down) dinner table. The women were running around serving everyone. I had brown rice, fresh milk, fresh butter, apple butter, and homemade bread . . . the sun was beginning to go down. Delores and I walked hand in hand a quarter of a mile to a house where a campfire was going. There were people sitting around the campfire, singing songs and passing smoke. Delores and I sat down in the circle, and we said hello. We sang and discussed the nature of the world's plight while the embers turned red. Janet read to us from Winnie the Pooh by lamplight. She had good taste."

Today Tomas is married, lives in Marion, Kentucky, and is retired from a long, postcommune career in government. He maintains many websites, including a newsletter for former residents of Morningstar Commune, where he also lived briefly.

Making Do on Little

Most of us became adept at eking out the greatest abundance from the fewest possible resources. We learned to grow sprouts in glass jars inside the house. Healthful and very inexpensive, sprouts would grow anytime in any dark corner, which was crucial when the garden was fallow. Sprout and peanut butter sandwiches made a fine lunch.

Many homesteads contained bushes of wild strawberries, raspberries, blueberries, or blackberries. Or for pennies you could pick your own at a nearby farm. These fruits became jams, breads, and pies as well as frozen and canned preserves. Depending upon location and climate, many of us planted baby fruit trees so that we could look forward to harvesting apples, pears, or cherries and making an even wider variety of foods.

Most women I knew baked bread from scratch, as I did. I bought the grain in bulk at the Peak Mountain Food Co-op, and ground it into flour with a little grinding mill which I set up on the kitchen counter every Saturday morning when I baked bread. I poured a few cups of whole wheat grain into the top, turned the crank, listened to the crunch, and watched the stream of fine-grained wheat flour flow out the chute into the mixing bowl. Then I mixed the flour with the yeast, milk, butter, and salt, and stirred, kneaded, pounded, and shaped the loaves, a real workout for the arm and hand muscles. After the loaves had risen, I baked them and the house filled up with a heavenly smell.

Our land offered other dietary bonuses, including maple syrup, which we harvested by draining sap from the maple trees and boiling it down. We also picked fiddleheads, a wild fern that grew abundantly in our area. A bowl of fiddleheads boiled in water and flavored with butter and salt was considered almost a delicacy among locals and homesteaders. Comfrey, also a wild herb, was supposed to have healing properties, so many homesteaders drank it as a tea. Every growing plant had potential. One writer for an alternative magazine recommended daylily stalks as "a green vegetable very much like asparagus," and offered cooking directions. Daylily tubers could also be used in salads like radishes.

Naturally most of us had gardens, so we capitalized on whatever vegetable was currently thriving, and even when we got tired of rotating meals of spinach soufflé, spinach soup, spinach salad, and spinach tacos, we waited it out until another type of vegetable came ripe; then it was time for corn crepes, corn soufflé, and corn soup. One could make very interesting soups from a hodgepodge of vegetables.

Early Happiness

As basic as our lives had become, the payoff was adventure and freedom. In the early days most of us cut our wood, hauled our water,
washed our clothes, ate pared-down meals, and took our kitchen baths
with a light heart, believing this to be a small price for not having to
drive in heavy traffic or to sit numbly in an office chair all day.

Keddy Ann Outlaw, who homesteaded at the foothills of the
Adirondacks in New York state, loved living on her fifty acres of forest.
She and her friends cleared the land and planted it in small patches.
The early days on the land were uplifting. "Was there ever such optimism as we had for our first 'crops'? Every carrot and radish, every
splash of spinach leaf, was a miracle. Mother Earth had made herself
known to me, and I felt humbled to be her handmaiden. Also, I marveled at the wild food in abundance—pigweed, fiddlehead ferns, morel
mushrooms, blackberries and apples."

John Armstrong particularly remembers the initial joy of working
hard on his homestead but finding moments for picnics by the lake and
long walks through the woods with his wife.

Most of us can attest to the fact that, initially at least, going back to
the land felt very much like falling in love.

🌱 *By January 1976, Kent and I had progressed from the two plastic camping sinks on the wooden counter to a spacious thirty-dollar white porcelain
cast-iron sink with a real faucet and real taps, though they were useless since
we didn't have running water. But the sink itself, mounted permanently into
the wall, was sizable and sturdy and provided space for washing dishes or
shampooing. Now, instead of bending over the roasting pan and splashing
rinse water all over the table as I aimed it at my sudsy head, I could lean over
a real sink to shampoo my hair, and even better, let the grey water run down
the drain. Kent had built a leech field outside, so wastewater could now swirl
down the drain and flow out through pipes. We no longer had to carry the
wastewater, slopping over the sides of the bucket every step of the way, outside the front door to heave it toward the woods.*

Before the winter of 1976 had melted into mud season, we decided to have an artesian well drilled. The hand-dug well had been sufficient—but what could we say? An artesian well would supply more water, faster. We would also install a hand pump for greater ease in drawing the water up from the ground, though we would still have to lug it to the cabin in containers. Well-drilling wasn't cheap, but the two families ponied up some cash together, talked to a local well-driller who charged by the foot, and agreed to pay him to drill one hundred feet down and no more. We couldn't afford it. The water flow at that level would be crucial. To provide for two families, the water would have to flow at three gallons per minute at least. The man and his well-drilling machine creaked up the muddy hill to the clearing where the well was to be. The formidable machine roared on and, like a dentist's drill, bored noisily into the ground, seeking water. Days passed, with lots of loud whining and clanking, but the drill remained dry. At ninety-nine feet, the well-driller finally reported one and a half gallons of water per minute.

Because we couldn't afford to drill more than another foot, it appeared that we'd have to postpone the completion of the project until we could scare up more money. The driller, a nice local guy who was kind to the invading hippies, offered to drill to 101 feet, giving us the last foot for free, and at 101 feet he struck a vein. Water surged up at four and a half gallons per minute. Kent and I and Ken and Wendy celebrated at the site, cheering and laughing as we watched the clear cold water gush out of the hand pump we had installed.

Kent scavenged a thirty-gallon water storage container from the dump and secured it on the second floor loft of the log cabin. He also installed a funnel outside the cabin into which water hauled from the well could be poured. From the outside funnel, the water flowed into a twenty-gallon container downstairs, then a motorized system pumped it upstairs through a hose system into the storage container. Now, when we turned the taps in the porcelain sink, the water flowed down by gravity to the faucet. But we never knew for sure how much water remained in the upstairs storage tank. When it went bone dry, which it usually did in the middle of a shampoo or at a crucial stage of cooking, we knew that three trips to the well with two five-gallon containers would fill it to the top. But if we weren't sure of the water level and *wanted to top it off before doing laundry or something else, we'd have to guess how much more water could be poured in before it would overflow.*

One day I felt certain the tank could take ten more gallons. It had been filled the day before, but I had washed dishes and filled the wringer washer twice. So I hiked to the well and returned with ten gallons. I poured all of it into the lower container on the first floor and turned on the motor to send it upward. Distracted by the arrival of a neighbor, I forgot about it until I heard Derek and Shawn screaming. I looked up as the water spread rapidly across the floor of the top loft and splashed down as a waterfall onto the first floor. The kids continued to screech, and, as I noted in my writing that week, "Kent appeared and started giving me hell for not standing right at the fuse box and watching closely so I could turn off the motor the second the container was full. In all, it was a bum morning." Perhaps the nascent tensions that would eventually cause our split were beginning to reveal themselves.

Kent found a shower stall at the dump, carted it home, and set it up in the kitchen beside the wooden counter where I cooked. He found a second, smaller water-storage container and bolted it into place on the wooden walkway right above the shower stall. Of course we had to preheat the water on the woodstove, carry it up the steep ladder-stairs, and pour it into the container. But for a shower instead of a kitchen bath, I was counting my blessings. The boys started horsing around on the walkway one day and loosened the container from its moorings, causing the stored water to burst out of the drain hole and flood the wooden walkway. After many moments like those, you began to long for conventional plumbing (even though it wasn't P.C.) so you could take a shower the simple way—just step in and turn the tap, without constant complications and clean-ups.

As I reflect on the log cabin's plumbing, as well other areas of our lives, I find it revealing that Kent and I, who had intended to live simply and stay with the basics, kept advancing to more complicated systems. This is true for most people who went to the land. They started with outhouses and ended up with composting toilets, or started with wood heat and ended up with solar panels. One-room homes grew into five-room homes as additions popped up over the years. Kerosene lanterns gave way to electricity, and hand-dug wells were retired in favor of motorized pumps from deep wells. Either all of us had been irreversibly socialized by American culture to seek the next greater stage of comfort, or we could not escape our atavistic impulses to invent and explore, taking the simple and transforming it into the complex. Or possibly most of us, unlike truly impoverished people, simply had the wherewithal and connections to raise the capital necessary for home improvements if we wanted them.

CHAPTER THREE

The Height of Happiness

"I learned a lot that changed my life and how I looked at things. I continued to move a lot and travel a lot, but I always missed Wheeler's Ranch and Morningstar and what I had there, and was always sad about leaving. In my particular situation, I found unconditional love there, which I had never found before. It was hard to replace what I had there. I always missed it."—Jodi Mitchell

"If somebody was putting on a roof or if somebody needed help doing this or doing that, we'd go over and help them do that project. It was a real community."—Bruce Lemire

❧ *Each summer morning as the sun ascended over the Adirondack foothills, the three Engelhart brothers rose from their sleeping bags and cooked breakfast over an open fire. It was 1975. They were all young and free, living in a tepee on 159 acres in Peasleeville, New York, just west of Lake Champlain. Steven, the oldest brother, remembers how they spent their spring, summer, and fall days outside, cutting wood, gathering the stones they needed to construct their houses, or walking the length of the Salmon River, which flowed along on the property line. Steven loved exploring the land, which teemed with pine and hardwood trees. "We got to know practically every inch of the property—where the various stands of trees were, where there were old cellar holes, where the old roads and paths led, and where there were wild* blackberries and mushrooms," he says. At night the brothers and a rotation of visiting friends would lie in their sleeping bags in the fire-lit tepee, talking late into the darkness, telling stories, singing, sharing ideas and jokes.

Steven had dropped out of college, where he'd been majoring in architecture, to join his brothers on the land. "We had that luxury of time that as an adult now sounds so wonderful," smiles Steven. "Time to get to know each other and the place, without the rush of children or careers or anything really pressing."

For amusement as well as practicality, they invented new words for items that occupied their routine but had no name, such as the smoking but un-burned pieces of log inevitably left at the edge of the open fire. "These things would cause a lot of smoke in the tepee and would irritate our eyes. But there was nothing to call them," recalls Steven. "So we ended up inventing the term 'hon-yat ends.'"

In the warm months Steven and his brothers worked on the land; in the winters they took jobs pruning apple trees at local orchards. Although they earned agricultural minimum wage, lower than regular minimum wage, the money they saved provided for their minimal needs until the following winter.

"The winter was for earning money and saving money; the summer and fall were for making things happen," says Steven. "So there was kind of a cy-cle to it."

The brothers also got to know their local rural neighbors, who were al-ways friendly and helpful, never judgmental. They helped them cut wood, in-vited them into their homes, gave them meals, and talked politics with them. "They were very typical working-class north country people," says Steven. "I think two or three of the men in the family were prison guards, and in their spare time they worked in the woods and cut pulpwood. A couple of the wives were hairdressers—really basic everyday people. Here we were, with long hair, coming up there, initially living in tepees until we built our houses and barns, living unconventionally, growing food. They were amazingly accepting and tolerant. Some of those relationships, even though they haven't gone on over time, were among the things I remember most fondly—being taken into people's homes, fed, given milk. We argued about all kinds of things, but it was very open, and they were very accepting. Their generosity made a huge impression on us."

During his time on the land, Steven grew closer to his brothers and got to know his rural neighbors. Even more important, he discovered another side of himself. "We took really well to living that kind of life. We learned how to build houses and barns, keep farm animals, grow things, fix tractors, keep old vehicles running, dig for water, and work in the woods. Our old peasant stock came back to us. We all discovered this other side of ourselves that had never really been cultivated. There was a lot of joy in that."

❧ It's a rare back-to-the-land experience that doesn't embrace at least some pleasurable memories. Timothy Miller observed after conducting extensive research on communes that "those who lived the communal life have largely fond memories of it all. . . . overwhelmingly, the reaction of those contacted [for interviews] was great enthusiasm for the preservation of what they almost all thought was a high point in American history as well as in their own lives." Jeffrey Jacob, who researched back-to-the-land people over several decades, agreed that those he interviewed for his project responded with "the depth of their feelings about their back-to-the-land experiences." Like Steven above, many people I interviewed thought the entire odyssey was consistently agreeable, the rewards vastly outweighing any downsides. Although I was not one of this group, I recently wrote to a friend, "I still occasionally feel a surge of longing for that time and place, for the sound of the ice pellets beating at the top of the skylight, the smell of the woods in fall, the wonderful, beer-swilling potlucks every Saturday night."

Perhaps time has oversentimentalized it for many, but most former back-to-the-land people cite the feeling of community as the sweetest memory that remains with them today. Since the back-to-the-land movement was so widespread, involving an estimated several million or more participants during the 1970s, community fellowship was ever-present, whether it was within the same house, on the same land, or in the same region. We were younger then, and we had the free time; our friendships clicked more quickly because we had such easy access to so many kindred spirits of roughly the same age group, in the same stage of life, with the same goals and outlooks. One back-to-the-land person confessed that she has never recaptured the feeling of total acceptance and belonging that she knew with her community in the 1970s. "Community is and must be a deeply felt experience," writes Robert Booth Fowler in *The Dance with Community*. "Community goes deep into our souls and in the process helps us to understand ourselves. . . ."

It wasn't just our local friends who made us feel validated; we also knew that we were part of a much larger national energy, a coast-to-coast network of back-to-the-land people who were living out the same dream. Whether they were milking cows in Wisconsin or picking oranges in California or chopping wood in New Mexico, they were our kin too. Belonging to a large and significant subculture brought a strong sense of satisfaction. We were a part of something important. That felt good.

In addition to thriving as members of a community, we discovered and appreciated the splendor of the natural world, we learned survival skills and tested our proficiency with tools, construction, and a wide range of manual tasks, and we enjoyed freedom from the constrictive social expectations of the larger society. Who wouldn't enjoy at least some aspects of a life interval like that?

The strong post–World War II economy in the United States had set the stage for the confidence that allowed us to drop out. We were less concerned than our parents' generation about the security of a steady professional job commensurate with our class and educational level. We knew we could make a go of it in the country with what little money we could generate from cash crops or part-time jobs. We had what Paul C. Light refers to in *Baby Boomers* as "great expectations" for our lives. Having grown up in a time of economic abundance, we had already had it all, so we did not acquire a materialistic mind-set, he says, and were "free to think about other issues, like the search for a meaningful philosophy of life." Our confidence and temerity, nourished by our generally comfortable upbringings, may have given us a worldview that would not have been possible in another era. "Someone caught in a depression thinks about jobs and income; someone raised in economic abundance thinks about tolerance and free expression," says Light.

Robert Houriet, author of *Getting Back Together*, lived on a commune in Vermont in the seventies. He says he doesn't believe it was the "permissive" child-rearing practices of our generation, as some critics think, that gave us the idea the world was "an unlimited breast"; rather, it was the wealth. "You're talking about the height of the empire; you're talking about the most money ever available— everyone was ripping with money in the sixties. Before the oil crisis, foundations gave away money. The upper class as well as the middle had more money than they could deal with. There was a luxury for rebellion."

❧ An eight-by-ten photo, browned with time, captures the youthful energy and hope that filled our homestead in Maine. The photo is black and white, but my memory fills in the colors radiated by the shining sun, the blue sky, and the green pines. Kent and I, Wendy and Ken, and the three children are standing in a clearing at the perimeter of the "top garden," as we would later call it. It's June, warm enough to shed some clothing but cool enough not to sweat. A breeze surges through the woods, rustling the leaves of the maples, pines, elms, and other assorted foliages crowded together on our sixty-two acres of land. The noon sun shines perpendicularly upon our heads, casting shadows across our faces, as we prepare to plant. But first, a photo. We line up, standing on the rumpled rows of plowed earth, twisted in dried grass and roots, while Kent settles his camera on the tripod. Setting the automatic timer, he scurries back into the scene and waits, posing. The camera snaps, preserving forever that pristine moment of innocence when the four of us really believed we could live self-sufficiently, in peace and harmony with the world, on sixty-two acres of wooded land in Maine.

I stand on the left, wearing a halter top, tight jeans, and large, dark sunglasses, with my hair clipped up, long strands escaping around my face. I'm holding Shawn, just a toddler then, who has thick white-blond curls and pink skin. In those days we called him "Tankie" because of his short sturdy legs, brawny body, and assertive expression.

On a summer day in 1975, one month after Kent and I had purchased the land with Ken and Wendy, the four of us planted the first garden during a weekend visit.

Wendy stands next to me, her sleeveless tank top rolled up to bra level to expose her model-thin midriff to the noon sun. She is tall, slim, and glamorous, with red hair and a creamy complexion. Her hair is wrapped up in a kerchief, sunglasses perched on top. She is smart, well read, and down to earth, with a hearty guffaw of a laugh and a wicked sense of humor. She loves coffee and cigarettes. We sit in her log cabin drinking coffee at the wooden table beside the picture window that over-looks the larger of the two vegetable gardens. We gripe about how much we despise our wringer washing machines, how fast we think our husbands would run out and buy automatic washers if *they* were the friggin' ones who did the laundry. She jokes about life's amusing little moments, such as when her husband rolled out of bed early that chilly morning, swaggered stark naked to the woodstove, and squatted sleepily in front of

it to load a few logs into the fire. Stealthily the cat tiptoed over from behind and lunged skillfully at his family jewels, batting them back and
forth in a quick *one-two* before Ken leaped to his feet, screaming, "What
the F—!" We laugh about driving toward Unity one day and spotting
neighbor children Jenny and Timmy stomping and crying on the grassy
shoulder by the side of the road. Apparently our friend Judy, their mother,
had squealed the truck over and ordered them out, actually making good
on that universal maternal threat. A few moments later we met Judy herself driving serenely toward us in the other lane, a wide Cheshire cat of a
smile planted on her face, her shoulders relaxed against the front seat, all
from having spent the past ten minutes *alone* while she completed her er-
rand at the Troy General Store, free from bickering children.

Next to Wendy stands Ken, her husband, a moody vegetarian who
smokes cigarillos. He is shirtless, his white cotton garden hat casting a
dark shadow over his head and shoulders, a wry twist of a smile visible
above the beard he has grown out since quitting that albatross of a job
in New Jersey and moving onto the land. In his right hand he holds a
short board for tapping stakes into the ground around the garden; his
left hand rests upon the head of his and Wendy's six-year-old daughter,
who grins, squinting into the sun. I remember marveling in those days
at how easy one girl child seemed to be, compared to the two little boys
I had. Jennifer could lie quietly on the floor and color in front of the
woodstove while my wild sons continually rolled around in a cloud of
dust, punching, biting, pulling each other's hair.

Kent has just run back into the scene and posed, microseconds before the automatic timer of the camera has clicked. He stands on the far
right, unfazed, a strong, bearded personality with a deep deejay voice
and a gift of gab, quick with the repartee. He wears a beige work shirt,
bell bottoms, and a National Guard camouflage hat left over from his
six years in the Guard. His left arm is draped around our three-and-a-
half-year-old son Derek, a skinny waif with blond curls. The photo was
snapped on one of our weekend visits a month after we had purchased
the land in May 1975, seven months before Kent and I and the boys
moved there permanently in December that year.

That winter, when we finally moved to Troy after all those frustrating months of waiting, I felt jubilant, like a kid on the first day of school vacation, with the vacation stretching endlessly into the future. No longer did I have to report to the office daily to write formulaic stories for the newspaper. Each morning as I awoke in the chilly air, I lay on the mattress, huddled under quilts, as first light materialized in the skylight above us. I listened to the sounds outside of tree branches creaking under the weight of accumulated snow, the hum of the wind gliding through the thick woods, a distant dog barking. I felt peaceful and so thoroughly relieved that from this point on I could just be *me*, undefined by society's spurious rankings, free of the yoke of a career title to authenticate my worth.

On a December afternoon blanketed with a cozy grey sky, I decided to take Derek and Shawn for a walk in the woods. "Why don't we explore the land?" I suggested, as I pulled on their snowsuits, boots, and mittens. The metallic sky peeked through the awning of tall trees surrounding the cabin. We walked through the snow toward a wide cleared slope behind the house where Kent had harvested all the trees he'd used to build the log cabin the preceding summer, cutting them and hauling them up the hill on a chain with the help of a borrowed pony. The swath of his work had left an open, stump-filled passage through the woods to the bottom of the valley. We trekked down easily as the boys took fast little red-booted footsteps past brush, stumps, and disintegrating trees lying sideways in the snow, their branches sticking crookedly up. The brook at the bottom of the valley was covered with a layer of ice that barely muted the sound of the water rushing furiously beneath it.

"Be careful boys," I said, holding both their hands, "don't step on the . . ."—and before the words were even out of my mouth, Derek had broken my grip and had kneeled down on the bank, leaning on the ice with one hand to get a closer look at the water bubbling under the thin cover. As the ice snapped and broke, he plunged face first into the shallow brook. I grabbed his arm and pulled him out, but his face, head, chest, and arms were soaked.

The silent winter woods resounded with Derek's screams.

"Come on, boys, we've got to go *right* home."

Having read Jack London, I knew the problems caused by wet body parts in cold weather. I turned around and faced the steep white path we had so easily descended to get here. In retrospect, the metaphorical possibilities were endless, but at the time all I could think of was getting Derek home fast before he got hypothermia.

How would I ascend that path quickly with two slippery, snow-suited, thirty-pound Weebles? I tried to lift Derek, but his snowsuit, saturated with water, had doubled in weight. I couldn't carry him, drag Shawn (who by now had started to cry out of sympathy), and climb uphill at the same time. Being only two and four years old, they could only take small footsteps. "C'mon, c'mon," I said, pushing and pulling and tugging them. The ascent up the slope was protracted, to say the least. My heart was racing by the time we reached the crest. By now the children had stopped crying out of sheer exhaustion. Now, on more level ground, I hurried them along the yard to the cabin. Inside, stripping off their snowsuits, boots, and wet clothes, I brought them close to the woodstove to warm up, and wrapped them both in a comforter. Wow, I thought. This was just like I'd pictured it—the mother snuggled up with her children in front of the fire on a cold day, instead of rushing irritably to pick them up at the baby-sitter on the way home from work.

Soon after we settled on the land, the hip young people in our area began to invite us to their potluck dinners. Ron and Eileen Reed's weathered farmhouse on the corner of Route 202 and Myrick Road was a favorite location for bearded men and breast-feeding women to convene on Saturday nights. Dressed in overalls, flannel shirts, and granny dresses, we crowded into Ron and Eileen's toasty kitchen, which smelled comfortingly of wood smoke and simmering foods. We heaped our paper plates with baked beans, salads, sprouts, and home baked bread, and spread out into the living room, eating with plates on our laps. In the glow of the lamps' light, we drank beer or cider, passed

Derek and Shawn enjoyed their early years on the homestead.

around a joint, and later danced or sang arm-in-arm around the piano. One night, as Kent and I left the Reeds, the full moon shone radiantly, illuminating the snowy landscape into daylight, and I thought to myself, "It doesn't get much better than this!"

About a month after we moved to Maine, the editor of the newspaper I'd written for in Massachusetts asked if I'd like to freelance some articles back to the paper about our lives in the boonies. I began to write regularly for him.

In the spring our homestead community expanded as another couple from New Jersey bought in with us. Rista and Cami Salaranto, long-time friends of Ken and Wendy, had been yearning to break out of the city and move to the land with their two-year-old daughter. In addition, Bruce Lemire, a high school crony of Kent's, had recently been laid off from a promising career in a corporate lab in New Hampshire, so we leased him a portion of our land where he built a small house. It was gratifying to have additional friends on our land as well as a growing community of neighbors in the Troy area.

Learning Manual Skills

As a community, we did practical tasks together.

I remember participating in several wall-raisings. The following fall after we had moved to Maine, Ginny, a smiling woman with curly brown hair, spread the word that a wall-raising would be held at her site at one o'clock Saturday, followed by a spaghetti dinner.

"Don't worry," explained Bruce, who had helped Ginny build the house frame, "it's not dangerous if you don't drink *too* much beer before the raising."

The sun sparkled through the tall trees where Ginny's foundation sat in the naked patch of cleared woods, the smell of fresh lumber sweetening the air. New floorboards, still untrammeled by manure-smeared Bean boots, rested across the foundation, and twenty-foot wall frames made of two-by-sixes lay on the floorboards. Wood chips, tools, and nails were scattered across the ground. By one o'clock, ten or twelve friends had arrived. They milled around the foundation, joking about sudden death by wall-crushings, and discussed strategy while chugging cans of beer from the cooler.

Bruce told me to stand at one of the outer perimeters of the foundation. As the group on the other side pushed the wall up from the ground, I was to tug on one of the slack ropes attached to the wall frame, pulling the wall toward me. Empty beer cans flew into the garbage bag as everyone moved into assigned positions. A row of men and women poised themselves to lift the wall frame off the floor and push it upward, while those of us on the outside prepared to pull the ropes. Someone joked that I should get ready to sprint fast, in case the wall tilted too far forward and crashed down on me, but finally the woods fell silent as everyone grew as quiet as a church congregation before a prayer.

"One—two—three—GO!" yelled Kent, breaking the silence.

Wood creaked like nails on a blackboard. Voices groaned. Slowly the wall frame ascended from the floorboards. Leaning onto the ground, I yanked on the rope, my palms burning like fire, as the wall frame rose high and strong, among curses and yells. Sweat dripped and arms trembled as the wall at last stood upright. In just a few moments it was all over. War whoops mingled with hammering sounds as the walls were pounded into place. This was the first time in my life I had ever helped accomplish anything so physical and labor-intensive. I had been a lifelong reader, writer, and thinker but had never been attracted to tools or carpentry.

Many back-to-the-land people whom I interviewed remarked about the joy of discovering and developing their latent skills in construction, mechanics, and repair during their early years on the land. When John Matz, now the owner of Sunflower Glass Studio, bought his land in Ohio, he had been a program director for a Jewish youth organization for ten years and had little experience with manual skills. In the area of carpentry, he says, he was "nonfunctional."

"My father was always a tinkerer and a builder. Me, I had built a set of shelves. So I said, 'Well, *shit*, I could build a house!'"

So John went to work and methodically built a scale model of his future house out of balsa wood. "I must have put $150 or $200 just into balsam wood," he says. "I cut it with all these little ribs. I mean, it was bizarro."

When it came time to build the actual house, John was terrified. He couldn't commit to pounding in a single nail. He put telephone poles in the ground for posts. Ready to build a platform on top, he set the boards across on top of the nails.

"I was going to build the whole house without nailing anything. Just to make sure everything fit."

Other back-to-the-land people in his area were helping one another build their homes, so a friend of John's arrived to observe his progress. He walked up to John's house and, seeing the un-nailed wood, said, "What *is* this?"

John replied, "I want to make sure everything's level."

His friend said, "Give me a nail!" And he pounded the first nail in. John recalls, "I almost hyperventilated."

His friend commented, "Screw it. If it's screwed up, no big deal. You'll fix it later."

John and his friend plunged into building, correcting any mistakes as they went. After the house was finished, John's sixty-four-year-old father came to help him put the roof on. John had all the boards but didn't have roofing material yet, so he drove into Lanchester to get it. Before leaving, he said, "Why don't you stay here, Dad, and relax this morning."

"Okay," said his father.

When John returned with the materials, his father had put half the roof on.

"It had taken me three weeks to do what this old man did in a few hours," he says. "Me, I would have gone for perfection once again. It took me about a year to get up on the roof and get windows in." Building his house was just the beginning. Now, thirty years later, John can hammer circles around any novice.

Community Fellowship

In Maine, inspiration for successful rural living was all around us. On a chilly fall day in 1976 we attended the first Maine Organic Farmers and Gardeners Association's agricultural fair, called the Common Ground Country Fair. Attendance on the first day was recorded at six thousand people, with total weekend attendance recorded at between eight and ten thousand. When we arrived early at the fairgrounds on the first day, exhibitors were unloading trucks and setting up booths. Fair personnel in bright red "Common Ground Country Fair" T-shirts offered help and answered questions. Crafts booths, service and social-action booths, displays, films, speakers, demonstrations, and exhibitions filled the grounds, all supporting alternative living in the country.

The smell of cooking food warmed the nippy air. Fried bananas filled with cinnamon and honey mingled with the scent of salt and melted butter from the red popcorn wagon. Next to a booth of Chinese food was The Hungry Hunza, which made sprout, cheese, tomato, cucumber, onion, and pepper sandwiches on whole wheat or oat bread. Pinch of Love sold tacos, pizza, sugarless desserts, and cider. Kristina's Bakery was a dessert heaven. All day, lines of hungry people stood before the food booths.

A rustically attired clown wearing a red shirt, blue overalls, and a blue hat rode a unicycle across the grounds, with a gaggle of laughing children running behind. Two magicians in black suits sold helium balloons.

The exhibition hall displayed prize-winning vegetables. Blue ribbons lay beside a hefty tomato with its shiny skin stretched tight across the juicy inner pulp, and beside a colossal pumpkin and a hearty bronze-colored potato. I loved the idea of being able to produce superior vegetables that others raved over. But had I had any insight at the time, I would have realized that during the past growing season I had devoted precious little time to our garden. I may have relished the *thought* of producing prize-winning vegetables, but I had never really gone out of my way to work in the garden, to pluck weeds in the hot sun, spread chicken manure, or see to the dozen other duties involved with gardening. If Kent asked me to do a specific task, I might do it as a response, but I never took the initiative in trying to cultivate a bountiful harvest.

The famous homesteading couple Helen and Scott Nearing were at the fair to speak. The authors of *Living the Good Life* had seduced many a homesteader into trying an alternative lifestyle. They were also on the lecture circuit and seldom failed to appear at Maine's agriculturally related events.

Helen Nearing's colorful crafts display lured me over. I examined her stack of hand-knit products and tried on an attractive hat. Helen told me it looked really nice on me, so I bought it. It was a beautiful hat. But it also carried the significance of having been made by the woman known as the mother of the homesteading movement. When people asked me where I had gotten that hat, I could namedrop, "From Helen Nearing." Speaking familiarly about the Nearings was a subtle form of a status symbol among the rural counterculture.

As the day moved on, I watched a woman named Kathleen Hudson spin wool. She sat at her spinning wheel, surrounded by a display of natural-colored yarns, all dyed with plant dyes. "Would any of you like some wool?" she asked, holding up a soft mound of white fleece.

I held the soft ball and tried to stretch it into yarn. To spin a few ounces of wool took her three hours, she said. Then she spent additional time dyeing it. I admired her having the time and particularly the serenity to spin out those ounces of wool patiently, hour after hour. I wondered if she had children.

As she spun, Paul Birdsall worked his draft horses in the horse ring while Walter Litten analyzed toadstools. On the open green, Rob Johnston, the owner of Johnny's Selected Seeds, was swinging a grain cradle, demonstrating old-time harvesting methods. A blacksmith pounded metal into shape, and a dowser demonstrated the technique of locating water with a "magic wand."

Animals inhabited a row of stalls outside the exhibition hall, which smelled faintly of hay and manure.

"Look at that lamb!" someone said fondly. "They say it was born just this morning." In the straw near its mother shivered a tiny black lamb. Goats, beefalo, and horses occupied other stalls. In the horse show ring outside, Susan Stump was poised to stage a demonstration of "The Donkey as a Useful Homestead Pet." I leaned against the fence and watched three people try to coax the stubborn donkey into the ring. The animal balked and refused, but finally permitted its owner to lead it slowly around the ring. Then Susan Stump launched into her talk praising the donkey as a useful homestead animal that could haul water, vegetables, and even children.

Four or five men entered the Fiddler's Contest, each contestant climbing onto the stage and playing the fiddle with gusto. While these fiddlers sawed away at the front of the fairgrounds, the woodsmen contestants sawed away more literally at the back. Jeff Cox of *Organic Gardening and Farming Magazine* lectured on the United States' need for a third party to serve small farmers while Helen and Scott Nearing lectured on "Living the Good Life" to loud applause.

Many booths displayed alternative technologies. The "New Waterless Toilet, self-contained, non-polluting, odor-free" was a true innova-

In 1976, Kent and I visited Scott and Helen Nearing, authors of *Living the Good Life*, a book that inspired many people nationwide to go back to the land.

tion at that time, though its descendant today has been through several evolutions and is in more widespread use. This earlier model, a true novelty then, ran on electricity, had to be emptied only once a year, and used no chemicals. There was even a newsletter available entitled *The Compost Toilet News*, which served as "a clearinghouse" for information and ideas about brands of composting toilets. Back-to-the-land homesteaders were excited at the prospect of upgrading from a stinky outhouse to this new alternative.

❦ One of the highlights of our first year in Maine was our personal visit with Helen and Scott Nearing, bellwethers of the homesteading movement, at Forest Farm, Harborside, Maine, on Penobscot Bay. Sooner or later every disciple of the back-to-the-land movement who lived within driving distance made this pilgrimage. After writing the Nearings a note requesting a visit, Kent and I had been delighted to receive a handwritten response inviting us to come the following Sunday. We drove up north, around the edge of the peninsula near Bucksport, and back down again toward Harborside, arriving at Forest Farm and parking our Volkswagen at the bottom of their dirt driveway. A sign at the entrance declared, "Help us live the good life / Visitors 3–5 / or by appointment." The Nearings' farmhouse, adjacent to yellow fields and thick woods, commanded a beautiful view of the choppy ocean, from which the wind was blowing fiercely that day. Helen Nearing greeted us at the door.

"We followed the famous Helen Nearing into her very simple, wood-heated kitchen," I later wrote, "where herbs and vegetables hung drying from an overhead beam. Although Helen, testing the stove top for temperature and then sitting down upon it, was immediately as warm and homespun as an old friend, I just couldn't help but feel somewhat humble in [her] presence."

They were very nice people, and I returned home more determined than ever to learn how to be a good homesteader. I admired their well-oiled machine of a homestead generated by a rigorous self-discipline—that I would later find out I simply did not have.

❦ Memories of many random, cherished moments come to mind when I remember the years on the homestead. One chilly morning, when the first layer of white crystals covered the ground, I stepped out of the cabin in my nightgown, jacket, and Bean boots to pick up a few logs for the woodstove. Then I saw our calico cat, Griselda, her swollen stomach deflated, prancing up the porch steps. She'd been hugely pregnant, but now—! As she purred and rubbed against my leg, I heard high-pitched mews. I crunched down the steps and followed the sound across the yard. It originated in the tangled pile of logs that had been tossed haphazardly at the edge of the yard. I yelled to the boys, who scrambled out the door.

"Guys! I think Griselda's had her kittens in the log pile!" I yelled excitedly.

Derek, a take-charge kind of kid, scaled carefully up the mountain of crisscrossed logs, lay flat across the top, and thrust his skinny arm down the narrow hole in the middle. He groped around and extracted a damp, newborn kitten. Its eyes were sealed, and its mouth was opening and closing with indignant mews. "Look, a grey one!" cried Shawn, jumping up and down with an ear-to-ear grin.

Derek handed the first kitten to me. Soft and warm, it smelled of pine. I held the tiny thing against my chest while Derek reached into the woodpile again. He pulled out another, this time a calico. When we finished, I cradled five wiggling kittens in my arms. We carried them inside, with Griselda following, and found a cardboard box in Kent's storage room. Lining it with towels, we placed it near the wood stove and arranged the kittens in it. Griselda climbed in, paws mixing, circled once or twice, and lay down with the kittens, purring. I put some logs into the woodstove and stoked the fire. It was a heartwarming start for a leafless November day.

❧ Just as I can still light up with the good memories of the days on the land, the people I interviewed for this book loved talking about it, regardless of how long they stayed. Many saw their experience as totally positive.

Farming in Upstate New York

Valerie Summer belonged to a group of women who convened at every full moon during the seasonable months. Outside on the land, under the glow of the moon, they would light a fire and hold a full moon ceremony. On May Day they dressed up and held a big celebration. "I remember driving a whole hay wagon full of women out there," she says. Valerie is one of those back-to-the-landers whose experience was overwhelmingly positive, which is why she stayed for twenty-one years, first at Birdsfoot Commune, then on a farm.

Born and raised in New Jersey, she had married young to escape that area, she says, but by the time she and her husband had settled on a thirty-six-acre "farmette" in New York a year later, the marriage had dissolved. When a friend told Valerie that one of the cabins at nearby

Birdsfoot Commune was empty and that she ought to move in there, she did, in 1975, residing in a tiny nine-by-twelve-foot house, warmed by wood, lit by kerosene, perfect for one person. The group of seven adults came together for meals in the main house, a ten-minute walk from Valerie's cabin.

Valerie enjoyed using the farm machinery and spent "many happy long hours" driving the tractor through the fields. She saw beauty in the patterns made by the plow's disk. Haying was equally fun for her. "I really loved haying so much," she said. "As hard work as it was, and as much pain as it was for the machinery to break down, it was such a wonderful way to spend a long hot summer day—driving the tractor and watching the bales come out at the end of the baler. It was really good. I miss it. I miss spending a day in the field like that in the summer time."

She also worked in the barn milking the cows, and enjoyed it so much that a year after moving to Birdsfoot she enrolled in the local technical college to take animal husbandry courses. In 1979, with two other members of the commune, she started a yogurt business which continued until 1996. At first they sold yogurt to the nearby co-op and health-food store, and later to the colleges in the area. Over the years the business expanded. A distributor picked it up and conveyed it to markets in Syracuse and Rochester.

In the early years she doesn't remember ever worrying about money. "It astonishes me how little money we lived on," she says. "I worked in the barn, and initially all we did was sell some milk to the neighbors. Another of the members was always growing vegetables, so we had a vegetable stand, but how much money could that have ever brought in? It never felt like we were doing without, but you would never, for instance, buy a tomato in winter. Or lettuce. You just ate what was there. We always had plenty to eat. I think I was the only vegetarian there. Somebody would slaughter a steer or a pig every so often, and the meat would be in the freezer, though I guess I just kind of ignored it. We just really didn't use much money."

By far the highlight of those happy years was the home birth of her daughter in 1979. "It never crossed my mind to go to a hospital," says Valerie, who had witnessed another woman's remarkable home birth two years earlier. Valerie's labor started early in the morning, and as the day progressed, twelve or fifteen people, including children, gathered in the room.

"It was a great, easy labor," she says. "One friend sat in the corner, and when he wasn't photographing, he was strumming the dulcimer. My daughter was born at five in the afternoon, so it was really great, and I felt very much, in those days, that my whole life was so intertwined with everybody else's that it seemed perfect to do that. I was very, very happy with how my birth went. It was a really good decision."

Raising a child in a communal environment was delightful too, Valerie recalls. "It was so easy! Because there were two other mothers there who had given birth to their children on the commune, it was a completely supportive environment. They were there, and after about two months, I could start going back to the barn and leave her with either her father, who was there at the time, or with one of the other women. Oh my God, I got so much help. For me it was the perfect situation."

In the early eighties Valerie left Birdsfoot and moved to nearby Meadowsweet Farm, where she lived for fifteen years. She makes it a point to say that she is not trying to give the impression that her years on the commune and farm were absolutely perfect every second. The experience was embroidered with frigid winters, stalled vehicles, sick cows, and the usual farming problems. But for her the joys far outweighed the difficulties.

"I don't know why I was blessed with that general sense of well-being," she says.

In 1996 Valerie left Meadowsweet Farm and moved into town because of a decision about a relationship. She now works as a massage therapist. She calls it "a huge difficult decision and a huge loss for me to be leaving the farm. I really really felt the loss of the land very deeply. I was connected to the land. I miss that."

Making Pottery in Oregon

The short guy in their group built the house, which is why Gordy Stewart, who is tall, remembers "many things to hit your head on." Gordy was in his early twenties when he left southern California to join his group of friends in cool, mountainous southern Oregon.

"We were all craftspeople," he says. "I was a potter, and the others were jewelers and woodworkers. It was a lot more about lifestyle and independence than it was about anything else." The short guy worked at a mill too, so he dragged mill ends back to the property and transformed them into four-by-fours, building the entire house with them. Another construction-related discovery Gordy made that first winter in Oregon was that the house, shadowed by the mountains, got no sun for three months.

"It was a classic city-kid thing. We grew up in the flatlands in southern California. We had no idea," he says.

They built a dam and trickle irrigated from it. They also did "hippie logging type things. I can lay claim that I cut the cedar trees, dragged them to a friend's mill, and then built my own hot tub out of them."

Gordy's life was serene and unstressed. He earned his living selling his pottery at crafts fairs. He and his group attended the Eugene Saturday market regularly, and also trekked up and down the West Coast to crafts fairs.

"The whole time we were just scraping by," he says. "Which was fine. If you could make it to the Christmas season, when you got most of your income, then you had some money left over to get through the winter. That was the seventies."

Gordy laughs as he recalls the one occasion when everyone else left the land for two weeks and he was suddenly alone on the property.

"There were multiple sets of chickens, multiple sets of rabbits, and it took me, like, *six to eight hours* to take care of everything, right?" he chuckles. "Plus milk the goats twice a day. I went from one thing to another. But I remember after the shock of it, I adjusted to the pace, and I was plenty happy just wandering around taking care of one thing after another.

"The second week a giant rainstorm rolled in. We had the dam half built, but the culvert wasn't stuck in it. I had to go up there for an afternoon by myself, with the CAT, and get this giant culvert stuck in the dirt with mud around it. But then I became quite happy out there by myself. I think that was my favorite two weeks. Then everybody came back," he concludes with a laugh.

After two and a half years on the land, Gordy wanted to begin wholesaling his pottery to stores, so he moved to Eugene to continue with pottery and go back to school. "I could make some money doing that. But when the eighties recession hit, it turned the whole market off. So I decided I would become a machinist. I wasn't doing that very long when a friend was starting a business and needed some help. The next thing I knew, I was wearing a tie and a shirt and driving around in a shiny car."

He returned to California, where he still lives.

He reflects, "Back in Oregon, we were young, our demands were very low, so we had a lot of latitude. If you could make a few bucks, you could buy something with it. It was great. I could go to the Saturday market and sell a hundred dollars' worth of pottery and come home a hero. All I needed was a little bit of food, something to smoke, and an interesting *and* interested woman. My thoughts never really went any further than that. It was really easy to be happy. Back then, my son wasn't asking me to fly him to San Francisco to spend four days. Oh yeah, sure, there goes two grand." Today Gordy runs a small software company, does contracting work, and is building his own product to sell.

Just Getting By in Atlanta

Originally from Miami, Janice Walker dropped out of the University of Georgia in 1970 to join the Athens branch of the Atlanta-area commune.

"We called ourselves 'the Athens family,' and we had to explain to people that it was not the Manson family. We had houses in Athens, in

Atlanta, and a working farm out in the country, and we could just go from one to the other. Many of the people who were in the commune changed nightly. But we would share the work. My husband and I visited the farm, though we didn't actually live there. We'd go out there and work sometimes, because if you wanted to eat, you helped."

Time flowed by in a dreamlike state of laughter, music, and friendship. "There was always music," she remembers, "in the commune, walking down Peachtree Street, in Piedmont Park, wherever. Our music was always playing, it was always there, piping out of the cars driving by or from stores or bands. It was like a movie soundtrack to your life."

Shortly after joining the Athens family, Janice had the ultimate hippie wedding, which the local television station broadcast on the six o'clock news. They married in a vacant lot on the corner of Tenth and Peachtree, with the Reverend Mother David Durette, one of the first openly gay ministers, officiating. Barefoot, Janice wore embroidered jeans and a T-shirt while her husband wore a leather loincloth and moccasins. Although the marriage didn't last, it was a wedding to remember.

At that point in her life, the last thought on her mind was building a career. "We didn't want to—it was selling out, you know? What kind of society were we contributing to in those jobs? When you had to dress the way they wanted you to dress, and you didn't have a say over the time and how you spent time? Besides, a real job wasn't needed. All you needed was a place to live, something to cover your body, food to eat, and friends. And you didn't need to work for that."

Occasionally, for pocket money, she sold *The Great Speckled Bird*, an underground Atlanta newspaper, or panhandled from tourists who thought it such a novelty to see a real hippie up close. "We knew we were a show," says Janice. "All of the straight people and rednecks would drive up and down Peachtree Street very slowly, especially weekends, to gawk at the hippies." Panhandling was so easy, she continues, demonstrating with a seductive, panhandling smile, a demure voice, and a wink: "Spare change?" she asks. "I was cute, you know. I used to do real well. Be a girl and be cute."

Falling in Love in New Mexico

Naked, her breast milk spurting, Pam Read caught the eye of Findley Hanna, who had been lying in his tepee watching her make mud bricks outside. They were living at Morningstar Commune in New Mexico.

He looked out at her, transfixed. Then he stripped off all his clothes and came out of the tepee with only his hat on.

"I was still nursing Psyche, and I was standing there, naked as a jay-bird, spurting milk like the Mother Goddess," Pam remembers. "Findley had this white Irish skin, with freckles, and he looked naked. The rest of us were nude, right? I mean, we're as brown as berries, and we're nude, but he looked naked. He looked like something you'd see when you pushed over a rock. That was our first meeting. He'd never even noticed me before! He wouldn't give me the time of day. So he came out, and he was helping us. Nobody knew at the time, and I found this later, but it was just because of me."

He "paid her court," she says, and when the dust settled eight months later, they were a couple.

Was Findley's wife upset? No, actually she was relieved, says Pam, and she went off to Mexico with another guy, leaving their four children behind. Pam had her own two children. "So Findley and I had six kids in a tepee for about two months."

Some couples' romance might have been tempered by several months in a tepee with six children, but not Pam's and Findley's. They're still married today, thirty-four years later, and have grandchildren. Thinking back on their early days with the children at Morningstar, Pam recalls that it was not all that difficult.

"The kids were older; actually, one of them was Psyche's age, and they were used to the whole thing. It's a little easier to deal with kids when you're not out around streets and cars. So we did okay. Then Findley's wife came back from Mexico and took the kids back. When she did, I kind of missed them."

Pam remembers that time as "my halcyon days" and still keeps in close touch with her friends from Morningstar. She is a cultural creative who reads and writes prolifically.

Dairy Farming in Wisconsin

In 1972 Michael Doyle moved to a former dairy farm in west central Wisconsin. In exchange for doing chores and feeding the cattle, he lived on the farm rent-free. He describes it as "a splendid place," with a four-bedroom frame house that was heated with wood, and a barn that the farmer used as a feedlot for beef cattle. Living rent-free allowed him to reach his goal of simplifying to an income of $1,500 a year, which he earned doing odd jobs as a hired man on area dairy farms.

Michael enjoyed the company of the local farmers and was fascinated by their family histories. As the farmers lent him history books about the area, they were amused that this young man with hair down to his waist was so interested in their history. Michael loved the farmers' stories so much that he began to tape-record interviews and take extensive notes. He wrote articles that were published in the local alternative papers, and began to gain a reputation as "the hippie historian."

In 1975 Michael joined a group of four couples who bought Yaeger Valley Community Farm in Waumadee, Wisconsin. Everyone contributed a share of money for the 20 percent down payment. "We bought our 180 acres of land for $39,000, which a neighboring farmer thought was exorbitant," he says, "but was really a very fair price."

A 1920s farmhouse with four bedrooms still stood on the property. The first year they all lived in the farmhouse together, except for one couple who stayed in the renovated milk house attached to the dairy barn.

Michael describes Waumadee as beautiful, rugged country in the Driftless area, a region bypassed by glaciers during the last Ice Age, forming a plain that has been carved up into *coulees*, or shallow ravines. The slopes are excellent for raising dairy cattle, and the topsoil in the valley floors, sometimes up to three feet deep, has been made extremely fertile by deposits of a wind-borne silt called loess.

The other men worked out as carpenters and ran one of the first chimney-sweep businesses in the area. Four of the women, inspired by Ina Mae Gaskin at The Farm in Tennessee, became lay midwives. The group rented out their pasture and raised a cash crop of sweet sorghum. They conceived of themselves as a spiritual community which sought truth through a variety of religious traditions, including Zen, Yoga, Sufi, and Native American practices. Michael practiced Bakti Yoga and for seven years fasted every Wednesday. The only single member until 1980, he continued to work at the food co-op. He was happy with the work and even happier that he could walk to it every day.

Skinny Dipping in the Eel River

When her parents came to visit and saw the dwelling she was living in, they held each other and cried. Cynthia Frost laughs at the memory. "It was hysterical," she says. "But I loved our way of life; I was just into it so much. I just loved it. I was happy."

In 1971 she and her partner, Ted, had moved to the Rio Dell/ Scotia area of California, about 250 miles north of San Francisco, and were living for $5 a month near the Eel River. The landscape had big rolling hills where other homesteaders were raising sheep; the view made Cynthia feel as though she was in Scotland.

"The Eel River was shallow all the way across," says Cynthia. "So everybody would come to our place. We'd all take off our clothes and go swimming in the river. It was wonderful."

Ted had constructed their first home himself by removing the camper top from his truck and building a room underneath. On one of the nearby hills was a big spigot of clean water, so Cynthia and Ted would carry their five-gallon milk containers there and fill them up for drinking water.

Inside the house they used a wood-burning trash burner for cooking. Later they replaced it with a three-burner gas stove plate and eventually graduated to a gas oven. They used kerosene lamps, which also helped warm the place with the heat they generated. A year later they bought a small house trailer to replace the first home.

Cynthia planted her first garden and successfully grew an abundance of vegetables. She was in charge of their tiny income. Ted received the GI Bill because they were both taking courses at the local community college; in addition they worked occasionally at a tree-planting job. By purchasing flour, brown rice, and soybeans in twenty-five-pound sacks, and carefully cooking all their meals, Cynthia fed them on a minimal amount of money. Their biggest expense was kerosene. Their living arrangement was rustic by most standards, but when they went tree-planting, which they occasionally did as a source of income, they camped even more seriously.

She remembers telling a friend who was coming to visit on a certain date, "Well you can't come then, because we're going camping." When the friend did arrive, she laughed like crazy and said, "And you're going *camping?* That's what you're doing now!"

Cynthia and Ted lived about a mile and a half away from their friends Steve and Sunshine. Together, using one of their old chicken houses, the four of them built a two-level sauna. They placed a woodstove in it and constructed a pipe the length of the room. In the winter they would fill the big five-gallon plastic buckets with water, carry them to the sauna, and enjoy a steam bath.

"You just started throwing the water on the stove and on the pipe to get it real hot and steamy in there," recalls Cynthia. "It was just wonderful. We loved it. If we went out on a Friday night and drank a lot of beers, we could have a sauna afterward. You'd come out an hour later, and you weren't even drunk any more."

Sometimes they would treat themselves to a shower in a big, ancient bathhouse on the coast, which was once used for people coming in on boats from Scandinavia, or sometimes they would shower at Steve and Sunshine's house.

Cynthia particularly remembers Delia, her mixed-breed goat who had one big and one tiny teat, and ears that hung down.

"But she was a character, let me tell you," says Cynthia. "The idea was to get her pregnant and then be able to have milk, but we were never able to get her pregnant. We had spool tables out in the yard, and she'd get up on one of the spool tables and dance. When we sometimes walked over to Steve and Sunshine's house to use the sauna, we would

Cynthia Frost loved cooking on the wood-burning trash burner in the one-room house constructed by her boyfriend beneath their truck's camper top.

try to sneak away so Delia didn't see us, because if she saw us leaving she would bleat loudly. Sometimes she wouldn't see us until we were quite a ways away, and then she would start, making all these goat noises. She wanted to go with us. Sometimes we'd all go together, and it would be so funny—Ted and I, and Delia, and the dog Scout, and two cats all walking down the road together."

Today Cynthia is a university librarian. She maintains an impressive vegetable garden in her backyard and still enjoys cooking.

Perfect Climate All Year Round

Rob Morningstar was seventeen when he arrived on the Kona side of Hawaii in 1971. In those days old abandoned coffee farms, teeming with fruit trees and coffee, were available free for the taking, so he and his friends settled on one in the hills and named it "God's Free Universe Commune."

The climate was perfect the year round, so they seldom wore clothes unless they hitchhiked into town. Then they wore "lava-lavas," any wraparound cloth that made them decent enough for public exposure. They subsisted on coconuts, mangoes, guavas, passion fruit (lilikoi), bananas, citrus, avocados, papayas, and macadamia nuts, which they foraged. They also caught fish at the shore. Although some people in the group occasionally had to purchase food items, Rob says he lasted for two years without using money because his needs were so minimal.

"It was as though we lived in our own garden of Eden," he remembers. "How can one not have an overall happy memory of this? It was all good."

They reconstructed a coffee drying deck on one of the old buildings and built a pavilion structure where they would sit together each evening to celebrate the sunset.

"Sunsets in Kona are world famous, and for very good reason. Nowadays the sunsets are often muted by Vog—volcanic smog generated by Puu O volcano that has been erupting ceaselessly for over twenty-five years. But back then there was no continuous eruption, and our sunsets were the kind you could see for a thousand miles. We would begin to sing Sanskrit chants like Hare Krishna and Om Namah Shivaya, and a host of others. Some would be playing guitars and others tapping finger cymbals. A few drums were always present. As the sun touched the vast horizon, some of us would start blowing these big conch and Triton trumpet shells, and this incredible sound would ring out across the hills."

Life was indeed grand. Until the toothaches began. But that's another story for later.

❦ *The farm animals we brought to Middle Earth Homestead were a source of discovery and joy. A colorful bantam rooster strutted confidently around the yard, his tail feathers fanned and sleek. He was handsome, and he knew it. He crowed at dawn every morning, his "Ur-ur-Uuurrrrr!" heralding the new day. A tired, lusterless black hen from a chicken factory got her second wind when we brought her to our homestead. Fresh air and sunshine filled her out. Her feathers began to shine, and she went broody, a phenomenon I had never seen. For twenty days she sat rigidly on her pile of eggs, her beaked face staring stonily ahead, getting up once a day to refresh herself and then returning to her state of near hypnosis. The ten chicks hatched, nine yellow and one black, and soon they were out of the nest, marching in straight-line formation behind the hen as she waddled, free-ranging around the homestead.*

We decided to raise turkeys too, and ordered eggs from a mail-order company. The eggs lay under the bright lights of an incubator we had borrowed until the day the wet chicks pecked their way out of the shells and wobbled on rubbery legs as they got their bearings. Soon the poults were outside pecking the earth; within months they had expanded into enormous birds with fanned-out plumages who marched formidably around the property in an intimidating flock, warbling loudly as they made their rounds. A small child was peering out Ken and Wendy's picture window one day when the army of stern-faced turkeys came advancing around the corner of the driveway. He let out a resounding scream of terror, his mouth a black O of fear, and burst into tears. With their size and noise, these turkeys probably looked like the creatures that inhabited the child's worst nightmares.

Ken and Wendy bought a pregnant goat, Emily, who didn't look pregnant so they thought they'd been scammed—but then she came through, delivering adorable triplets. No bigger than house cats, with buds of horns, they jumped right up from the straw and began to butt each other playfully. Emily provided milk for a while, and when she wasn't doing that she was free-ranging the homestead searching for edible items on the clotheslines. If you caught her chewing clothes you could shoo her away, but she'd stand nearby, head tilted, a smirk on her face, merrily awaiting her chance. You had to be careful. You couldn't just turn and walk away. Playful as she was, she would lower her head and charge, ramming you from behind in the rear.

We also bought two large beautiful California rabbits with soft red-brown coats. Raising rabbits was supposed to be easy and cost-efficient, requiring just two cages, straw, and feed. Rabbits ate little and required almost no care. Their meat was supposed to be tender and delicious.

Having dutifully consulted Mother Earth News on the proper methods and timing for rabbit reproduction, we built the doe a nesting box and put the buck in her cage for visits. When no litters appeared after two or three cycles, I became discouraged and told everyone we had an infertile rabbit.

But then one spring evening I visited the rabbit quarters at sunset and saw that the doe had built a nest in her box and lined it with her own down. Cautiously I reached into the nest and felt body heat and movement. I extracted one newborn rabbit and held it in my hand, marveling at how satiny its flesh felt and how unearthly the pink head looked, with the sealed eyes, the prominent nose, and the hairless flaps of ears. As I replaced it in the nest, I pulled back the fur and hay and counted eleven in the litter. "Awwww!" I thought.

My adoration rather than indifference toward a litter of animals destined to become my future dinners may have been a clear warning sign of my lack of readiness to master self-sufficiency.

CHAPTER FOUR

Getting Close to Nature and Natural Processes

"We would invite friends for a dinner of chicken and dumplings. The only stipulation was that they had to butcher the chicken. This usually worked once. They wouldn't come back again, but we'd invite some new couple the next time. And they would take care of the chicken that time."—Thomas Kidder

"Three winters spent upon an isolated farm had taken all the romance out of the back-to-nature life for a young author. The roads were either deep in mud or cut with the tracks of sleighs, so that the only place to walk was up and down in a field, along the lee side of a fence. Also, four summers had taken the romance out of agriculture as an avocation for a literary man. The cows broke into the pear orchard and stuffed themselves and died. . . ."—Upton Sinclair

"A plow had been purchased, and they set about 'breaking' prairie. But alas! they knew not how."—Albert Shaw, author of a history of the Icaria Community in Texas, which failed in 1864

🌱 *In Arkansas, at about the same time Kent and I were admiring our first litter of rabbits, Jim Carlson and his wife were also raising rabbits on* their farmstead. They had bought nine acres in the Ozarks in 1975 and moved into the small house that Jim describes as "built completely outside of any building inspector codes." The land itself was beautiful, though. A little pond shimmered behind the house, and about two-thirds of the wooded property sloped up into hills. They heated with wood, grew vegetables in their garden, and kept animals. Like many of us who had read the popular books about overpopulation and future starvation, Jim had felt mildly apprehensive about societal collapse and believed it was important to learn how to grow food and become self-sufficient. Once they arrived on the land, he plowed almost a third of an acre with a neighbor's self-propelled, walk-behind plow.

Successful as gardeners, Jim and his wife grew an abundance of crops, including potatoes, onions, cabbage, broccoli, green beans, wax beans, kidney beans, pinto beans, English peas, corn, tomatoes, bell peppers, yellow squash, acorn squash, and zucchini. In addition they raised melons, pumpkins, peanuts, and strawberries. The grapevines on the property generated a few grapes too. "We planted corn, then went back two weeks later and planted pole beans so they would climb up the corn. That was kind of neat."

"I wanted to do everything," recalls Jim. "I wanted to cultivate fruit trees and grow everything I could grow. We had a lot of success with green beans, potatoes, and corn. We canned and we froze a lot of stuff, and we put potatoes in a bin on the side of the house with a little chicken wire around it to keep the chickens away. So we did eat pretty well, I think."

For Christmas one year, Jim surprised his wife with two young horses, who grazed behind the electric fence at the back of the property. He also kept dogs, cats, ducks, chickens, and, of course, the rabbits. The chickens laid eggs while the dogs, cats, horses, and ducks enhanced the aesthetics. But the rabbits posed a greater difficulty.

Although seasoned hunters and farmers don't think twice about it, many of us who went to the land never got past our discomfort with slaughtering animals. At Middle Earth Homestead in Maine, Kent gritted his teeth, pulled out the hatchet, and butchered our rabbits, teaching me how to do it as well. Jim abhorred it as much as Kent and I did.

"I was not a vegetarian then, and I thought if I was going to eat meat, I should take responsibility for it," says Jim, who no longer eats meat of any kind. *"With our vegetables, by and large, we didn't use pesticides. So I thought, same thing with meat. We'll raise our own and they won't be mass-produced and injected with chemicals. So I did butcher rabbits. But I did not like it at all.*

"I was a terribly inefficient rabbit raiser," continues Jim, who is now a college professor in Georgia, *"because what you're supposed to do is raise those little rabbits for about eight weeks just to fatten them up, and then kill them. Meanwhile you're constantly breeding new crops of rabbits. Well, I would put off the slaughtering—and put it off and put it off. I put more feed into those rabbits than we would ever get back out of them. We finally did sell them."*

🌱 More than any other generation before, those of us who went to the land in the 1960s and '70s had been sealed off from prolonged exposure to the natural world. Before World War II, 30 percent of Americans still lived on farms, but between 1930 and 1954, 1.8 million farms disappeared, and by the 1960s, when most of us were growing up, postwar prosperity and the expansion of the consumer culture had lured many middle-class American families to the suburbs, where their lives were eased considerably by new technologies and conveniences.

So we grew up longing for the land. But far from being original, the back-to-the-land philosophy was a reincarnation of several long-standing American traditions—the idealization of nature and the valorization of agriculture and manual labor, which have persisted as threads of the cultural consciousness since the founding of the nation. Americans began to mourn the loss of the natural landscape, of farmers, and of the old ways almost from the beginning of their decline in the nineteenth century.

The American mythology of nature as an edifying and benevolent force originated in colonial times. When the first English colonists arrived in the New World, they were thrown into an immediate relationship with the natural world such as they had never experienced before in civilized England. They had no choice but to be "scrutinizing events in Nature and finding them to be unquestionably . . . meaningful." To the Puritans, Nature was credited with being a teacher "sent by God for man's profit and instruction. . . . Natural processes were his intimate and intimately known mentors." Later, during the American Romantic literary movement of the nineteenth century, Emerson also "insisted that Nature is man's benefactor" and that "in the woods we become one with God." This was reinforced by Thoreau's *Walden*, a "classic text of self-discovery through Nature." The arcadian movement of the late nineteenth and early twentieth centuries reflected Americans' continued national longing for nature, which was disappearing faster than ever as the United States became increasingly urbanized and industrialized. As "the rattle of iron wheels on cobblestone streets or soft-coal smog" got on people's nerves, more middle-class people "longed for contact with the natural world," writes Peter J. Schmidt in *Back to Nature*. The result was a surge of periodicals and magazines that celebrated country life. Like many movements before us, back-to-the-land people yearned for a newfound intimacy with nature that had been blocked by the intrusion of industrialization.

Beyond the pull of nature, farmers, craftsmen, and manual laborers have been held in high esteem in American mythology, juxtaposed as romantic figures against the evil forces of progress and industry. In early America the agrarian myth was advanced by Thomas Jefferson, who believed that "America's virtue" depended upon farming as "the only true form of wealth." Farms fostered self-sufficiency and resourcefulness, and therefore "nourished the personality type needed in a democratic political system." Followers of that school of thought feared that the presence of manufacturing might usurp the honored status held by farmers, craftsmen, and skilled laborers. As soon as industry began to make inroads on the agriculturally based U.S. economy in the late eighteenth century, Americans struggled with the moral ramifications. They had seen how the Industrial Revolution in England had turned farmers into a badly exploited underclass of unskilled factory workers. Despite the misgivings of skeptics, the Industrial Age in America took off to meet the demands of a growing and expanding population. By the end of the nineteenth century the country had been transformed. Rural workers, no longer needed on the farms, had flocked to the cities to find work in factories, where they had indeed metamorphosed into an underpaid underclass of workers. Factories, textile mills, meatpacking plants, and steel industries covered the landscape. Improved transportation systems now distributed manufactured goods throughout the country. New sources of energy appeared as coal replaced wood, followed later by petroleum, natural gas, and oil. The uses of electricity multiplied.

With big business and industry overtaking small farming in the United States, it did not take long for Americans to sentimentalize the earlier way of life that had been lost. By the mid-nineteenth century, the rise of the middle class created "a certain amount of anxiety" among middle-class men because they were becoming separated from manual labor, which was virtuous and provided "a source of bodily and spiritual health for the producer." Through physical exercise, middle-class men could once again access "the ideological virtues of the independent farmers and artisans residually valorized within the middle-class cultural domain."

Our back-to-the-land ideology revived these deeply rooted underpinnings of the American consciousness, enabled perhaps by our comfortable, mechanized childhoods which protected us from seeing beyond the myths. The affluence of the postwar period enabled even a modest paycheck to go far, so parents of the 1950s and 1960s moved to the suburbs in droves, bought houses, cars, appliances, and televisions, and, "to the playtime repertory of earlier years—swing sets, sandboxes, tricycles, bicycles, balls, and bats—. . . added Frisbees, hula hoops, and Barbie dolls, plastic playthings" for their children. Middle-class suburban children who grew up watching *The Lone Ranger* on television and playing "Mother May I?" in the backyard on summer evenings had little experience with the harsher side of life and lacked firsthand contact with the back-to-nature existences they would later crave.

Cultural legacies may have played a subconscious role, but the deluge of 1970s back-to-the-earth books and articles inspired us very consciously. "Today we're living in Alberta on 160 beautiful fertile acres," reads one *Mother Earth News* profile, "70 in hay and 40 in timber—with a one-and-a-half story log cabin, barn, a couple of other buildings, and a creek running in front of the place. There's a one-acre dug-out reservoir which gives us great water . . . and a 25-acre pond behind the house. Lots of ducks and geese land there . . . we even have a muskrat! . . . I'm stocking up on wheat, honey, potatoes, and beans. We've got a cow giving us fresh milk, and in the spring we'll have chickens."

Thus when the longing for the land stirred in our hearts, as it had done in the hearts of many Americans before us, our particular vision may have been more myopic than that of previous generations. We imagined ourselves under blue skies with cotton white clouds floating by as we wielded our axes and hoed the garden. We anticipated the spiritual and aesthetic as well as the economic benefits of hard physical work, fresh air, and sunshine, hands-on tasks caring for soil, trees, vegetables, and animals. The relationship with nature "remind[s] us daily of the chain of life . . ." reads the statement of one back-to-the-land community. "We believe that man is more whole if he lives so that he is able to observe and relate to his natural environment. We must not lose sight of man's relationship to all life, nor his responsibility toward it."

Hence we moved to the land planning to amalgamate with the beauty and the seasonal rhythms of nature, as we imagined them to be, having learned about their virtues through reading Emerson in our English Literature classes, or from an afternoon matinee of *Cimarron*, where the characters wore nice outfits and kept all their teeth. Of course, in most cases going back to nature did fulfill one of the anticipated promises: immersion in beautiful, natural surroundings.

Bill Pearlman, a poet who lived on a commune in New Mexico, still remembers the stunning landscape—"a land of great space and beauty, mostly untrammeled by modernity. The communes were often built in mountainous areas close to the sun, not unlike ancient cities where inaccessibility and the brilliant light marked a place where the soul could find an earthly paradise. The light in New Mexico has meant a great deal to me. There was and is a sense of splendor and energy in the New Mexico landscape. There was a heart and mystery there."

Living outside the mainstream required grit. Homesteading friends of ours, pictured above, lived in conditions similar to ours.

June Holley, executive director of ACENETS in Ohio, lived in a nine-by-twelve-foot shack on top of a ridge in West Virginia, overlooking deep wooded valleys. "I remember waking up in the morning and doing what we would call 'watching the dragons coming up out of these deep valleys.' The dragon-shaped clouds would float out of the valley every morning, up over the hemlocks, and it was just breathtaking, just beautiful," she says.

But we discovered nature's darker underbelly too. Sunsets and new calves *were* beautiful, but to the uninitiated, natural processes, agrarian activities, and survival in the wilderness had many downsides. The natural world could be intimidating; farming could be daunting. How many of us had ever watched the blood spurt from a slaughtered animal before, watched the light fade from its eyes—by our own hand, no less? How many of us had scraped ice off the floors and walls of our homes as the temperature plummeted and we frantically threw logs into the woodstove and turned the flue wide open? Or spent a day under the blistering sun, back stiff, bent over rows of crops, brushing away gnats that flew up our nostrils, only to come out one chilly morning in September and find a killing frost shrouded like powdered sugar over the rows of plants? Although some of us achieved a lifetime proficiency at gardening, construction, or animal husbandry, the amassment of taxing work, as well as the abhorrent facets of nature, hit home after a few months in the trenches.

The life was hard. As the realities of daily homesteading unfolded before his eyes, Simon Shaw, producer of the popular *Frontier House* series—in which three families reenacted a nineteenth-century homesteading life for six months in Montana—was shocked. He had previously idealized this way of life. "Gone is the romance those movies and television shows once promised," he wrote. "Instead I see a world of daily challenge, danger, and near impossible odds. The facts speak for themselves: barely 40 percent of homesteaders ever succeeded on their homestead in the West. For the remainder, the encounter was simply too harsh. . . . I suspect if [those original pioneers] could take a glimpse at the world we inhabit, they would be mystified at our purpose. Why would we, having come so far, even wish to spend a day in their shoes? For me, at least, this has been a sobering experience." No wonder five million of the seven million nineteenth-century homesteaders failed. John Martin Campbell, author of *Magnificent Failure*, reports that a large number of these failed homesteaders were "citified dreamers . . . [who] failed within weeks or months of trying their hand at homesteading, mainly because they had not the foggiest notion of what farming was about."

The moral of the story is that there is indeed a gap between the idealized theory of pastoral life and the exhausting reality, a gap which some of us couldn't bridge.

Weather

The weather loomed as a more personal foe in our country milieus, where we spent more time outside doing agricultural chores and construction. Its capriciousness could easily destroy our plans, big time.

"A wild southwestern prairie in the flowery months of May and June seems a much more inviting and hospitable place than under the withering sun and scorching winds of August," observes Albert Shaw in his history of the nineteenth-century Icaria Community. That community was soon abandoned.

Cold weather especially, with its hazardous consequences of frozen pipes, stalled cars, slippery paths, and hypothermia, was particularly intimidating in the country, where we were more isolated from goods and services. Since most of us had moved happily into run-down houses, or had built our own maybe just *slightly* below the inspection codes, cold weather was a potentially serious adversary.

David Starnes will never forget the brutal Colorado winters on his farm. "The first winter I was there was the worst in any of the neighbors' memories. The short walk to the outhouse was Siberian. The wind sang through the utility wires like sirens. I was huddled by the smaller woodstove, a 'Hot Pot' in the kitchen covered Indian-style by several blankets. My friend Tom, whose living space was upstairs, stepped into the kitchen. He was wearing his heavy overcoat, an old bearskin, stagecoach driver's gloves, a watchman's cap, and a furrowed brow. Frost covered his mustache. We looked at each other, praying to survive until spring—still months away. Tom's humor was consistent: 'Let's call our mothers,' he'd always say."

At Slaughterhouse Creek commune in Salida, Colorado, Marty Rush describes the snow as "brutal. . . . Equipment and woodpiles and [outhouses] could disappear overnight, then had to be located and dug out. If you stepped off one of the packed-down trails between the cabins, *you* could disappear. Snow drifted over second-story decks—*entire cabins* could disappear. It was an eerie feeling, being slowly entombed in your house as the inexorable snow got deeper and deeper."

One former homesteader in a northern region remembers how the temperature often plummeted to twenty below zero for days on end. "We didn't have our systems together at all," she recalls. "We had cars that wouldn't start. We had tractors that wouldn't start. The manure gutter cleaner would freeze. Everything would freeze. The pipes would burst. Oh, man!"

My first Nor'easter in Maine left a strong impression. I had driven into Waterville in the Volkswagen that afternoon. The appointment had taken longer than expected. When I emerged from the building, the sky was ashen. Snowflakes blew sideways toward the ground, accumulating rapidly. Cars crept along with headlights on, sliding as they ascended streets. I brushed the snow off the windshield of the VW, started the engine, and felt the tires spin as I tried to pull out of the parking space. Pumping the clutch, pressing the gas pedal, I rocked the car back and forth, but it sat stationary, wheels twirling, until finally it lurched forward into the street.

"Oh my God," I thought as I slid along the streets of Waterville, "I've never seen a snowstorm like this one!"

I crawled timorously along, the wipers beating furiously across the windshield, eyes squinted toward the white void ahead. On the way I had to pick up Kent, who had been waiting at a friend's house (no cell phones in those days!). By the time I arrived, the steering wheel had left red imprints in my palms, and I happily turned the wheel over to him. He drove the rest of the way to Troy while I braced my hands against the dashboard as we headed straight into an endless white tunnel of snow. We arrived, at last, at the turnoff to Bagley Hill Road, the deep valley of a road that rose to a huge crest of a hill. To pick up speed for the uphill climb, Kent gripped the steering wheel, pressed boldly on the gas, and roared down the hill, gaining a speed of fifty by the time the car reached the bottom of the valley. We progressed about ten feet up the other side before the speed dropped abruptly from fifty to ten. Soon the car vibrated, whined, and finally stopped in its tracks, wheels spinning.

"Get in the back seat, El, so we can get more weight there," Kent said. Awkwardly I scaled the top of the front seat and dropped into the back. The redistribution of weight didn't help. The sleet beat against the windshield as we sat bewildered in the car, wondering if we should start hiking. We were still about half a mile from the house, a long hike in a Nor'easter. Luckily Derek and Shawn were staying at Ken and

Wendy's house that day, so they were safe. Then two lights beamed through the blurry white mess. Two snowmobiles, riding side by side, glided up beside us, their runners soft on the snow.

The drivers were James, a local farmer from whom we bought our milk, and his brother Steve, from whom we'd bought the land. Offering to help, they both jumped on the back fender and bounced while Kent slammed on the gas. We climbed twenty-five feet farther up the hill.

We realized, finally, that the car would not make it. The three men shoveled a path to the side of the road and pushed the VW out of the way.

"Well, whadya think, Ellie, you still want to live in Maine?" laughed Steve. Down East winters were old hat for these two lifelong residents of Troy. Kent and I still had a lot to learn.

I climbed onto the back of Steve's snowmobile while Kent boarded James's. The two snowmobiles soared gracefully up the hill with the two greenhorns riding behind the two veterans, clutching their waists.

James, with Kent behind, passed Steve's snowmobile and sailed off Bagley Hill Road to the right, flying down the dirt road. A hundred feet later, James and Kent turned onto our driveway, shot up the little hill by the top garden, and disappeared around the corner into the woods. Steve and I trailed behind. But his snowmobile couldn't scale the tiny but precipitous rise of our driveway.

"Well, this is the end of the line, I guess," he grinned.

"Thanks!" I said gratefully, climbing off and sinking into a drift.

It was now late afternoon, and darkness had fallen. I hiked the last eighth of a mile to the cabin. Killer snowflakes stung my face like airborne needles. Without a flashlight, the hike was laborious. With difficulty I climbed up the crest of the driveway and slogged past the top garden, now buried under a thick white cover, the site where Kent, Wendy, and Ken and I had posed for our first photo on that summer day. Then the sound of an oncoming snowmobile assailed the quiet as James came roaring out the woods, dead-on at me. With a little screech I jumped off the path into a snowdrift as he flashed by in a blur. "Ya hooo!" he yelled happily.

I climbed out of the drift with snow-filled Bean boots and trudged across the clearing by the top garden, around the curve of the driveway, and down the darkened path toward the log cabin. Alone in the woods, tall trees swaying over me on all sides, with the wind wailing and the snow pelting and swirling around me, I felt as never before the eternal power of a blizzard. One hand-built log cabin, a woodstove, and a pile of logs were now all that stood between us and death-by-storm. We were nestled in the woods miles away from the nearest small town, even farther from any hospitals or shelters, with no telephone and a car, for what it was worth, that lay buried in a snowdrift at the bottom of Bagley Hill Road. The sensation of living so close to the edge of danger hovered somewhere between fear and total exhilaration.

Natural Wood Heat

As I neared the log cabin, my hair thick with snow, I thought about the protagonist in Jack London's short story "To Build a Fire"—the man hiking across the Yukon in sub-zero weather, whose spittle froze in midair. Trying to reach camp before dying of hypothermia, he desperately attempted to light a fire to save himself, but his fingers were too numb to hold the matches. With the last match he nursed a tiny flame to life, but then a clump of snow fell from a tree above and smothered it. The man died. I thought about that story as I climbed the snowy steps of the log cabin and pulled open the front door. Kent, dripping with melted snow, was feeding logs into the woodstove, and I hurried over to stand close to it.

Many of us who went back to the land heated with wood. During the most horrific cold spells, our ability to start a fire and keep it alive was crucial. Most of us had already learned the basics of starting a fire back in Scout camp, but successful wood-heating actually began long before the first match was struck. A good model homesteader would know enough to prepare the firewood well in advance. Back-to-the-land people who hadn't done their homework about firewood preparation faced an unpleasant surprise come winter.

Cutting, chopping, and stacking wood in preparation for winter was a year-round job at our homestead.

The ideal firewood came from hardwood trees that had been cut down and left under a cover for several months to a year. If the wood was any younger than two or three months old, it would be considered green. You could put ten crumpled newspapers into the woodstove, add gasoline, start a bonfire in the woodstove, and then add green wood, and the fire would fizzle out as soon as the paper had burned. You could cut green wood into one-inch pieces of kindling and throw those into a raging fire, and the fire would eventually go out. A homesteader needed to cut logs and split wood from full-length trees that had been cut and left to dry for the longest possible time, even up to a couple of years. If the wood was green, it couldn't be cut or split easily.

Once the wood was aged, cut, split, and stacked, keeping it covered was imperative. As soon as a winter thaw sent rivulets of melted snow flowing down the woodpile, the water settled around the logs and then froze again when the temperature dropped. On a frigid night when the fire was dying, a desperate and unprepared homesteader would find herself using a sledgehammer to dislodge frozen logs from an ice castle of a woodpile. Even worse, a spaced-out homesteader who didn't accumulate enough wood by winter or who ran out during the cold season probably ended up buying a couple of cords out of sheer desperation, or worse, cutting down green trees on the spot and passing them off as firewood for lack of anything else.

The stovepipe that ran from the woodstove through the roof of the house had to be elevated high enough off the roof to be able to catch wind currents. If it was too low, the roof blocked it from receiving proper air flow, so the fire would suffocate. On the other hand, too much stovepipe exposed to the air might cool its temperature enough to cause creosote buildup, which could be dangerous. A tarry residue that built up like cholesterol in human blood vessels, creosote tended to accumulate in stovepipes anyway, and could cause a serious fire. One had to tap the pipes continually to release the chunks of creosote and send them sliding down the pipe. The fire had to be kept hot enough and with enough air current to prevent buildup. Another reason not to use green wood: it contributed to creosote buildup.

Like heating with wood, cooking with wood was also more energy-efficient and natural than using an electric or gas stove, but I can tell you from experience that the cook couldn't walk away and do other things while waiting for water to boil or a chicken to bake; she had to plant herself in front of the blazing hot monster and continually feed kindling through the top holes to keep the fire hot enough to bake or boil dinner and ensure an even distribution of heat throughout the body of the stove. If the temperature soared in one corner and fell in another, the food, obviously, would cook unevenly, perhaps burned on one side and raw on another. Having suffered through several of my own badly cooked woodstove meals, I truly admire the back-to-the-land women who could do this well.

Wood heat was as close to natural as you could get. But it was not simpler.

Outhouses

Outhouses were the commode-of-choice for those who built their own dwellings. Cheap, easy to construct, and environmentally sound, they appealed to homesteaders because they were throwbacks to the pre-twentieth-century anti-technology. Harmless to the environment, they didn't waste gallons of water and didn't require complicated plumbing systems. In other words, they allowed for more natural processing of human elimination. The drawback was 1) they often stunk, 2) they attracted flies and bugs, and 3) they were situated outside of the main house, which was inconvenient for nighttime emergencies.

"Last night I woke up, and Jim was sitting on the edge of the bed, groaning, with his face all contorted, struggling to pull his boots on," one back-to-the-land woman recalled during one of our coffee klatches. "He was trying to make it to the outhouse." Poor Jim, hit by an attack of diarrhea, had torn out of the house and run awkwardly through the snow to the little building with the half moon carved in the front. Similar outhouse stories, too delicate to be discussed outside the closed circles of back-to-the-land friends, were shared during many gabfests.

Even in nonemergency situations, some people felt uneasy traipsing out into the pitch darkness, carrying a lantern or a flashlight that illuminated only six feet ahead, to make that nighttime trip to the outhouse. The night sounds, real or fantasized, could put a person's imagination in high gear. Was that a mountain lion or a bear that just moved over there in the bushes? What about the little critters and insects that lived in the outhouse while it wasn't in use and might not be expecting company at night?

Different types of indoor and outdoor commodes, quite frankly, inspired varying degrees of uneasiness. Inventive homesteaders constructed imaginative arrangements, such as an open bucket beneath a chair in which a hole had been cut, with perhaps—but not necessarily—a curtain draped around it for privacy. This type of primitive toilet, which required the continual emptying of a waste-filled bucket, was not, in the opinion of many a woman who did it, an enjoyable task. Even some of the sophisticated, store-bought commodes had to be manually emptied. Although the storage container was sturdy plastic and closed off with a sealed cap, it had to be carried to a leech field, opened, and emptied onto the ground. The most fortunate among back-to-the-land people could afford composting toilets right away, though the seventies prototypes of today's composting privies fell short of perfection. "Issues of shoddy construction and overoptimistic designs plagued both the manufactured and build-it-yourself models, and users struggled with odors, flies, incomplete processing and hard-to-empty systems," notes a recent *Mother Earth News* article.

But even those early composting toilets, whatever their flaws, did not assault one's sensibilities quite as much as other accommodations that some back-to-the-land people invented. Those who could not afford the composting privies had to put on permanent hold any squeamishness they might have felt.

Construction and Repairs

Building a house from scratch is a labor from hell. Homesteaders who had never tried it before or had imagined it to be like the time-lapse versions depicted on *Little House on the Prairie* were in for a shock. For a start, consider what it's like to clear the land before building. One former homesteader describes his experience:

"The site where I envisioned my home was beautiful, surrounded by four perfectly placed sugar maples that were reminiscent of gates to a kingdom—two in front about thirty feet apart and two in the back about the same," he recalls. "The house *had* to go there. Between the four main trees, there were dozens of little pine trees between ten and fifteen feet tall, one about every five feet. Just to clear that house site of about three thousand square feet, I cut down over a hundred trees, leaving a hundred stumps about two to three inches in diameter. When I started digging to put cedar posts in as a foundation, I realized that for each hole placed six feet apart, I had to cut through thick tangles of in-tertwined roots, twisted around rocks. The ledge was two feet under the ground, so each hole took about four hours. Anyone who has ever done this type of work can relate to what it means to be truly exhausted!"

Construction commences next. Peter Matson had read *Walden Pond* before going to the land. After facing far greater sweat, cost, and aggravation than Thoreau had led him to believe he would experience, he observed wryly in 1977, "You'll say I'm envious of his strength and daring, his opportunity. He well may have dug [his cellar] in two hours, it's certainly possible in sandy soil if your hands are not given to blis-tering, you have borrowed a good sharp shovel, you are young and pur-poseful. . . . In [my] case the shovel is only the start: a lot more work should be done with a pick, as I had already found out. Pieces of the bed rock keep breaking off the granite, and because of the effect of wa-ter and changing temperatures, work their way to the top. I reckoned that if H.D. could dig his cellar hole in two hours, mine would take thirty-six. On the other hand, Henry's picture of himself in other parts of his writing is not compatible with this. His reputation in and around Concord, a community that surely put a premium on work, was that of a sometime layabout."

Patricia Foley spent the summer of 1972 hand-digging the 22-by-26-foot, two-foot-wide, four-foot-deep foundation for their stone house before retreating to the toolshed for the winter. "We did it with picks and shovels," says Patricia. "The soil was removed only with great diffi-culty because it was so full of blueberry roots. Underneath that was a very heavy yellow clay subsoil, and underneath that, about one foot down, was the most obdurate hardpan you ever saw."

She and her husband then committed a major error while digging the foundation. "In addition to not knowing how to grow gardens and things like that, we also didn't know how to build stone houses," Patricia says. "We thought we'd dig out this big trench and throw stones into it. Then we'd put the stone wall on top of the stones. You can't do that! We learned this *after* we'd thrown all the stones in. After this *huge*, Siberian effort at rock-hauling, which went on all summer, a more experienced person informed us, 'You can't do that. Water is going to get into that trench, it's going to get between the rocks and it's going to freeze in the winter. Then it's going to heave the rocks, it's going to heave your wall, and the whole wall will fall down.' We had to take every rock that we had put in the trench out of the trench. By hand."

Even when a homesteader survived the clearing of the land and the construction of the house, there was always something waiting to go wrong. Jane Kirkpatrick observes that "Murphy—as in Murphy's Law—must have been a homesteader." In one month's time on her homestead, heavy winds blew the two-hundred-pound septic tank down the hill to a river. The tractor broke. The mules escaped. Water accumulated in the tiling beneath the floor insulation. "With turkey basters, Mom and I began sucking the water out through the woodpecker sized holes."

Going back to the land made most of us first-rate carpenters, tool operators, and mechanics. We had no choice. Our survival depended upon it.

Our second winter in Maine, the weather was wild. Snowstorms and ice storms whipped through the woods, splattering themselves against the house, burying the cars, blowing down trees. The waterline burst twice, sending volcanoes of water splashing over the floors. Soon after, when the pipes froze, the water wouldn't flow at all. The car and truck broke. The chainsaw needed a new bar. An ice storm hit one Monday and the electricity, which we now had, flashed on and off all day. By evening, the power came back, so I settled down in bed with a book. I dozed off about nine with the book open across my chest. I was jolted awake by an unearthly boom that made the house shake. I hurried out of bed and rushed to the top of the stairs. Kent was below, throwing logs into the woodstove.

"What was that?" I yelled.

"What was what?"

"That noise!"

"Ah, probably these logs hitting the back of the stove when I threw them in."

"It was really loud!"

By December 1975, Kent had completed the log cabin enough for us to move in, but he continued to make structural improvements and replaced the window that was shattered when the ice storm ripped out the upstairs wall.

"Then probably a tree limb falling on the roof. Go back to bed. I'll be up in a moment."

I returned to bed and fell asleep immediately. Then Kent's shouts started me awake.

"El! C'mere! Hurry! Come on down!"

I rolled out of bed, groggy, and descended the ladder-stairs. Kent stood by the opened front door, pointing outside.

The side of the house was ripped out. An ice-covered tree had fallen over the electric line that was attached to the side of the house, this wrenching the boards right out. A gaping hole exposed Derek's and Shawn's room.

"What'll I do, what'll I do?" Kent was muttering nervously, pacing. "Guess I'd better prop up the wall with a log."

"We'd better call Central Maine Power," I advised. "That electrical line is almost touching the ground."

After placing a call to Central Maine Power (we now had a phone too), I watched from the window as Kent propped the sagging wallboards under a tall, thick log. Within half an hour, flashlights appeared at the top of the driveway as the crew from CMP arrived, their chain saws at the ready. As Kent prepared to join them, glass shattered loudly as the log propping the wallboards slipped out and smashed through the window. The earsplitting noise didn't wake the two boys, who had slept through the commotion in their wall-less bedroom, now exposed to the winter night air. Chain saws roared, boards creaked, and hammers pounded. The house shook to the rhythm. The boys continued to sleep soundly.

At 1:30 the men completed the repair, which included chainsawing down the tree which had fallen on the line, helping Kent nail the house back together, and attaching a new type of bolt onto the electric line. As they left, Kent invited them in for a cup of tea, but they declined— they had so many more calls to handle that night.

Kent walked inside, hung up his coat, and took off his steamed-up glasses.

"Shit!" he declared. "That was terrible. You know, that was the first time in my life that I've been really scared. I could envision myself frying, with those wires."

Animal Husbandry

Most of us had much to learn about animal husbandry. "Little did I know how much milk a goat would produce," says Lucy Joseph, who lived on a commune in Illinois. Her group had thought it a brilliant idea to purchase a goat, but they couldn't keep up with the copious milk supply. "I couldn't drink it, and neither could many people," she says. "It was impossible to keep yogurt cultures going, to turn gallons and gallons of milk into yogurt. We had more milk than we knew what to do with. Even our many yard dogs had stopped drinking it, so only the cats would touch it. Meanwhile I milked and milked and milked, while Sarah the goat mostly wreaked havoc around the place."

Linda Clarke loved managing her animals, but raising her goats also meant no days off. "A half a day was a big adventure," she said, "unless you could find a neighbor you could barter chores with, which we did a couple of times. But you always had to 'dry off' two or three animals because the neighbors didn't want to milk more than one," she sighs. "Going away wasn't something I did very much. At all."

When Jane Musser's goat gave birth to twin kids, one of them developed bloat. She treated it using a *Mother Earth News* remedy, which at first appeared to have worked. Thus she was crushed when "we found one kid dead and blown up like a balloon. . . . To make matters worse, the other baby had a slight swelling on its left side." The second kid survived. But their plan to raise two pigs was foiled before they even got started: "Unfortunately, the whole venture started out as a catastrophe. We bought two six-week-old piglets from a neighboring farmer and brought them home in burlap bags (around here, the standard method for transporting the animals). By the time we got them to our place, one of the little porkers had died. We were awfully upset by this. . . ."

On our homestead, our ignorance about animals caught up with us one spring when we decided to buy mail-order ducklings to raise for meat. After the twenty-four cute birds arrived, we placed them in the boys' plastic wading pool, believing that ducklings would, of course, prefer to be in the water. When we returned to the pool an hour later, they were all floating facedown, having drowned. We were heartbroken (another sign, perhaps, that we were not true farmers). Perhaps we should have read *Mother Earth News* more closely that year. How else would we have learned that baby ducks can't stay afloat without a special oil their mother secretes into the water?

We were also naive about pest management. Living close to nature meant living close to a large population of mice who moved into our cabin the same winter we did. One evening, as the kerosene lanterns cast a ginger flush across the ceilings and walls, I heard an unfamiliar noise coming from inside the thick insulation on the low ceiling above me. I didn't recognize the sound of skritch, skritch, skritch and the mewing squeals, so I paused and listened. I started as something dropped out of the ceiling and landed at my feet. I squatted down and found a little nest containing a dozen pink baby mice, tiny feet and arms kicking. They looked like little pink aliens with horselike heads. Their satin skin and sealed eyes could only evoke pity. What were we supposed to do—hurt them? Uncertain about the proper protocol for handling unwanted baby mice, we promptly stuck them back into the insulation, for lack of a better solution. All that winter the sounds of unseen mice spread out like tributaries from a river to the four corners of the house. At night, as we lay in bed, we could hear the nervous little footsteps racing frenetically through the insulation, crinkling the aluminum covering as they went. The squeaks and squeals left no doubts.

We responded the way all good homesteaders did; we bought a Havahart mousetrap, which simply cages the mouse without killing it. We smeared peanut butter inside, and set it up on the kitchen floor. On the first night it clanged shut. Kent rolled out of bed with the flashlight and groped his way down the ladder to the kitchen. A trembling field mouse cowered in the corner of the trap. Kent opened the front door of the cabin and released the mouse into the front yard. He reset the trap, smeared more peanut butter, and climbed back up the ladder to the loft. The trap resounded twice more that night. Kent got up twice more and freed both captives, shooing them out the front door. The next clang didn't awaken us. In the morning, as we came downstairs, the boys had discovered a new mouse in the trap and were yelling excitedly. This time Kent drove half a mile down the dirt road and dropped the mouse off in the woods.

For as long as we could, we used the humane Havahart mousetrap. But honestly! Chauffeuring mice to a new location every day was not only insane and futile but tiring. And it finally dawned on us, I guess, that every mouse we escorted out of the cabin had probably moved right back in by nightfall and brought all its friends too. Weary of the squealing, sick of the ugly piles of hard black poops that amassed daily on the cupboards, we retired the Havahart in favor of a Maine coon cat named Jethro and several traditional mousetraps.

Fellow homesteader Rista Salaranto helped us butcher our pig.

Animal Slaughtering

If we had trouble disposing of pesky mice at Middle Earth Homestead, you can imagine how upsetting it was to slaughter chickens, turkeys, rabbits, or, the annual pig. I abhorred it. But the purpose of raising these animals was to eat them. That was what self-sufficiency was all about. It had to be done. Like most other back-to-the-land people, however, I hadn't been born into a farm family and had already been irreversibly socialized to feel repelled at the sight and smell of the blood, guts, and feathers that flew far and wide when a squawking chicken or turkey was slaughtered. One fall we did a number of turkeys. After the slaughter outside, which Kent did with an axe, the bodies were brought inside the cabin to be defeathered, a messy and smelly process that leaves your body and hair crawling with remnants of feathers. The nauseating smell hung in the air long after the turkeys were finished. Some good friends of ours in Troy raised turkeys too, and they wrote an article for an alternative magazine describing the slaughtering process. They wrote, "We have never mastered the method of killing poultry by piercing the brain through the roof of the mouth, so we stick to the good old hatchet. One person holds the turkey with his head on the chopping block . . . and the other chops the head off, hopefully with one merciful blow, although we have had our failures when the bird ended up being bludgeoned to death." I doubt they liked it any more than I did.

The pig was the worst. A *Mother Earth News* article describes the process so matter-of-factly of how a two-hundred-pound hog was "shot in the head with a .22 and promptly stuck in the throat with a double-bladed sticking knife." Then the body was dipped in hot water so that the scalded hair could be scraped off. Conveyed to the barn, the hog was then "hung from a big beam with a block and tackle . . . his head was removed, and he was gutted."

On our homestead we raised a pig each year for three years. The first year we sent it out for slaughter. The meat was returned to us neatly packaged in large cardboard boxes. The second and third years we slaughtered it ourselves with the help of friends. I remember the dining room table in the cabin, covered with newspaper, on top of which bloody innards were strewn alongside the sections of meat that we cut and packaged. The smell of guts fouled the air. I particularly remember the third and last year we raised a pig. A friend arrived with a rifle to shoot it in the yard. Standing five feet away, he raised his rifle, aimed right between the animal's eyes—and missed, hitting it in the head off-center enough to wound it but not kill it. That pig let out a squeal of agony that could have pierced Hell. The sound haunts me still. It charged aimlessly around the yard emitting a sound much like a human scream for a full two or three minutes until our friend, cursing, had reloaded his gun, aimed again, and this time hit the mark. The woods fell silent. The grim reality of self-sufficiency was tarnishing my original vision.

Raising Crops

An ominous disclaimer is buried at the back of the popular seventies book *Farming for Self-Sufficiency: Independence on a 5-Acre Farm*. How many hopeful homesteaders with country dreams in their eyes ever read those last few pages of a book so thick with hope and rich with advice on self-sufficient living? There the authors write, "Unfortunately, these people [coming to the country] don't seem to have the slightest idea what to do when they get into the country. . . . Some of them try to grow some of their own food. 'Of course we're going to produce all our own food,' they say, pointing to three square yards of ground half dug up and planted with dying cabbage riddled with flea-beetle." Our inexperience, naiveté, and idealism may indeed have blinded us to the problems that would face us while growing our own food and cash crops. Imagining that food just sprouted naturally from the ground and the trees, as it had since the beginning of time, we underestimated the frustration of raising crops.

Miriam Ross, her husband, and three children bought their dream farm in Arkansas in 1978. "We fell in love with it, but we bought a piece of *rock*," she says. "We had to plant our fruit trees with dynamite. I'm not kidding. We drilled and blew holes and planted trees with dynamite."

Gail Adams and her family raised tobacco as a cash crop on their Virginia farm. Tobacco required arduous exertion, for after it matured it had to be stripped, tied, and packed by hand. "That was the most miserable job," she says, "because it's cold, and you can't really heat the barn because then it would cause the leaves to dry out. So you're in there, cold, you're pulling on tobacco, and your hands get stained. It wasn't real pleasant physically."

In the Ozarks, Jane Fishman was serious about gardening, "But the Ozarks are *tough*," she says. "It's rocky. I tried to garden, but we had to terrace because it was on a hill. Then one big rain would come and wash out all your terrace and your topsoil that you'd brought in."

The setbacks in crop production may have hit us in the pocketbook as well as in our pride. We were raising food not only for our own consumption, but as a cash crop for the income we were beginning to need. Don Wirtshafter remembers the droughts in Ohio. In the seventies he was living on $600 a year, so he really depended upon the produce from the garden. "The gardens around here are spectacular, but we lived through some summers where there was absolutely no rain. I remember when things just turned brown, the earth cracked up. And this is when I was really counting on money from the garden," he says.

Pierce Walker, a real farmer from Indiana who was interviewed for Stud Terkel's book *Working*, sums it up: "Farming, it's such a gamble. . . . Weather will make ya or break ya. The crops have to have enough moisture. If they don't have enough, they hurt. If you have too much, it hurts. You take it like you git. There's nothing you can do about it."

❦ *Paw Paw, West Virginia, 1973: Pat Manuele and her boyfriend Brad had at last signed a contract to sell their peaches to a fruit broker for six dollars a bushel, more money than they had made since they had arrived at Spring Gap Orchard, a fifteen-hundred-acre peach and apple orchard about six miles west of Paw Paw, West Virginia. Pat had begun her back-to-the-land venture with high expectations in the summer of 1972 when she joined Brad, whom she had met in college, and two other friends at Spring Gap. She was in love with Brad and with the land. Peaches were to be their main cash crop. "I learned to love peaches in any form," writes Pat. "I learned too that peach fuzz was to be abhorred: peach fuzz got into your neck and elbow folds and itched for hours."*

That summer of 1973 the peach crop looked extraordinary. After struggling for income the previous year, they were so proud to at last have landed a lucrative contract. Pat describes the unexpected loss that followed:

"What happened [a few days later] was far beyond our imaginings. I went outside to take in clothing that had been drying on the line. Black clouds appeared to rest atop our mountain. The sky was very dark, as if it were nightfall. As I stood there, a gust of wind blew one of the shirts out of my hands. The backs of the poplar leaves up the hill were showing. All this gave clear signs we were in for another rainstorm. A bright bolt of lightning lit up the sky over the mountain. Almost immediately I heard the first crash of thun-

der close by. I had not gotten to three in my counting, so it was probably within two miles.

"Drops began falling as I ran to the porch. Big drops. I stood there for a minute watching the rain come in at a sharp angle. When I went into the kitchen to start dinner, the room was so dark that I turned on the lights. Unexpectedly, the metal roof was ringing. We looked out the window: half-inch balls of ice bounced off every level surface. Lightning and thunder were everywhere. The hail seemed to be getting larger and now accumulated on the ground. Without warning, there was simultaneously an extremely bright flash of light, a deafening explosion of thunder and, overhead, lights fizzled out.

"Hail kept pounding relentlessly and thunder rumbled insistently overhead, although now a slight distance away. The hailstones appeared to be an inch in diameter. I had never seen any so large! Abruptly the hail turned to rain, still beating against the house, but blessedly quieter. Indoors the silence was complete.

"Over breakfast the next morning, Brad said, 'I have to go out to the orchard to see if there's any damage.'

"He left, but returned soon. He had found nearly all of the ripening peaches nicked in one or two spots. Nothing could be done or said to make things right, to repair the harm. Within the next three days, brown rot, a fungus that lived in the wood of the old trees, migrated into the wounds of the damaged peaches, causing them all to rot on the trees."

The unexpected hailstorm had ruined the peach crop, and the contract had to be dropped.

Pat reflects, "That tempest was a turning point for me. I never again held the optimism that we could make it financially working the peaches."

CHAPTER FIVE

Not-so-genteel Poverty

"The poverty portrayed by left-wing intellectuals was . . . romantic. The poverty I knew was dreary, deadening, and shameful." —Dorothy Allison, author of *Bastard Out of Carolina*

"I had given up having kids, a home, a car, a viable job, a low cholesterol count, new clothes, decent medical insurance, a retirement plan, peace of mind, or any of the other mysterious things that people consider part of a normal life. Meanwhile, the next generation had stepped into the void and was making a lot of money."—David Manning

🌷 *Paw Paw, West Virginia, 1972–1974: After the hailstorm and the ruined crop in the summer of 1973, Pat Manuele and Brad faced insolvency. They had struggled financially since May of '72, when Pat moved to Spring Gap Orchard. They had worked industriously that first peach season. Pat's arms ached from picking peaches and loading them into crates, which weighed about forty pounds each. Blisters formed on her hands, and bugs ravished her legs.*

"Little no-see-ums that got in my eyes, solitary wasps and flies were everywhere. Half-inch bright green bugs leapt out at me from everywhere; some were treehoppers, others June bugs. The sum total was audible as a constant buzzing hum in my ears." But Brad's praise and compliments

pleased and validated her. She yearned for his approval. His ambivalence about their relationship made her feel alternately loved and unloved. That first summer of '72 they had trucked twenty crates of peaches to Washington, D.C., to sell at the farmers' market. "Unfortunately the hydro-cooling hadn't worked as well as desired. We lost some to overripeness, the soft syrupy blobs of mush leaking out the sides of the slats. But the first housewives of the morning bought the last solid ones at half-price for pies, and we were on our way home." They had grossed $200. A second trip to the farmers' market grossed another $200. The waning summer months saw the end of the income-producing season. Their annual rent was $2,000, though they were being charged half that since they had arrived and started managing the orchard halfway through the year, in June. Still, $400 fell below their expectations and their needs.

But Brad kept insisting that peach sales would be lucrative. They opened their orchard to the public for peach-picking, as a desperate last attempt of the 1972 peach season. Not many people came. Although Pat loved her life on the orchard and treasured the "crystal-clear days, glorious sunrises [and] magnificent sunsets," as well as "the swims, the work, the walking, [and] fresh meat and produce [which] nourished our strong healthy bodies," dejection shadowed her as solvency remained elusive. All that first winter, they ate peach jam, peach bread, peach wine, canned peaches, and peach cookies made from their surplus of unsold fruit. They traded peaches to neighbors for zucchini, tomatoes, potatoes, and onions. To round out their diet, they shot deer and cooked the venison. They even ate baked or oven-roasted snakes. The endless winter finally faded, the snows retreated, and the buds reappeared, and with that their hopes for a better season returned. That is, until that summer afternoon when the sky grew black and the hailstorm slammed mercilessly onto the peach trees.

Pat and Brad picked apples for twenty-five cents a bushel. They applied for and got food stamps. When the second winter began, desperation dogged them once again. Remembers Pat, "Brad was depressed about the hard economic times we had fallen into despite all our efforts. Although selling pick-your-own in the orchard gave me a temporary escape, it didn't free me from his black mood." Financial setbacks persisted. At the end of the peach season

in 1973, for example, an organic food co-op in Washington, D.C., had offered to buy fifteen bushels of peaches, but when Brad delivered them, the
manager of the co-op reneged because the peaches had been sprayed with sul-
fur, which Brad insisted was not a pesticide.

Of course, on the return trip from this venture, Brad discovered a leaking gasket on the van, the first of nonstop vehicle troubles.

"I was frustrated by the economics of our life," says Pat.

1970s Trickle-down Inflation

By the 1970s, the golden years of the American economy had come to
a screeching halt. As the U.S. Office of Management and Budget reported cryptically in 1983, "In the decade of the 1970s, the economy
failed to perform as well as in the 1960s." Throughout the seventies,
prices rose, white-collar layoffs broke records, interest rates climbed,
and inflation stayed high. Between 1967 and 1973, according to a report in the *American Economic Review*, the cost of necessities rose more
than the cost of luxuries. In 1978 all prices rose 12 percent, and the
next year they rose 13 percent. The automobile—virtually all of us
owned one—was a big casualty of inflation. We depended upon vehicles more than ever in isolated areas, so we too felt the impact of buying, maintaining, gassing, and repairing our cars. Another spiraling expense was food. Few of us were entirely rid of the supermarket. Besides,
price increases in just a few areas of the economy created a ripple effect,
as "an upward ratcheting" of across-the-board prices occurred. Even
with a simple, no-frills budget, back-to-the-land people were hard
pressed to stretch modest and sometimes sporadic incomes to cover sky-
rocketing costs.

Pat's story is typical. Many of us had believed, as she had, that we
would thrive on the land with trifling incomes. The books and counterculture magazines had said so over and over. We had read all the
Mother Earth News articles on how homesteaders could generate money
without going to work. Many of us had anticipated earning our smidgen

of income through crafts or cash crops. Two issues of *Mother* in 1973 and 1974 included the articles "Raise Worms for Fun and Profit," "Finding Part-time Work in the Country," "Invest $8.95 and Harvest $200.00 from a Garden," "How to Double $2,500 in Two Months," "Farming for Self-Sufficiency," and "Ralph Borsodi's Constants: Money You Can Count On." In addition to establishing such cottage industries, we would supply our own food needs, heat with wood, share with our groups, or offer "country payments"—bushels of tomatoes or the like— in exchange for goods and services from the outside world. It went without saying that we would no longer be buying the frivolous toys and gadgets we had once believed to be necessary and now knew to be pointless, such as makeup or new shoes. Once in the country, though, we discovered that our theory of counterculture economics was a bubble ready to burst.

Miscalculations

The first thing that threw us asunder was our distorted perception of just how far a low income would stretch. Twenty years earlier a modest income *could* have provided most of life's necessities. In 1950, for example, a man earning a working-class wage of $1,800 a year could buy a three-bedroom house and provide for a family. But those days were gone by the early 1970s.

Second, our critical stance toward the American economic system had been nurtured by a one-dimensional perception that capitalism was nothing but a system designed to create "the rise of the most ruthless, cunning, avaricious, self-seeking individuals, lacking in sympathy and compassion," and that we could dissociate ourselves through self-sufficiency.

But, explains Copthorne Macdonald, an engineer and author of many books, self-sufficiency as many of us envisioned it was almost economically impossible. Macdonald wrote a column for *Mother Earth News* from 1973 to 1983, and through this came into contact with many back-to-the-land people. He himself had believed that American society would collapse but later began to change his mind. "Industrial society was not only *not* falling apart, but it was strengthening in a lot of ways," he says.

"Alternative society never grew large enough to be really separate from the mainstream society. If it had been large enough, maybe it would have been possible to buy your farming tools from somebody who created them in a forge. But in fact you had to buy them from some company in the mainstream economy. If you had a chain saw to cut your wood, you had to buy gasoline for your chain saw. There was never a real separation from the mainstream's economy, even for the sort of purists in the movement who wanted to be really, totally self-sufficient. That was never really a possibility. You might get close, but you could never be there because the infrastructures, the support systems that are needed to make an economy work, just weren't there."

He continues, "Subsistence living was very, very difficult. I can remember reading an article in *Mother Earth News* by some fellow either in Minnesota or maybe it was one of the Dakotas, who had figured out how much an hour he got paid for making flour, and it was less than ten cents. Living self-sufficiently was very hard, very difficult work. At some point, back-to-the-land people looked around and saw that other people were out there having more fun."

In *The Nature of Economies*, Jane Jacobs compares economies to natural ecosystems. Using a desert and a forest as metaphors, she compares the energy flow resulting from sunlight shining on a desert to the energy flow resulting from sunlight shining on a forest. In the desert, "the passage of energy is swift, simple, and vanishing," but in the forest, "energy flow is anything but swift and simple, because of the diverse and roundabout ways that the system's web of teeming, interdependent organisms uses energy."

In other words, the larger capitalistic system, because of its complexity and diversity, channels a healthy economic energy through itself and creates self-renewal and growth. Individual economies, such as communes or homesteads attempting to be self-sufficient, do not have the size, complexity, cash flow, or diversity of goods and services to survive very well independently.

Our rejection of American free enterprise and widespread consumerism had lost something in the translation, spinning off into the con-
viction that money itself and the accrual of money was ignoble. But consumerism and cash are clearly different things. Timothy Miller recognizes
this "confusion," as he puts it. "Most people confuse the artificial construct that is money with wealth, which is 'the sum of energy, technical
intelligence, and raw materials.'" While renouncing wealth and the acquisitive, dishonorable mind-set that we believed was attached to it, we
imagined that a life without consumerism could logically be a life with little cash, overlooking the fact that even the very leanest existence still required many necessities that could not be grown or built. In fact, a rather
dicey challenge was, and still is, to define what is "necessary" versus what
is "extravagant." Interestingly, the counterculture contained its own
streak of reverse snobbery and one-upmanship about the degrees to
which any individual had successfully repudiated the purchase of material possessions that were "not necessary." But who could define the
boundary between the two? We had declared, "We'll give up all luxuries!"
without first defining clearly what a luxury or a necessity would be in our
back-to-the-land lives. We had assumed the difference would be obvious,
but it wasn't.

"While we speak about luxuries and necessities as if their meanings
were self-evident, it is difficult to make a real distinction between them,"
writes Thomas Hine, author of *I Want That! How We All Became Shoppers*.
"If I came to your house and declared, 'You have too much stuff,' it's very
likely that you would agree with me. If, however, I start ridding your house
of things I deem to be unnecessary, before very long we'd be arguing."

In one of the few scholarly essays on the subject, Michael Maniates
thoroughly analyzes today's voluntary simplicity movement (VSM), a
watered-down evolution of the back-to-the-land financial philosophy,
and points out that purists who ridicule others' purchases as being "too
luxurious" are being simplistic. He points out that as members of a society we often have to purchase expensive items that could be judged "luxurious" by others, but are not necessarily. "If everyone else is wearing an
expensive suit to that job interview, you have got to as well if you hope to

send the right message, regardless of your feelings about consumerism or your leanings toward frugality. Likewise, the presence of more behemoth vehicles on the road ratchets up the arms race on the highway; standing a fighting chance against one in a collision requires buying a larger vehicle yourself, no matter how much joy or dismay driving it brings."

"Often," says Hine, "it seems that our definition of a luxury is something we don't buy for ourselves."

Similarly, how does one distinguish between *vanity* and necessity? Was deodorant really necessary on a farm, or was it a luxury? What about other implements of traditional grooming? In an ideal world of simplicity, no one would care what she or he looked like or what clothes she or he wore. Much as we might have liked to, however, most of us were not able to shed our vanity entirely when we moved to rustic settings. Furthermore we could not change the way the larger society judged people based on smell, appearance, and grooming. If any of us worked at a job outside the homestead, we could hardly expect to appear at work stinking from lack of deodorant, or wearing manure-stained jeans. And each degree of investment in appearance left an added strain on the limited budget. No matter how poor we might have wished to become, breaking out of our earlier socialization of vanity and grooming, as well as from current cultural expectations, was tricky.

Frank Levering and Wanda Urbanska recognized this tension after moving to an orchard in West Virginia. They wanted to elude the culture's shallow preoccupation with outward appearance. But they needed money and they needed to sell a visibly pleasing product. "As orchardists, we sell fruit in a marketplace that demands a measure of perfection—not a pockmarked peach or apple with worms inside, but one worm-free and with a visually appealing exterior."

And what about simply *wanting* a new goody once in a while? Back-to-the-landers had agreed that consumerism was bad, that *wanting* things was a sign of weakness, but some of the items money could buy began to look mighty good after a few years of lean living. "Sooner or later, we are going to have to acknowledge the uncomfortable fact that this amoral commercial culture has proved potent because hu-

The idea of living simply had seemed noble at first, but sparse surroundings, combined with little cash flow, took the wind out of many sails.

man beings *love* things," writes James Twitchell in *Lead Us into Temptation: The Triumph of American Materialism.* "In fact, to a considerable degree, we live for things. Humans like to exchange things. In all cultures, we buy things, steal things and hoard things. . . . We create ourselves through things. And we change ourselves by changing things. We often depend on such material for meaning. . . . Being able to buy what you want when and where you want it was, after all, the right that made 1989 a watershed year in Eastern Europe."

The Middle-class Myth of Poverty

Many of us had clearly romanticized the idea of low-income living because of our lack of exposure to it. Author Dorothy Allison, who grew up in a poor white family in South Carolina, wryly observed the difference between the middle-class myth of poverty and the real thing. In her essay "A Question of Class," she writes, "The poverty depicted in books and movies was romantic, a backdrop for the story of how it was escaped. The poverty portrayed by left-wing intellectuals was just as romantic, a platform for assailing the upper and middle classes. There was an idea of the good poor—hard-working, ragged but clean, and intrinsically honorable. The poverty I knew was dreary, deadening, and shameful." As refugees from the middle class seeking asylum within the peaceful shelter of genteel poverty, many of us had a rude awakening. Instead of the poor-but-happy lifestyle we had anticipated, we got tension, sporadic or nonexistent income, and broken cars.

Perhaps we had been influenced by our culture's association of "genteel poverty" with intelligent, exemplary individuals such as artists, writers, musicians, professors, or priests, too focused on the life of the mind or humanitarian works to care about their humble surroundings. Thoreau, in fact, is described in an encyclopedia entry as having been raised "in genteel poverty," where he "placed nature above materialism." He had done it with such aplomb; why couldn't we? But many of us had not thought about the fact that, as most sources confirm, "Walden was not a wilderness, nor was Thoreau a pioneer; his hut was within two miles of town, and while at Walden, he made almost daily visits to Concord and to his family, dined out often, had frequent visitors and went off on excursions."

In the post–World War II United States, severe poverty was a widespread reality that existed alongside affluence. By 1964 President Lyndon Johnson had declared War on Poverty. But in those days of stronger social stratification, most middle-class people had little to no contact with severely impoverished people. For that very reason, in his 1962 book *The Other America*, Michael Harrington referred to the millions of low-income people as the "invisible poor."

Our inadequate firsthand knowledge of low-cash lives had allowed us to idealize them before we actually tried living them. The renunciation of money that had been built into the counterculture was, according to Timothy Miller, "either blue-sky romanticism or evidence of social privilege." Like most of my peers across the nation who sought genteel poverty on the land, I too had grown up in a middle-class family, insulated from any conspicuous connections between work, money, power, and class. My father disappeared into the sliding doors of the commuter train each morning and reappeared hours later at the dinner table. Any relation between his daily rides into the city and my safe, clean, comfortable surroundings was all but lost on me. If Dad had worked third shift in a plant and dragged himself home at dawn with exhaustion and grease all over his face, if my parents had spent evenings quarreling over bills, or if I'd had to take a job at an early age to buy my own school clothes, I certainly wouldn't have romanticized the low-income lifestyle or the physical labor associated with it. Instead I would have grown up obsessed with entering the middle class rather than leaving it. But those of us who rejected the values and practices of our class heritage as well the capitalistic system that had advanced them, had little understanding about what insolvency entailed. One woman I interviewed for this book had briefly joined a Socialist Workers party on a university campus before going to the land. A blue-collar man chided her at the last SWP meeting, accusing her of abandoning her blue-collar friends to go live with a bunch of "dirty hippies." The man was furious that she wanted to "reject the very material things that the workers wanted and worked so hard to get: dishwashers, deodorant, and, I think, he may have mentioned electric toothbrushes," she said. The man obviously knew more than she did about what it meant to do without.

Perhaps subconsciously, part of our willingness to actively seek the privation we would end up resenting was our desire to "redeem [our] souls," as Paul Berman suggests in his article "The Moral History of the Baby Boom Generation." Privileged baby boomers, he writes, realized on some level that they had done nothing to deserve the inheritance of comfort and abundance their parents had gathered for them by suffering through the depression, World War II, and other major events. As a result, these young adults who came of age in the

1960s were dogged by spasms of conscience and sought to "leave behind the privileges and comforts of middle class life and go fight . . . for a better world."

But when the crop sales and the crafts fairs failed, while the bills for taxes and used car parts piled up, we no longer felt redeemed, only frightened. Barbara Ehrenreich, author of *Nickled and Dimed*, calls poverty "not a place you would want to visit for touristic purposes; it just smells too much like fear."

Counterculture Economics

Statistically, those of us who could sustain ourselves well or even get ahead financially on the land were in the minority. Jeffrey Jacob's research on back-to-the-land people revealed that only 3 percent of back-to-the-landers subsisted from a combination of cash crops, bartering, and resources on their own property; only 2 percent survived through "intensive cultivation of cash crops"; and 15 percent were able to generate a major source of income from entrepreneurships at home. On the other hand, 44 percent worked full-time away from the homesteads, 18 percent had pensions and investments, and 17 percent survived on part-time or seasonal work. Some back-to-the-land people prospered over time with their cash crops or crafts turned into entrepreneurships. In Maine I knew a couple, Seth and Deena, who seemed to make an adequate living selling handmade leather goods on the crafts fair circuit, and another couple, John and Sue, who maintained beehives in the backyard and sold enough honey to the local co-op and other stores to stay solvent. John Matz was able to start and maintain a successful glassworks studio on his land.

In my observation, these successful entrepreneurs were the minority. It's also possible that successful back-to-the-landers are merely more visible today than the others who couldn't stand the destitution and disappeared off the radar and into professional attire somewhere.

Some back-to-the-land people survived much longer because they arrived in the woods with larger cash reserves—discreetly downplayed, of course, since having too much money broke the implicit rules of the counterculture. We were, after all, trying to set an example for the larger avaricious culture that lived and breathed cash flow and materialism. Our purpose for going to the land was to strip away the excess. Yet an inherent conflict in the back-to-the-land ideology was that money and its accumulation was bad, but that low-impact technology and environmental awareness was good. On a low budget the continued discomforts of outhouses, lanterns, or water-hauling attenuated many people's initial passion for the principles. On the other hand, back-to-the-landers who had the money to buy composting toilets or solar paneling could continue their mission to preserve the environment and hold true to the values with much less personal inconvenience.

Rival emotions (alas, those split-second surges of jealousy) had been known to flash through a homesteader's mind when it became obvious that the back-to-the-landers down the road had trust fund dividends flowing in regularly yet continued to put on a façade of being nobly poor. But of course they had to. Being financially secure in an opulent way was taboo. Those lucky idealists who also happened to have a nest egg were careful to keep it quiet and spend it unobtrusively. If it became necessary for financially secure back-to-the-landers to make a sizable purchase, such as a new four-wheel drive or top-of-the-line woodstove, the expected rule was for them to downplay it, waving it off at the potluck get-togethers as having being found at a steal price somewhere or given for free by a brother-in-law in the city.

Of course, as long as one had no money to speak of, it was considered perfectly okay to apply for and receive food stamps, to patronize government-subsidized medical clinics, and to take advantage of government programs for the poor. For back-to-the-land people there was generally no shame in being open about this; for some, in fact, it was a semi-status symbol demonstrating their sincerity about having downsized to the bare bones. But after a while the freebies couldn't make up for the rising cost of living.

"The stress points of a life off the land center to a large extent on the elusive quest for 'enough' money. With few exceptions . . . back-to-the-landers also find themselves preoccupied with money, and as a consequence their relationship to tranquility becomes a precarious one," concludes Jeffrey Jacob.

Instant Poverty at Middle Earth

As you may recall, Kent and I had an Economic Plan, on paper at least, before moving to Maine. According to this plan, we would sell the city house in the spring for more than the mortgage payoff, use that profit to pay off the credit cards, and have enough cash free and clear to move immediately to Maine and get through the first growing season. Our log cabin would be paid for, the wood heat was free, the well was full of water, the garden would provide much of the food, the hens would lay eggs. Any extra money would be a king's ransom, in yesterday's dollars.

But the plan ripped apart the moment our Massachusetts house failed to sell on the timetable we had scheduled. As the months dragged by with no offers, Kent, determined to build our log cabin before winter closed in, left his job, moved to the land, and started building. My job kept us afloat meanwhile. When we accepted the low offer in late November, we were able to pay the mortgage and the credit cards; but when the dust settled, after moving expenses and the purchase of that second woodstove, we had barely any money left. Neither of us was employed any longer, and the garden was buried under a foot of snow and ice. Kent was able to file for unemployment from his previous job, and six weeks later the first check arrived. Others followed sporadically. Soon I had to look for the first of several dead-end jobs (which I talk about at greater length later). But because we started out in the hole, we never quite climbed out. Somehow, for nearly five years until I left, we got by, but barely. The income from low-end jobs, unemployment checks, and the rare sale of a batiked T-shirt, balanced against the expenses of broken car parts, taxes, and other emergencies and sundries, kept us wobbling precariously on a financial tightrope.

Cost-saving Measures

At Middle Earth we utilized many cost-saving measures to hold poverty at bay. For example, I baked all the bread at home. We bought only secondhand clothes for dimes at yard sales. We bought cheese and honey at the local co-op. We gave each other kitchen haircuts and would never have considered going to a real barber or hair salon.

After all, Scott and Helen Nearing, role models for the back-to-the-land community, had created a solvent and self-contained economy on their homestead. They worked only four hours a day, doing what they referred to as "bread labor," and then had four hours a day of leisure, to read, write, play music, do whatever they wanted. They "felt as free . . . as a caged wild bird who finds himself once more on the wing." As they explained in their book *Living the Good Life*, "The basis for our consumer economy was the garden. By raising and using garden products . . . we were able to provide ourselves with around 80% of our food."

Little did I know at the time that all was not as it appeared. The Nearings were not entirely free of cash flow, for all their appearance. According to Vivien Ellen Rose's well-researched doctoral dissertation, Scott and Helen Nearings' income from 1954 to 1972 "consisted of speakers' fees, net book sales, and donations. After 1955, the [Social Science Institute] paid Helen Nearing a nominal wage so she could report social security income to provide for retirement. . . ." In addition, the Institute's board of directors, which included the Nearings, "promoted the Nearings' books and offered financial contributions as well. Their revenues varied from $2,000 to $10,000 each year, with small deficits often being made up by board member donations. [The Nearings] published nine books, traveled throughout the United States, Europe, and Asia, and lectured in venues from living rooms to churches to international vegetarian conferences. . . . In 1971 and 1972, thanks to increased sales of their homesteading books, the Social Science Institute took in a little over $12,000 and $18,000 respectively, but still spent nearly what was earned on books and travel." Not that I begrudge the Nearings their income, whatever it was, but they always projected the impression to their followers of having and needing so little cash. Implicit in their model for homesteading was the negation of money. A good, solid bankroll contradicted the dogma of the Good Life.

On our homestead, unlike theirs, the garden did not add up economically, as it was supposed to. I remember one beautiful August day when I made ketchup for the first time. Outside the pine trees were swaying against the blue sky. In the kitchen, where I was working, the steam from a pot of boiling water had misted the window. Sweat ran down my face, leaving clear lines through the red stains across my cheeks. My fingers, hands, and arms were sticky and red as I sliced, pulled, cut, and quartered. For two hours I worked with a *Mother Earth News* article on "How to Make Ketchup" propped open in front of me. The nearby walls were plastered with seeds, stains, bits of pulp. Rivulets of juice flowed from the growing piles of damp tomato skins and cores on the counter, splashing onto the floor. Each time I carried another Ball canning jar to the cauldron of water on the stove, I stepped on tomato juice and tracked it across the floor.

When I finished this hot, endless task, the result was one canning jar, only half full of homemade ketchup, upon the counter. ONE JAR!! The whole process, from gathering the tomatoes to admiring the results, had taken three hours. After leaving the sopping red mess, I walked outside onto the front porch. The pine-scented breeze cooled my sweating face as I thought about having just spent a perfectly good summer afternoon making half a jar of ketchup. The Troy General Store sold whole bottles of ketchup for seventy-five cents. I was supposed to be saving money by harvesting, canning, and freezing the goods from our garden, but how much was it really saving, compared to the salary I might have been making at a real job? Had I saved enough from my homemade ketchup to pay for the new gaskets that the seven-year-old car now needed?

Car problems, in particular, seemed to plague us. One can jettison almost all the clutter of life, simplify right down to the two-seater la-trine, the lanterns, and the eggplant meals, but a car is almost always a necessity, especially in isolated areas. Some back-to-the-land people who lived on well-planned communes or land cooperatives created sys-tems for sharing a car or two among the whole group, as well as tools, expertise, and income, which reduced the need for individual owner-ship. Others, let's face it, had anticipated how expensive it was to be poor and brought inconspicuous bank accounts with them to the land and were therefore able to maintain their cars. One homesteader I in-terviewed told me that her father "freaked out when he saw what we were driving and bought us a four-wheel drive, so we were in pretty good shape vehicle-wise after the first year."

I too had been the recipient of a new car seven years before we had gone to the land. I remembered when my parents had bought it for me, brand new, as a college graduation present. My mother and I had entered the Volkswagen dealership that sunny May morning after graduation, she looking properly middle class in a skirt and top, with well-coiffed hair, pulling out her checkbook and casually writing out the full amount for the car on the spot while I stood beside her struggling with my clashing feel-ings of contempt, envy, and gratitude. True, Volkswagens didn't cost all that much in those days, but I felt contempt toward her ability to scrawl out a check and outright own a car. It seemed so bourgeois, so representa-tive of what my friends and I all felt was wrong with our overly materialis-tic society. I also felt stirrings of envy at how wonderful that must be. And I felt deep gratitude. After all, she was buying me a car! The gratitude won out, of course, and I could barely contain my excitement, sycophantically thanking her over and over. The car's overpowering smell of newness; its purring motor, its fresh blue exterior, un-dinged by hardships of the road and the seasons, catapulted me into a lovely postgraduation high on that blue-skyed summer day. The world lay at my feet! I was a college graduate with a new car, a new job awaiting me, and a bright future.

But now, seven years later, by the winter of '77, my mother was dead, my career was over, and the car was beginning to stall a lot. The floorboard was collapsing, assailed by long winters and rock salt on the roads. Ice-cold drafts blew up from the open floorboards as I drove; the speeding ground was visible below. Kent was very handy at car repairs when he could find the right parts at the dump. Fellow Middle Earth homesteader Bruce Lemire said, years later, "I can remember the way Kent fixed the car. He'd say, 'I'm not sure what's wrong with it, so I'm going to replace this part.' Then he'd say, 'Okay, it still doesn't work, so I'm going to replace that part instead.' So he'd replace parts until the car worked," laughed Bruce. "I used to say, 'God, Kent, why don't you figure out what's wrong with it. It's cheaper.' But I guess that's just a way of attacking a problem."

Since the VW was declining fast, Kent found an ancient Jeep somewhere in town and bought it for a song after a lucky postal delivery of several unemployment checks at once. The reason for its bargain price was that it had no functional reverse gear, and one of the doors would not completely shut. Although Kent tried to repair it, the door would swing open without warning as we drove down the road. The time the door swung open and deposited three-year-old Shawn along the snowy road is another story; suffice to say he survived it, and as a grown man now he can laugh about it. While I may have acted sanctimonious about my mother's ability to run out and purchase a car as one of the morning errands, I was beginning to appreciate the practical advantages of financial security. Money wasn't just about buying frivolous, useless things; it was sometimes about buying safety.

So now we owned two unreliable cars instead of one, and our car problems multiplied. I'm sure over the years we spent more on car parts and repairs than a new car would have cost—had we had the money or credit. One day while Kent was repairing the Volkswagen's broken floorboard, he accidentally cut through the car's brake line. There went the brakes! The car had also begun to leak a quart or two of oil every day.

He said to me one afternoon, "I need to drive the Jeep into Waterville to get the parts to fix the VW's oil leak and brakes. I guess you'll have to plan on taking the Jeep to work tonight when I get back, because I'm going to have to take the VW apart to fix it."

Our seven-year-old VW bug broke down frequently. We could barely afford the parts to repair it, let alone a new car.

"Okay," I said, aware of the maneuvers needed to avoid needing reverse gear. Later that day, when I was ready to drive into town, the VW's innards were scattered across the yard. Kent's face was covered with grease and sweat as he clanked the wrench against metal car parts.

When I got into the Jeep and turned the key, the motor clicked. Furiously I turned it again. No sound except a click.

"Oh shit!" I screeched. "Not this one too."

"Hell!" exclaimed Kent, getting up from the ground with his wrench and stepping around the VW engine parts. He lifted the Jeep's rusted hood, stuck his head in, poked around, and moved back and forth between the engine, the ignition key, and his toolbox.

"Wait a minute," he said optimistically, clinking onto a part under the hood. "I think I may have the problem. Right there." He hopped into the driver's seat, turned the key, and listened to the ignition click.

"Dammit!" he exclaimed, throwing the wrench onto the ground. "Okay. If I can't get this one started, maybe I can get the other back together," he sighed.

Covered with leaked oil, he emerged from under the Volkswagen fifteen minutes later. As I sat behind the wheel accelerating at intervals, he checked the oil level in the engine.

Kent said, "The oil leak's fixed. For the time being. But those brakes aren't so good." He said that if I pumped them a lot and downshifted the gears as I was approaching a stop, I'd be okay. If all else failed, pull the emergency brake. There was only one stoplight between here and Waterville, so I'd be fine, he said. He'd find the parts to fix the brakes tomorrow.

With a headache moving up the back of my neck, I got into the VW and started driving up the slope. I hadn't gotten five feet when I heard Kent yelling, "Wait! Stop!" Beneath the car, a gasket lay in the snow surrounded by a puddle of black oil. Such were the car problems that beleaguered us for, it seemed to me, a good part of the time I was there.

The following week Kent replaced both the Volkswagen's brake line and the master cylinder. After that the car started most of the time and ran fairly well. At other unpredictable times it wouldn't start at all. Then the engine seized up one day as Kent was returning from Belfast. The car wouldn't go more than thirty miles per hour, the engine clunking ominously. We had no choice but to drop it off at a local mechanic. It needed a repair job that not only would take several weeks but would cost $500, which in yesterday's dollars, and at a dead-end job income of about $100 a week, was insurmountable. It was a blow.

We started driving the Jeep again, which had aged severely since we had first acquired it. The northern climate is not kind to cars, and in addition to having no reverse gear, the body was now badly rusted, with the doors, floorboards, and back flap hanging by metal threads. Aesthetics was the least of my concerns. I just didn't want my children falling out on the road, as Shawn had.

Obviously cars grow old, break down, and wear out everywhere, not just on farms, homesteads, or communes. But they cost the same to repair or replace, whether they are parked in the muddy yard beside a log cabin, where the inhabitants are scraping by on substandard income of unemployment checks and waitressing tips, or whether they are parked in a penthouse parking garage. The necessity for a reliable car is pivotal to economic success or failure, more than ever in rural areas without public transportation, where jobs are miles away. An eternally ailing vehicle can become the linchpin of perpetual financial hardship. In proportion to the number and frequency of car problems, you become more and more deeply ensnared in the capitalistic trap of needing to go to work in order to pay for the last car part you needed in order to go to work.

If I'd had money to spend on a car in those days, I assure you I would only have wanted a new car so that it would run reliably, a car that would start every time I turned the key, and maybe even have a decent heater. Never, ever would it have occurred to me to want a new car for status or show. In fact, never would it have occurred to me to want money for any reason other than to fend off the aggravations and discomforts that were beginning to mount.

Struggling Financially in Virginia

In 1978 Gail Adams, her husband, and three children bought a farm in Bristol, Virginia. They had been living in Washington, D.C., and the ills of city life troubled Gail and her husband Larry. He had a long commute through heavy traffic, the price of real estate in the D.C. area was astronomical, and the schools were overcrowded and drug-laden. Something was missing from their lives. Furthermore Gail had always wanted to get back to her roots by moving to the country. "Most of the women I was friends with seemed to want to gossip or talk about shopping all the time. I just wanted more. And I loved gardening. I more or less wanted to do organic gardening and just live a simpler life."

Some days Larry would say, "I just want to grow a big field of corn." They decided to move to the country. They left Washington and moved into a two-story farmhouse with a big front porch. Never expecting to live entirely off the land, they counted on a full-time income from Larry. But they hadn't expected it to be so much lower.

When Larry told an employer how much salary he wanted, the employer responded, "There's nobody here makes that kind of money." So Larry took a salary cut, and they tried their best to live on it. The house was not well insulated, a fact they became aware of as soon as winter set in. They raised cattle and occasional pigs, and grew tobacco and some corn. They canned and froze vegetables and fruits. Despite the cost-saving measures of growing and preserving food, they struggled financially.

"Larry did not make the money that we were used to having, and we found that it wasn't that cheap at first to live on the farm," said Gail. "Up in Washington you could do better cost comparing, and get better deals; down in Bristol the food was a little more expensive, clothes were no cheaper—the only thing that really was cheaper was taxes and land. Everything else cost the same. You go to an eye doctor and get glasses, just anything like that, it was very expensive."

Gail soon had to go to work too, but they remained insolvent. The old car with the peeling vinyl roof was always breaking down too, which was a source of embarrassment for the three daughters.

One time Gail was driving a daughter and her friends to a school function twenty miles from the farm. "The radiator had broken, and we had to take jars of water and fill it up on the way up there. One morning, I'd taken the girls over to Bristol. They had a real big intersection where four main roads came together, and we were starting to cross there, and my car died right there," says Gail, recalling how the mortified girls had cried, 'Mom!' Someone finally stopped and pushed us out of the way, but it was horrible.

"I was always devising ways to make the money last, and it got to the point where I had the reputation in the family of being the stingy one, the one who wouldn't spend anything. I wrote all the checks and paid the bills. I would always be the one to say, 'We do not have the money; we cannot afford it.' Eating out, for example. I would say, 'I could buy three days of groceries for this; we can't do it.' I was always the one who had to be the person to say no. I used to buy butter in a lump and cut it in pieces rather than buying it in sticks already cut, just to save money.

"It did get to the point where I didn't have clothes to go out, so I was content to stay home and not try to go out and do things, because of the clothing situation. After I went back to work, the employees in that office all wore white pants and some kind of little top, so I still didn't buy nice dress clothes. For several years I hardly had anything I could go out and look nice in."

Because Gail was a smart clothes shopper and bought only quality clothes when they went on sale at 75 percent off, one of the girls told her, "Mom, people don't know how poor we really are."

She always devised low-cost ways to go out with her husband. Sometimes on Saturday evenings she and Larry would go over to Bristol and buy a box of day-old fried chicken on sale and a bottle of cheap wine, and they'd go ride around the back roads. "Depending on the weather, we'd get out and walk, go down to the creek, or just ride around. That was our entertainment, our date."

Gail says she felt desperate about money on several occasions when things went wrong. "We had a couple of twenty-year or fifty-year floods that did some damage to our barn and some of our crops. The water from the creek that encircled the house and barn rose to within twenty feet of the house." Gail could see the valuable topsoil running down into the creek. "I always felt that topsoil was worth more than money," she said.

As the water flowed into the barn, ruining all the hay, they had to release the two pigs, who they assumed would stay around the garden area. The next thing Gail knew, a state policeman was knocking on the front door later that morning, asking, "Ma'am do you own a hog?" The pigs had trotted off to the highway, so Gail had to send the girls out there after them—"embarrassing for teenage girls," she notes—to herd them home.

Gail loved her years on the farm and has no regrets. Deprivation never affected her during those lean years, "but I did feel it from my children."

Affording college for their three daughters was difficult. Gail and Larry had set aside some money before going to the land, "but honest to goodness," says Gail, "we didn't have any idea that the cost of college would go up so much during the '80s." Although Gail and Larry could help out, the girls had to work their way through college.

Their oldest daughter, Christina, was a teenager when her parents moved to the farm. She deplored the poverty. "We were dead broke," she remembers. "Sometimes we didn't have enough heat. One winter there was a big blizzard. We didn't have enough oil in the tank, so my parents had to shut up all the rooms and all the upstairs except for the living room and the kitchen. My mom would turn on the oven and open the door. We all slept around the woodstove and the open oven for a few days. It was *so* cold and *so* miserable, and I thought, 'I can't believe we're living like this.' I was old enough to know that this wasn't the way it should be. I was really angry at my parents then for what they did. I was like, 'How could you move here and let us do this? How could you do this? How could you not get enough oil in the heating tank?' I was really mad at them."

Tightening the belt, her mother used to mix items together to stretch them. "If there was a little bit of shampoo left, she'd mix Palmolive in it, then add water. You were washing your hair with this splashy, thin concoction, which I just totally hated back then, and which I would still hate today. Even if I were broke, I wouldn't mix products."

The cupboards at home were stocked with food, but on the road the family could rarely afford fast food. If the girls got hungry during a trip to town, they either had to wait or make do with a partial snack. Famished, Christina and her sisters might ask their mother to stop for food. She might say, "Okay, I've got four dollars, and it's got to feed all of us." So each of the girls would choose one item off the fast-food menu—Christina might get a burger, another sister the french fries, and the third sister a salad—and their drink would be water.

One Saturday, Christina grew very hungry on a shopping expedition to Bristol. Her mother said, "You either can wait till we get back home because we have food there, but right now this is all I have," and she handed them one dollar. "Maybe you can get a snack." She dropped the girls off at K-Mart.

"We were *hungry*," explains Christina. "My mom wasn't being mean or anything; that was all she had. So we went into K-Mart and got this bag of really cheap ham sandwiches, three ham sandwiches in the bag for like fifty-nine cents. Then we found one container of chocolate milk. Everybody got one sandwich, and we shared the little container of chocolate milk. We all three got to eat something good for lunch, for a dollar."

Christina admired her mother's ability to buy quality clothing on such a restricted budget. They shopped at the best store in Bristol, but they shopped only for sale items. Christina, her mother, and sisters would "circle that lone sales rack." Any desired clothing had to appear on the 75-percent-off sales rack before Gail would buy it.

"I think that was a really, really good lesson, in retrospect. It was very difficult back then, though. We went through a lot of times of never having enough money for the little things teenagers need."

Christina left the farm with strong career aspirations. She couldn't wait to get a degree and move into a profession. Did she consciously aspire to a well-paying job? "You bet I did. I absolutely did," she responded.

College proved to be a financial struggle. Christina worked her way through, sometimes working three jobs. "I had very, very lean times, but I knew it was temporary. Because then I was doing it for the greater upward movement. Yes, I did vow never to be poor again," she says emphatically.

❦ *In a photo taken at my brother's wedding, my sons, Derek and Shawn, pose beside me on the dance floor at the reception. The boys, six and four, are happily oblivious to their mismatched little jackets and pants, probably all Kent and I could find in their size range at the Troy Annual Flea Market. Derek's jacket is an odd pink or salmon color; Shawn's is camel. Their sleeves hang to their knuckles, and the trousers, one plaid and the other solid, fit loosely.*

We barely made it to that wedding. When the invitation arrived, Kent decreed that there was no way we could afford to drive to Rhode Island and stay in a motel for two nights. Period. We didn't have any money. All those brilliant ideas about cash crops and cottage industries had been the pipe dream of some editor at Mother Earth News, apparently. I phoned my father to tell him we couldn't attend. I pictured him at the other end, mouth pursed, as he offered to pay for our trip. I accepted. He would pay for the motel in advance and send a check to pay for our drive down. But in a later phone call, as we ironed out details, he grew momentarily irritated and asked, "Shouldn't you be ashamed at your age that you need to ask for money to get to your brother's wedding?"

The knife twisted as this comment hit the mark swift and true. After hanging up, I was beyond mortification. I cried and decided we wouldn't go to the wedding after all. But we were already committed, the reservations had been made, the local mechanic had just put a rebuilt engine in the VW (for which we'd had to take out a $500 loan), and the car appeared to have no impending breakdowns. My sister intervened and campaigned to convince me that Dad hadn't really meant it—don't be foolish, take his money and go to Rhode Island, he could easily afford it.

We drove to Providence in our banged-up VW. The foliage brightened the landscape. I felt as though a lifetime had passed since I'd seen people driving up-to-date cars that weren't splattered with mud. I feasted my eyes on the women sporting salon haircuts, wearing makeup and jewelry, the children in fresh, matching clothes. As we drove past glass-tinted skyscrapers and malls into neighborhoods, I watched houses glide by that did not display frozen long johns flapping on a clothesline.

At the wedding reception we ate catered food and drank cocktails rather than home-brewed dandelion wine. We mingled with relatives and friends who were well dressed, taking off in their careers, and who apparently hadn't yet died of pesticides in food. Envy stirred, for I remembered dressing well once, wearing makeup, buying new clothes. I remembered going out for dinner in restaurants with Kent on Saturday nights, going on vacations, buying things just for fun, none of which we could do anymore. I know how shallow that sounds, but I have to be honest. What haunted me most, however, as we drove back up Route 95 to return to Maine, was the shame. I was still cringing at the knowledge that I'd had to accept money from my father in order to travel to the wedding. I was still stinging from his remark, "Shouldn't you be ashamed at your age that you need to ask for money to get to your brother's wedding?" Chances are, he hadn't meant to be supercilious or cruel; all parents say things they don't mean in the heat of the moment. In general, Dad, rest his soul, was always kind and supportive.

In The Stigma of Poverty, Chaim Waxman writes that "poverty is a special type of stigma which attributes to the poor a status of being 'less than human,' and that stigma has taken various shapes at different historical stages. . . . The basic stigma was poverty as a manifestation of moral defect. The classification of the poor indicated that there were perceived to be gradations or levels of moral defect among the poor. In general, however, poverty was seen as due to the moral failure of the individual."

The fact that Dad's words had struck a nerve in me indicates that deep down, right or wrong, I had internalized this unspoken stigma. I was thirty years old and a financial deadbeat. A failure in the eyes of my father and the whole wedding party, no doubt. And most important, in my own.

CHAPTER SIX

Generating Cash Flow

"The pressures of moving back and forth between farmstead and job make the allure of convenience all the more seductive."
—Jeffrey Jacob, *New Pioneers*

🌱 *Bracing himself for the cold, Bruce Lemire rolled out from under his three or four thick blankets and hurried across the darkened room to the woodstove. Outside, the night wind howled. Ice crystals had formed on the nail heads on the plywood floor. Opening the stove's metal door, he quickly stirred the glowing embers with the fire iron and stacked kindling and a few logs onto the dying fire. Blowing gently, he waited, quaking with cold, as the tentative flames rose from the embers and caught. Latching the woodstove door, he rushed back to his bed, reset his alarm clock, and crawled gratefully under the covers for another interval of sleep. Because Maine was in the grip of such a potent cold spell during Bruce's first winter on our homestead, the fire had to be fed every two hours throughout the night, like a hungry baby.*

Bruce had moved onto our land in Troy after he was laid off from his job at the CROP *Protection Institute in New Hampshire, a company that tested chemicals. He had entered the company at the bottom and moved up fast. By the time the company closed, he had taken over the job of manager of his division, planning the experiments and writing the reports. But the company had folded at about the same time Bruce and his wife had divorced. "I was* out of work. Out of marriage. It was an opportune time to do something different," he said. "I came up to Troy just to simplify everything." So Bruce moved onto the land and set about finding a more serene existence.

"I remember that the only permit I was required to get was for a septic system," says Bruce, "and I remember clearly that it cost $75 for a guy to come over. He told me I had to dig a hole four feet deep, and when I got down to two feet I hit bedrock because it was built on that cliff. So for the $75 he drew out a plan for a leach field and a septic tank and all this stuff—and—I never saw him again. So I put in an outhouse, as I'd planned to do."

Bruce had never constructed a house before, but he had built smaller things, so he was confident a house would pose no problems. A local woman offered him the wood from her old, collapsing barn, so he spent his summer days tearing the ancient structure down, loading the wood into his pickup, and driving it back and forth, load after load after load, to his construction site at Middle Earth. He completed his home before the winter weather paralyzed the region. Except for the foundation. The house was still up on blocks; the floor consisted of 5/8-inch plywood, which was all that protected him from the outside air.

"That first winter was hell," he recalls.

He received a ninety-dollar-a-week unemployment check, which did not stretch far beyond survival. This was fine in the summer. He had lived frugally, planting vegetables and eating from the garden. But by winter he would have welcomed more cash to purchase "things to make life more comfortable," such as tools, furniture, a better refrigerator. Many of the counterculture people in the area collected unemployment checks without an iota of guilt and learned how to work the system so that they did not have to discover a replacement job until the last unemployment check had been cashed. Bruce, however, felt guilty living on unemployment, so when the Waldo County Unemployment Office landed him a job in Bangor, he soon found himself working at Eastern Maine Medical Center as a respiratory therapist for $1.65 an hour.

Now he rose each morning after a night of fragmented sleep, dressed in the dark, and bumped down our potholed dirt road in his truck, breathing out clouds of air as he waited for the heater to kick in. Bangor was a thirty-mile *drive on slippery roads, so he left his house an hour before punch-in time. He worked his shift aspirating the lungs of very sick patients, a job for which his earlier work experience had not prepared him.*

"I had a hard time with it because many of my patients were terminal, and I was just keeping them alive until they died," says Bruce. "There were several that I unhooked from the support systems. There was this third floor over in the corner of the Medical Center, the building that we would take them to die. That was rough. It was stressful. Mostly old people, and I enjoy old people. I remember one elderly lady that I took up there and unhooked, and she said cheerfully, 'Goodbye!' I said, 'Yeah, goodbye.' She didn't know. She was dead come Monday morning when I went back to work. To watch some of these people deteriorate . . . there were just some things that were too hard, you know?"

Bruce was earning only $91 a week at his job, from which he had to buy gas for the commute and pay for other needs. His shift at work, plus the two hours of commuting, devoured his time too. Six months was all he could stand before he resigned from the job. Soon after, he left Maine and moved out West.

❧ As the U.S. economy continued to decline in the 1970s, along with our dreams of getting by on cottage industries, cash crops, and occasional odd jobs, many of us began to "work out," as we called reporting at a legitimate over-the-table job where the employer reported taxes and wages. Before moving to the land we had told our city friends, our parents, and especially ourselves that if we ever did have to work out, we would prefer random, non-career-oriented jobs, whatever we stumbled upon. We had gone to the land to escape the trap of a hollow, fast-track occupation in some office. White-collar careers were stifling and limiting. They sucked all the life's blood out of you, and if you reached age sixty-five, the boss gave you a gold watch, kicked you out the door, and forgot about you; that's how impersonal it was. But lately, the way the economy was going, you might end up fired and out on the street long before your retirement. The 1970s saw the first massive white-collar layoffs and downsizings in any of our memories, which gave us further reason to distrust the idea of investing ourselves in a career.

On the land, when it came time to work out, we were initially drawn to blue- and pink-collar jobs. For one thing, white-collar opportunities did not abound in places like Troy, Maine. But low-impact jobs were just what we wanted. A plain old job would just be a *job*. It would not stress us out. We would have little to no emotional investment in our stints at the local general store, the restaurant, or the hospital ward, and that suited us just fine. It would be easy. No hassles, no gold watches. We could quit any time we wanted, without guilt.

In 1979 Daniel Yankelovich referred to us as "the New Breed," whose strange new work ethic had overthrown the "old value system" of careers. Under that system, people had identified themselves almost entirely by their careers. In particular, a man's sense of responsibility and masculinity was strongly tied up with his occupation.

Yankelovich notes, "In many surveys conducted in the 1950s and 1960s, most men (75 to 80 percent) would say in response to direct questions that they were indeed satisfied with their jobs. However, when one probed for the reasons, most would, in effect, reply, 'Well, it's really a lousy job, but at least it's a living. As long as it lets me take care of my family, I'm satisfied.'"

But the young people of the new generation were different. Unlike our elders, we were not motivated by money or success. We were motivated by self-fulfillment, whatever situation brought that about.

"In the New Breed," continues Yankelovich, "we see the beginnings of an ethic built around the concept of duty to oneself, in glaring contrast to the traditional ethic of obligation to others."

In the 1970s, agrees Amitai Etzioni, the scholar and founder of American Communitarianism, millions of people began to "devote less zeal to their work and more toward improving their understanding of self and others, toward cultivating their 'inner space,' and pursuing leisure activities. . . ."

The very point of work-out jobs was that they would not become focal points for our identity, fulfillment, or social life, as professional jobs might have. As one former commune dweller reminded me, "Back then, when you worked out, there were people you worked with, but your *friends* were not necessarily the people you worked with. You made your friends outside of work. During those years you went to work, and then you came home to be with your friends. We didn't necessarily socialize with people we worked with; we spent more time with them just by dint of how many hours we worked, but then you would go and make friends elsewhere." On the other hand, work-out jobs had their disadvantages too.

Work-out Jobs

The jobs that substituted for our entrapping city careers often turned out to be as dissatisfying as the professional gigs we wanted to avoid. And paid a lot less too. The "mindless" jobs that we imagined we wouldn't bring home with us came home with us anyway, at the very least physically, in the form of aching feet, sunburn, or back pain, if it was an outdoor job. Robert Acuna, a real outdoor laborer interviewed for Studs Terkel's book *Working*, describes the difficulty of "bending and stooping all day. Sometimes you would have hard ground and by the time you got home, your hands would be full of calluses. And you'd have a backache . . . There were times when I felt I couldn't take it any more. It was 105 in the shade and I'd see endless rows of lettuce and I felt my back hurting. . . . I'd just go home and fall asleep and wake up just in time to go out in the fields again."

Kent learned this when he took his first work-out job at a seed company called Johnny's Selected Seeds, where he earned a little above minimum wage. During the growing season and harvest time, he toiled under the hot sun (yes, even in Maine) in the unshaded fields. He came home sunburned and sore from the constant bending and standing, with dirt-stained, callused hands from plucking and digging. Quite a different story from radio dee-jaying.

To the surprise of many of us, work-out jobs had psychological repercussions too, in the form of boredom, frustration, anger, and other negative emotions: in other words, the same feelings professional people have after a bad day at work, only for far lower pay. Kent discovered that any boredom he had felt at the radio station in Massachusetts was downright electrifying compared to the monotony of the winter tasks he did at the seed company. During the cold months he and the other workers sat all day in a chilly warehouse sorting and packaging custom-bred seeds that were mailed to customers around the country.

It's true that some back-to-the-land people who needed to increase their cash flow were fortunate enough to live within driving distance of gratifying jobs in fields they liked. But because of our isolation, a large number of us worked in positions not commensurate with our talents, goals, and education.

Waitressing at the Waterville Steak House

One of my favorite scenes from the play *The Glass Menagerie* is Tom's outburst to Amanda about how much he hates his job at the warehouse: "I'd rather somebody picked up a crowbar and battered out my brains—than go back mornings! I *go*! Every time you come in yelling that Goddamn 'Rise and Shine!' 'Rise and Shine!' I say to myself, 'How *lucky dead* people are!' But I get up. I *go*! For sixty-five dollars a month, I give up all that I dream of doing and being *ever*!"

Whenever I teach that play now, I always linger at that scene, asking the students, "Did you ever have a job you hated that much, the way Tom does?" Secretly I'm thinking of my *own* stint as a waitress at a steak house in Waterville, Maine.

Very soon after we moved to Maine, I had to work out. Kent and I desperately needed the cash. Establishing a simple life was more expensive than we had realized. As one ex-homesteader friend of mine remarked wryly, "It took *money* for a tiller, a chain saw, a woodstove, a pickup truck. Everything cost *money*. It took a lot to be "*self-sufficient*."

So the next thing I knew, I had my hair in a bun, with wisps springing out on all sides, and now stood, donned in a checkered uniform, white apron, and white orthopedic shoes, taking orders from surly parties of four at the Waterville Steak House. I was now driving twenty-five miles over country roads into Waterville, the nearest small city, to work as a waitress in a restaurant that specialized in steaks and seafood. The upside of the job, and the only one, was that I was able to scavenge seafood from the Pu Pu Platter, the house specialty, whose items I salivated for. The tiered wooden platter held an assortment of baked and fried seafood whose smell intoxicated me as I conveyed it across the dining room to the lucky party who would eat it. I particularly loved the breaded jumbo shrimp. At twenty dollars a plate, I could never afford to pay for a platter, but like all the waitresses I surreptitiously slipped an untouched jumbo shrimp or two into a napkin as soon as I waltzed past the swinging doors into the kitchen, slipping them into my purse to enjoy later at home. As unhygienic as this sounds, you must realize how hungry I was. I was always so hungry! The tantalizing smells of the food during the long evening shifts made me crazy. And chronic exhaustion exacerbated my hunger. Remember, I never slept past dawn in the mornings. Before leaving for the restaurant at three in the afternoon and driving an hour on the potholed roads into Waterville, I had already put in a full day on the homestead, feeding the woodstove, hauling the water, doing wash in the wringer, and taking care of the children while Kent worked outside. By the time I climbed tiredly up the steps of the log cabin at midnight after working my shift, I was limp with cold, hunger, and exhaustion. As the soft snores of Kent and the boys drifted down from the upstairs loft, it was my own private luxury to settle onto the couch across from the woodstove and savor two cold jumbo shrimp. They tasted heavenly, especially when combined with a tall glass of cheap red wine which I gulped down rapidly to help wash away my memories of the evening.

Now—of the many downsides to the job: First, I was ungraceful and awkward carrying trays. Second, I was never one to remain serene under pressure. When three or four parties were yapping for me at once, yoo-hooing, snapping fingers, demanding more ketchup or faster service, I quickly grew panicky, unlike the other waitresses who seemed naturally laid back, unfazed by restaurant annoyances. I was overly sensitive and unable to take it in stride when customers acted cold, crabby, or belligerent. I approached a booth, for example, where a husband and wife sat drinking. I didn't realize how drunk the man was until I smiled ritualistically and asked, "Are you ready to order now?" The man, hefty and middle-aged, reeking of alcohol, turned his whole body ninety degrees toward me and mimicked my voice as he responded mockingly, "No, we're not ready to *order now*, so take that stupid *schmile* off your face and get out of here."

During rare quiet times I'd loiter with the other waitresses in the corridor between the kitchen and the dining room and listen to them monologue idly about their boyfriends or husbands. One eighteen-year-old girl with bouncy dark curls complained a lot about her husband, and the signs were so obviously there, to me at least, that her marriage was already as flat and sour as an old beer. Sure enough, she soon was bragging about dates with one of the dishwashers, which turned into overnights (she shared all the details). Her divorce was not a surprise to me.

I easily picked up on the subtle signals among the girls and sensed that they didn't like me. If they mocked me because I wasn't a good waitress, well, they were right about that. I was a *terrible* waitress. It was a wonder the management kept me around. I lacked a Maine accent, so they knew I wasn't "from around there," but my husband was now collecting unemployment checks, just like Rhonda's husband, and I was working there for the same reasons they were, because I needed the cash. Was I really any different? I didn't think so. At this point, we had no money saved, low-income jobs, and no other place to go except back to the cabin in the woods.

I suppose if we'd really wanted to, we could have packed it all up, driven down to Portland, and begged Kent's financially secure parents to take us all into their comfy upper-class home until we regrouped and got back on track, and that was a choice the other waitresses at the restaurant probably didn't have. But how could we give up now? We had a financial and even greater emotional investment in living where we did and the way we did. We weren't starving or homeless, just frightened and frustrated by the severely narrowed choices the lack of cash flow had brought.

Other Work-out Jobs

I wasn't the only one to work out at a horrible job.

Soon after he and his wife had settled on their land, John Verlenden had to seek work. "I did so many labor jobs I can't remember them all," he says. "I had one job for a while digging out swimming pools, which is some of the hardest work I've ever done in my life." Then John received a call from the city of Terra Alto, which wanted to hire him under the CETA program to run the sewage treatment plant. After all, he had an almost completed undergraduate degree.

The person hiring said, "You're the only person who has this much education who isn't running banks around here. You're the only person we can ask to run this sewage treatment plant."

John replied, "I'll be glad to help, but I have no knowledge whatsoever." The man said, "Well, there's a manual out there."

"Is the plant running now?" asked John.

"It runs pretty much by itself," explained the man, "but it does need somebody to do tests, and also to maintain things and just keep an eye over it."

John asked, "Well, how long does it run by itself?"

"It's been a couple of months that it's just been out there running itself. There was a real good man who had the job before you; he knew that plant up and down. But he committed suicide."

John now says, upon reflection, "I tried to fit this together with maybe one of those not-so-great side benefits of being a lone sewage plant operator for eight hours a day. Nonetheless I went out there to this room with a huge impeller-driven motor. I did find the manual. On the table. Right where the guy had left it, no doubt. Right before he went off to shoot himself, which is what happened. He shot himself. Yeah, he was a loner. And really smart; everybody said he was the smartest guy in town. But a loner.

"I never could figure out the manual," continues John. "As for the tests I was supposed to be making, I couldn't figure them out either. It was just over my head. Before, I'd thought I could learn anything in the manual. This simply was not so. You really had to have a background that was deeper than I had in chemistry. Either that or the gumption to go to the local library and read up on chemistry every night for six months until you actually understood those concepts. I had that job for probably nine months, and it was tremendously, incredibly loud in that little house where I had to be in the winter, especially, because it was so cold and there was a lot of snow on the ground. It was so loud in that little house that I could stay in it only for the minimum amount of time. So I would spend my time walking around the sewage treatment plant grounds, outside, and learning animal tracks."

"There were a lot of animals in West Virginia," he adds with a laugh.

For four and a half years, Jim Carlson, who lived on a farm in Arkansas, worked in a factory as a weaver, operating the looms. He started working the graveyard shift and later worked the swing shift. "Have you seen that movie *Norma Rae* with Sally Field?" he asks. "It made it look like you just stood there and ran one loom. No, you had about thirty to fifty, depending on what kind of machines they were. And it was very noisy. There was this cotton dust in the air all the time. There were almost no worker rights there. It was a real anti-union climate, and the company controlled it pretty heavily. I worked there at the time there was a union vote. And we lost," he laughs. "They never unionized. Anyhow, that was all to make it possible to live in the country."

An Abusive Workplace

Her parents' move to the country had caused a sharp drop in income, and the effects carried over into Christina Adams's college years. Although her parents pulled the money together to send her, Christina lived on a weekly college allowance of five dollars. "It got so desperate that I said, 'Mom, you have got to send me some money,' and so she started giving me ten dollars a week," remembers Christina. "That's all I had, for all of my needs. So I was always scraping up jobs. I started cutting guys' hair for five dollars. I was really good at makeup and doing hair, so for dances I'd charge the girls ten dollars to do their hair and makeup. One night I had seven clients before a big Homecoming dance. So I made seventy dollars that night."

During the last year of college, Christina's parents couldn't afford the required hundred-dollar fee for her to eat in the school cafeteria, which meant that she had to work three part-time jobs. The one she disliked most was waitressing. Because of the stressful schedule, she lost a lot of weight.

"Waitressing was really an abusive environment. The supervisor once tried to tell me a dirty joke, but I anticipated his punch line, and he got this spoiled, pouty look on his face because I'd ruined his dirty joke. Then he flashed a big bankroll and asked me to run off to Vegas with him. The work was extremely difficult too. You'd serve people these huge dinners with prime ribs, salad, all this stuff, and the standard tip was a dollar," she recalls. "And that horrible side work. They won't even let you sit down. Yet, I was lucky to get that job. There was a woman there who'd been a coal miner, but she'd lost her job. She lived two hours away. This was the only job she could find. She'd drive almost two hours every day, through the winding mountains, to come over and be this waitress, then go back to her home."

Some People Liked Working Out

On the other hand, some back-to-the-landers recall the work-out jobs they held with some nostalgia, just short of fondness, saying that some of these short-term jobs weren't bad. They liked the freedom of knowing they could quit any time, with no regrets.

Carlyle Poteat, a video producer, remembers taking many uneventful short-term jobs while living full-time on her farm outside of Chapel Hill, North Carolina, during the seventies. Some were fun. She particularly liked the job as a house cleaner for a wealthy professional couple. Carlyle managed their household, shopped, ran errands, and managed appointments with maintenance people who came to the house.

"That job actually felt like a good deal to me at the time. They paid me really well. It was enjoyable work, and it gave me freedom too. I had a fair amount of time for myself," says Carlyle.

Many back-to-the-land people say they gained priceless experience from spending time with people from working-class backgrounds. Don Wirtshafter, now a lawyer, went to the land in 1972 and made an effort, on principle, to live below the income tax level of $600 a year. He did haying and other odd jobs for the neighbors. "It was really valuable for me to be able to hang out with these old farmers, who'd pay all of a dollar and a quarter an hour and treat you in a very formal way, except that they'd invite you to eat a great country lunch. I learned a good deal of farm sense, especially from Ed Sheridan, a local auctioneer farmer and horse trader, who was quite a character. Being able to hang out with people like him and John Lewis taught me farm *sense* that I wouldn't have learned in any city job."

Michael Doyle, now a college professor, feels the same way. From 1973 to 1975 he worked as a hired man on various dairy farms in Wisconsin. As a young man with hair down to his waist, living in an area of Republican dairy farmers, he was "the anomaly," he says. But the farmers, socially progressive and fiscally conservative Lincoln Republicans, accepted him without question. His reputation as an assiduous worker had gotten around. "They knew I was dependable, and they kind of tolerated me as a local character," he remembers. "The farmers used to stop by all the time to chat because they were always lonesome for someone to talk to, and it was an interesting way to exchange ideas, for me to find out where they were coming from, and for them to learn a little bit more about the wider world and wider ways of living that I was in touch with."

Kathie Weir grew close to her work colleagues at hotel resorts. Originally she had decided to seek a commune to live on, and she spent a summer visiting a few in northern New York, Vermont, and Virginia. But when the moment of truth came, she couldn't bring herself to join any. Instead she traveled widely, worked at odd jobs, and bonded with the workers she met there.

"I liked the camaraderie of hotel life," she notes. The places I worked in were large enough to house the staff, so they had the feel of a commune without the responsibility. A poor substitute perhaps, but I liked it. Among the resort staff, I met an odd collection of loners, drifters, losers, and people like myself, who were not quite sure where we fit in. Some of the waiters and waitresses were in their seventies and had never done any other type of job, but they were perfectly happy. The kitchen help in Florida was gleaned from recent parolees, homeless people, and teen runaways. There was a preponderance of gay men working in the resorts. Many of them became my close friends.

"While working in Florida, I dated a golf pro," she continues. "He couldn't believe that I was willing to live in the staff area with all of the 'deviants and degenerates,' as he called them. He worried for my safety, but I didn't. There was an odd pull to that lifestyle, one that I sometimes long for today. I think it was the excitement of always living in the present. I likened working in the dining room to vaudeville, because we all had our little schtick for coaxing more tips out of our guests. But if one set of guests didn't go for it, there was always another set coming in next week. The audience was constantly changing. Many of the people I worked with in the resorts are dead: from old age, AIDS, alcohol, drugs, generalized poor health, criminal activities. I like to bring them back to life in my stories. I miss them."

❦ I, on the other hand, was a lousy waitress. Little wonder I didn't take to it the way Kathie did. Besides, I had gone to the land seeking respite from my burnt-out career as a reporter, and waitressing had turned out to be ten times more stressful, with pay at a fraction of what I had earned before. Navigating the twisting, snowy roads late at night after a long shift, my feet frozen, I began to gain a new appreciation for the professional job I had had. But relief was in sight. Nine months after I started at the steak house, a friend in Troy who held a coveted secretarial job in one of the academic departments at nearby Unity College called and told me she had resigned. She suggested I apply. From my vantage point, the thought of being elevated not only to a *daytime* job but a *typing* job seemed like perfect relief from the misery of waitressing late at night! I applied and got the job.

Unity College, a small institution of higher education with an emphasis on environmental programs, was only seven miles from Troy. As a secretary, I now *sat* at a large mahogany desk in a quiet office with carpeting. I now received a steady, forty-hour-a-week minimum-wage salary instead of a sub-minimum wage and tips. What a luxury for me, as a morning person, to report to work at 8 a.m. instead of 3 p.m., sit in pleasant surroundings typing forms and documents for faculty, be home in time for supper, and go to bed early, as befitting my biorhythm. What's more, the professors and staff were very pleasant. What more could I want?

The job itself was a good one. The problem was me. After a few months I began to chomp at my bit, restlessly. Acute boredom had set in. Eight hours a day sitting at a desk, typing items for others, had become frustrating. As a creative person, I would rather have been typing something for me. The days of monotony sucked all the energy out of me, leaving nothing for other pursuits. Each day I counted the minutes until morning break when for fifteen minutes I could read whatever book I'd brought with me, and until lunch break, when I could eat and read for an hour, and until afternoon break when fifteen minutes of reading would carry me through until quitting time.

The paycheck was low, but I was used to that. I crashed and burned on ennui alone, a fatal flaw that seems to follow me wherever I go. I lasted nine months at the job, a second failed gestation period which had not produced the rebirth of myself that I had been seeking. I was still finding my way, looking for a balanced life with equal parts meaningful work and carefree play.

I resigned from Unity College in May 1977.

That summer I wanted to give my crafts a shot. I was a batik artist who batiked designs on T-shirts. I loved creating scenes of nature on T-shirts and moving the shirts through the dyeing process to capture the colors I was striving for. I earned a few dollars at crafts fairs that summer, but probably I lost money if the overhead was factored in. Still, it had to be done. My creative side had been severely stifled during the last few years and needed to be released, even for a short time. But the more I did batik, the poorer we got.

In the fall of 1978 I got a "real" job again, this time as an associate editor at *Farmstead Magazine* in Freedom, which was more to my liking. Again, the salary was not high, but after the summer of batik, in which income was sporadic and mostly nonexistent, we needed a steady paycheck again. The tension between the joy of freedom and the keen anxiety of financial need tugged once more.

Working at *Farmstead* brought me one notch closer to a profession that drew on my natural proclivities for reading and writing. I may not have been good at delivering Pu Pu platters to drunken parties of four, but I was literate enough to read and edit manuscripts well, to write articles, and to communicate clearly with authors. Reporting to work at *Farmstead* was cool because the other workers were also semi-hippies or back-to-the-landers, so we had a lot in common. Each morning I was usually the first to arrive. I started the fire in the woodstove that heated the drafty building. Shivering in my Bean boots, I wondered if I'd ever be warm again. My house was cold in the morning, my workplace was cold, and then we returned to a cold house at night because all of us were gone all day. Now that Kent and I were both working—to finance the broken car parts, the electric bill, the tools, the gadgets, the grocery items—we had to put the boys into the only known day-care center in central coastal Maine, a state-funded operation managed by very sweet, laid-back area hippies on CETA salaries. Day-care costs added to our mounting expenses, which gave us all the more reason to work. By now it was clear that we were being sucked back into the big bad system like bugs swirling down a drain.

Yaakov Oved observes that most communes throughout American history failed because they were unable to carefully balance their ideologies of separatism with their need for interaction with the larger economy and culture. "Without a minimum of approval [from outside society] . . . they were unable to exist," writes Henry Near, yet too much interaction with outside society extinguished the fire of the groups' original reasons for separatism, thus causing a loss of cohesion that led to their demise. While "demise" may be too drastic a word to describe many back-to-the-land situations where family members began to work out, acquiring outside jobs marked an important step in the evolution away from the level of simplicity we had known in earlier days. It was a step toward rejoining traditional society. Of course the scale hadn't tipped yet; we still thought of ourselves as homesteaders who happened to have jobs, rather than as employed people who happened to live on homesteads.

Once we needed the cash badly enough to go out and earn it at a low-wage job, we lost the time and energy needed to effect our self-sufficiency. But if we didn't work, we'd be in even worse shape.

Jeffrey Jacob also recognizes this dilemma: "This issue of jobs and homesteading gets to the central dilemma of simple living in the country: time versus money. In order to develop a self-reliant farmstead, a family or couple needs time to build fences, weed the garden, milk the goat, and cut and stack wood. But at the same time, back-to-the-landers must earn some kind of income to buy, if nothing else, garden seeds, a nanny goat, or the cast-iron stove that burns the wood to keep them warm through the winter. To the extent they sell their labor in the local economies, they lose valuable time to improve their property. Working exclusively on the homestead, however, does not produce the cash to buy the durable resources like lumber, cement, and bricks that a microfarmer needs to prosper."

❦ *As soon as the VW headlights clicked off, solid blackness enclosed us, as though a coffin lid had closed shut. The absence of any artificial, city-generated light had been enchanting on summer nights, when every star in the universe, large and small, had sparkled boldly from all corners of the bowl-shaped sky. We would sit outside on lawn chairs, heads back, pleasantly dizzy from staring upward, admiring the breadth of stars we had never seen before moving to a location free of artificial light. But on cloud-covered winter nights, when we arrived home at 6 p.m. and parked the tired VW at the top of the driveway, the natural darkness was icy and hostile as we unloaded the boys from the backseat by flashlight. Kent aimed the narrow beam of light down the sloping path* that led to the log cabin; no reassuring smoke issued from the chimney. Beyond the perimeter of the flashlight's beam, solid blackness reigned. To me, the hike from the car to the cabin at the end of the day, which would have seemed like an exciting adventure in the early days of homesteading, now felt painful. Each of us carried or dragged one of the children, plus packages. We inched our way through the snow, down the slippery trail, past trees and stumps, following the flashlight's beam. Finally the cabin came into view, slumped in the snowy woods, dark and dejected from a day without firewood. We climbed up the creaky front steps while Kent unlocked the padlock on the front door. Inside he clicked on the inside front light. I'd asked him why we couldn't leave the front light on in the morning when we left the house. I hated returning to a black, cold house at the end of the day. But he argued that the electricity would run all day, and this, of course, would drive the bill up. When we came through the door at night, he went to the woodstove, opened the flue, crumpled newspapers, arranged kindling, and lit a match to get the fire going. It would take several hours for the temperature to rise, so we'd all go to the upstairs loft to keep warm. Although cold and tired ourselves, we then had to cook dinner for the boys, who were even hungrier.

It was beginning to dawn on me that I lived in Maine in a log cabin, with a few canned beans on the shelf, but was right back in the rat race I had left. Here I was getting up in the dark, in a cold house, dressing myself and dressing the children while Kent did chores, so all of us could leave in one cold car by 7 a.m. (the other car was, as you may have guessed, indisposed in the yard). We drove ninety miles a day, first dropping the boys off at day care outside Belfast, then dropping me off at Farmstead in Freedom. Then Kent drove on to Johnny's Selected Seeds in Albion. We reversed the circuit at the end of the day, driving home on the dark country roads to reenter a frozen house. The difference was that this new rat race was far more physically uncomfortable than the previous one in Massachusetts—and paid a helluva lot less too! Again we were living paycheck to paycheck. Oh Mother Earth News! Where was this comfortable income I was supposed to be able to generate from selling corn or dried worms?

CHAPTER SEVEN

Staying Healthy, and Paying for It

"Our landlady had said that the river water was clean. And we were stupid enough to believe her. That wasn't too smart. I didn't have any problem, but Ted got real sick with dysentery, and it took a while for him to get over that."—Cynthia Frost

"The muffins were made out of organic wheat flour, and my allergic daughter bit right into them because they were pretty good and immediately broke out in the rash she always got whenever she took anything like an antibiotic. Then I realized, 'It's the goddamned organic flour!'"—Patricia Foley

❧ *June 28, 1968: Outside the tent, the sky darkened and an evening breeze wafted through the trees and grass. The stars appeared. Pam Read Hanna could see them shining through the sides of the open-air tent where she panted through the contractions. She was about to have her second baby. Her labor had started sometime between seven and nine at night, though she could not be sure, for no clocks were used at Morningstar Commune, where she and her husband Larry had lived for the past fifteen months with their son, Siddhartha. For the next five hours Pam envisioned ocean waves and mentally surfed them, as the childbirth books had instructed. She had no intention of going to a hospital. Two years earlier, before coming to the commune, she had delivered her first child by herself at home on a comfortable floor mattress. She finally pushed him out after an eighteen-hour labor, caught him, cut the cord, cleaned him, and brought him to her breast to nurse. "It was really hard," she says, "but I learned a lot from that. That's probably what started me on being a midwife."*

She nursed her son for two weeks. Breast engorgement and fever cut it short. "I went to a doctor finally because I was so miserable," she remembers. "It was torture, just torture, to nurse the baby because it hurt so bad. Oh man, I was so miserable. I was also really anemic. The first doctor I went to was so nasty to me. He hated hippies, and he said I would be prosecuted if I had a baby by myself again. I was so pissed off. Then I found another doctor who was nice and kind, but he said because I had an infection I really needed to stop nursing, mainly because I was so anemic. So I had to stop. Oh, talk about shame. I had failed!"

This time, Pam knew what to expect. Alone in the tent with her husband, she knelt on her hands and knees when the moment came, and pushed out her new baby daughter, Psyche Joy Ananda, who had "bright coppery red hair and hazel eyes."

The birth had been beautiful and memorable, free of white, sterile drapes and an authoritative male doctor commanding her to push. No complications arose with breastfeeding this time; she was able to nurse the baby for a year and a half. Soon after the birth, however, Pam developed childbed fever, the primary cause of postpartum death only a century earlier. Under the circumstances, she was not at all averse to visiting a traditional doctor and receiving antibiotics. In her memoir she writes, "B. and G. must have paid the doctor because I know we didn't have any money." Asked if she had felt at the time as though she was selling out by seeking conventional medicine, Pam replied, "Yes, yes, as a matter of fact, I did."

❦ The counterculture demonized Western medicine in general and the American health care system in particular. The system was spiraling out of control. Hospital costs had risen dramatically in the 1960s, four times faster than any other consumer item, and by the 1970s a stay in the hospital cost as much per hour as it had cost per day in 1905. The cost of a hospital room alone had risen from $10.25 per day in 1940 to $50.10 per day in 1964, to between $72 and $110 per day by 1969. New hi-tech diagnostic machines and medical tests generated staggering bills. As specialists replaced general practitioners, the price of office visits soared too. The doctors themselves had become insufferable. Haughty, inaccessible, and untrustworthy, they now booked twenty patients per hour and ran two hours behind schedule, yet had the audacity to charge *you* if you missed an appointment. They looked you over brusquely, ordered expensive tests, and rushed toward the door, annoyed if you asked questions. Marcus Welby, M.D., no longer practiced in the United States.

Medicare and Medicaid, enacted in the sixties, had triggered widespread health-care inflation. Although general inflation had also contributed to rising costs, the medical community was "given their own ticket to write," Godfrey Hodgson observed. "They could, and did, expand their buildings, take on new staff, invest in fancy electronic equipment, make generous settlements with the unions—and could be paid whatever the bill came to by the feds, just as long as the friendly fellows at Blue Cross or at the insurance company said it was OK. The result was a bonanza not only for doctors and hospitals but for insurers, electronic data processors, surgical dressing manufacturers, drug companies, and all the other interests which feed at the $70-billion trough of the medical-insurance complex."

A backlash against Western medicine vibrated through the pages of *Mother Earth News*. The magazine ran a series entitled "Kitchen Medicine," which offered herbal solutions for everyday ailments ranging from parasites to infections. Rich corporations manufactured pharmaceuticals for profit, the magazine reminded us, so we shouldn't contribute to their wealth by buying their products. Similarly, doctors prescribed treatments and tests for profit, so beware. "Both you and your overworked doctor will be better off if you can prevent or cure your own minor ills," the article stated. And we back-to-the-land people set out to do just this.

Yes, living on the land was to serve as our insurance against health problems and medical costs. After parting company with the masses of overweight, stressed out stiffs in the city who languished in offices all day courting heart attacks, we hoped to dissociate ourselves from the bloated health-care system. We wouldn't need it. The fresh air, the hard physical labor, and the nutritious diet would all but guarantee glowing health and longevity. Why, look at the Nearings, still homesteading in Harborside, Maine, living proof of how the Good Life rejuvenated a body and mind. When Kent and I visited their homestead in 1976, Scott Nearing, ninety-three, and Helen Nearing, seventy-three, bloomed with good health and looked far younger than their years.

"Helen, short-haired and energetic, just can't be 73," I wrote at the time. "She has spent the past two years building [their] new stone house near the waterfront, which they'll move into next spring. . . . She designed it, and carried and laid almost every stone from the bottom of the cellar to the top of the chimney.

"The Nearings feel their longevity and good health is due both to their healthful eating habits, and the Good Life—a life free of tension, time clocks, and bills," I concluded, with sincere admiration for the couple who had successfully homesteaded in Vermont and Maine since the 1930s.

In addition to taking charge of our own health, many of us jettisoned health insurance. We were against the whole insurance industry. This philosophical stance conveniently coincided with our rejection of professional careers. My hash-slinging job at the Waterville Steak House, for example, had not exactly included a benefits package. Just as well. Expensive health insurance premiums only filled the coffers of the rich insurance companies. Insurance was for anemic organization men who smoked cigarettes and ate white bread. In the one-in-a-million chance that illness should strike and we had to be dragged, kicking, screaming, and penniless, to a doctor or hospital, well, creative solutions existed. We didn't need money or insurance, for heaven's sake.

One popular notion among back-to-the-land people—before we moved to the land—was that "country payments" were accepted in lieu of cash by doctors, dentists, or others whose services might be desired. A country payment was a noncash item, such as a bushel of tomatoes or a contribution of services. A rural legend or two was always circulating about a homesteader in Montana or California who had paid the $150,000 bill for his rare congenital medical condition (which even alternative living could not have prevented!) by building the doctor a second home in the mountains.

Be *creative* and you would never have to worry about health insurance.

In 1976 Eliot Coleman stood before an audience of long-haired followers who had driven from all over Maine and beyond to attend the Maine Organic Farmers and Gardeners Association Convention at the College of the Atlantic in Bar Harbor. Coleman, wiry and tanned, had purchased a portion of Scott and Helen Nearing's famous homestead and was gaining prominence as a junior leader of the movement. He was already a household name among back-to-the-land people.

Coleman said, "Look in any city and pick out the biggest, most pretentious, most expensive buildings. You can be sure they'll be the insurance companies. And you're paying for those fancy buildings." He and his family survived well outside the monetary system—eating off the land, selling produce at a roadside stand, and putting that money back into the farm. He said they had no electricity, telephone, or running water (though, according to Vivien Ellen Rose's research, he was already on the lecture circuit and was "sponsoring summer internships in organic gardening at his market garden home next door," suggesting that at least a modest livelihood involving transactions with the outside world must have been present, after all). To this day I remember Coleman's ardent position on insurance, having heard it at that conference and in several other speeches during my years in Maine. He was against it.

During that lecture a skeptical member of the audience challenged him, asking if abandoning life, health, and car insurance was really sane.

Coleman said he and his family had none.

"But what if a husband dies and leaves his wife with a couple of kids?" asked someone else.

"Well, the gamble is really quite heavily in your favor, especially at your age," he replied quickly—and he always had a quick answer for everything. "And the sick thing about it is that the insurance company is gambling that you're going to live, and you're gambling that you're going to die."

"But what if you were in a car accident and someone was badly hurt?" someone persisted.

"I drive carefully. Next?"

For a year and a half after moving to Maine, Kent and I had held on to some cheap health insurance from our previous mainstream life, probably yesterday's equivalent of a COBRA plan. We couldn't afford it, resented paying it, and questioned it constantly. Speeches such as Coleman's fanned the flames of our doubts. In the late winter of 1977, Kent had taken a job at Johnny's Selected Seeds, and a few months later Johnny's, a growing business, decided to enroll in a group health insurance plan. We dropped our private plan like a hot ember from the woodstove. Six months later the insurance company sponsoring the group plan folded. We had a few weeks' notice.

"Well, what do you want to do, El?" asked Kent. "Want to go back to a private plan?"

"Hell, no!" I replied. "We just can't afford it." By now I was working at *Farmstead Magazine*, and the owner had been talking about enrolling in a group health plan later that month.

"Let's just wait it out a few weeks and enroll in *Farmstead*'s plan," I said.

"Good! We'll do that," said Kent. "It'll only be a few weeks between insurances."

How sorry we were not to have health insurance a week later when we carried Shawn into the emergency room at Mid-Maine Medical Center in Waterville with a crushed finger.

It happened late one afternoon, as twilight hovered. I was sewing in the upstairs loft of the log cabin. Kent and the boys stood in the yard feeding apples into a hand-cranked cider press which Kent had borrowed from a neighbor. I could hear their voices outside as I stitched quietly, thinking how lovely it was to be alone in the house with only the sound of an occasional log crumbling in the woodstove. Then a wailing scream broke the silence. I dropped my sewing and ran to the window. Commotion, voices, crying and yelling grew louder. I rushed downstairs to the front door. Kent was running in from the side yard, crunching brittle leaves beneath his Bean boots, carrying Shawn, who was screeching maniacally, his hand red and limp. Derek was running alongside sobbing and frightened. "I didn't mean to!" he cried. "I was just turning the crank, and Shawn came along and stuck his hand in."

"His finger got mashed in the cider press," yelled Kent. "We've got to take him to the hospital."

Grabbing Derek by the arm, I ran like a demon up the leafy path to Ken and Wendy's log cabin, pulling him with me, falling on my face as I scrambled up their front steps. I picked myself up and pounded on their front door. Shoving Derek into their house, I explained the emergency to Wendy and ran back down the path to our car. Kent had wrapped Shawn's raw, bleeding finger in a handkerchief. We tore into Waterville. I drove while Kent held the screaming child for the forty-five minute drive. As we rushed through the emergency room doors in our worn-out jackets and muddy, ripped jeans, I remembered all the horror stories that circulated among the counterculture people about hospitals that slammed their doors in your face if you didn't have insurance—which only proved how cruel the big bad system was and how right Eliot Coleman was about boycotting it.

When the attendant took down the information, she looked up, pen poised, and asked, "Insurance?" I felt small. In rural Maine, with its seasonal workers and high unemployment, they were used to treating uninsured people, but my heart was still pounding like a bass drum as I shook my head no. For all I knew, the hippie accounts of uninsured people dying on the sidewalks outside the barred hospital doors were true.

Nevertheless they called in a surgeon for Shawn, pumped him up with Demerol and Novocain, and repaired his finger. He awoke and slurred to us about all his exciting dreams of giants and dragons. Six hours had passed since the accident. In the end, the hospital presented us with a bill for $400, an unmanageable sum for us. Having promised to pay it when we could, we walked out the door at midnight with Shawn sleeping over Kent's shoulder, his hand wrapped in a castlike bandage. Shame crept over me. I was sure we would never pay that bill.

Two weeks later—still between insurance policies—an accident befell Derek, who was now five years old and attending kindergarten at the day-care center. The teachers held kindergarten lessons in a conference room. The five-year-olds sat around a table learning their letters and numbers, reading, and coloring. Being a wiggly child in those days before attention deficit disorder was known, Derek lost his balance and fell over against the teachers' urn of coffee, which overturned, drenching him with scalding coffee. A teacher swiftly wrapped Derek's burned arm and leg in gauze while another one carried him to his vehicle and drove him to the emergency room at Waldo County General Hospital in Belfast. He suffered second- and third-degree burns. Although we brought him home that night, he had to return to that hospital four or five times to have the burns checked.

Accidents

Obviously, as many of us learned, a healthy outdoor life did not liberate us after all from doctors, hospitals, or colossal bills. Living on the land in fact may have increased the odds of accidents. A homesteader in robust shape who used a chain saw daily was at equal or higher risk for injury than a professional who sat at a desk. A chain saw's chain could snap, or the tree could fall the wrong way. Tractors were notorious for flipping unexpectedly and crushing the user. A range of catastrophes could occur. "Occupational injuries and accidents are more prevalent in rural America. Rural areas have an overall rate of disability and death from accidents 30 to 40 percent higher than urban areas," reports the *Congressional Record*.

Norma Cobb, an Alaskan homesteader, had hoped that a well-balanced life of exercise, good diet, plenty of sleep, and "the open country with its natural surroundings" would contribute to her family's wellness. But when "the bullet ripped into my seven-year-old's frail little chest" in a freak accident, the child had to be airlifted to a hospital 150 miles away, where he underwent two surgeries and stayed in intensive care for five days. "Doctors said they would arrange payment of Sean's medical bills since Les and I were without jobs and low on money." Several years later, when her husband injured his eye, "I did everything I could, but it wasn't enough." He nearly lost the infected eye. They were so low on funds that Norma and the children had to remain on the homestead while he returned to his parents' house in the lower forty-eight to receive treatment.

In 1978 Marion Ross and her husband bought a twenty-acre farm in Arkansas. "We felt that San Jose was polluted as far as air, water, and morality," she says. "We just wanted to get our kids out, where things were kind of more pure and wholesome. And we were readers of *Mother Earth News*."

When Marion was away for the day, her eight-year-old son asked his father, a mechanic who ran a home business, "Can I light that cedar tree on fire?" Because the cedar tree was less than a foot tall, his father assumed he just wanted to hold a match under a branch, so he told him that it wouldn't ignite anyway.

"Unbeknownst to him," says Marion, "my son had stolen some of my husband's waste lacquer thinner from the shop. So my son gives the waste lacquer thinner to his sister, and he says, 'When I say *go*, you throw the lacquer thinner on the tree and I'll light the match,' not taking into account that the wind is blowing. So he says, 'Okay, *now!*' My daughter dumps the waste lacquer thinner, the wind pours it all over my son, he strikes the match and *voila!* He's on fire! My husband is on the phone in the shop and he goes, 'Oh, excuse me, I've got to go, my son just ran by and he's on fire!'"

The fire singed her son's eyelashes, eyebrows, and a little of his hair, but fortunately there was no permanent damage.

Marion's son also suffered terrible injuries in a car accident, which occurred during the one year they carried health insurance. The bills came to $7,000, an obscene amount of money in those days, but the insurance covered most of it, and the family's church helped with the rest.

"When more bills came due, we started selling tools," Miriam says.

Clean living didn't always prevent ailments of other natures. Soon after Sallyann J. Murphey and her husband Greg moved to a forty-two-acre farm in Indiana to practice the simple life, she observed an improvement in their health and well-being. "Gone is the driven, nervous man I was once married to," Murphey notes in her 1994 memoir, *Bean Blossom Dreams*. "My tall, skinny Greg has filled out: his shoulders widened from all the outside work, his tummy a tribute to an abundance of fresh food." But farm life did not thwart Greg's later illness, which culminated in emergency surgery to remove an abdominal "abscess the size of a large grapefruit."

Disconnecting ourselves from the health-care industry was far trickier than simplifying in other areas. We may have hated the oil industry and chosen to heat with wood; we may have disliked retail stores and chosen to buy secondhand clothes; but when our appendicitis flared or our wounds bled, we flung ourselves back at the feet of modern medicine.

Adrienne discovered a breast lump while participating in the Frontier House experiment in Montana, where three families reenacted the lives of nineteenth-century homesteaders. Filming stopped while she, now very much converted back to a twentieth-century woman, rushed into town to seek hi-tech medical attention. The lump proved benign. She said, "You think about a woman's options in 1883, though, and she'd have been so busy, what are the odds of actually seeing a doctor? What could he do if he found anything? I'm so glad I could come to 2001 technology." We may have denounced the rampant flaws of the health-care industry, but most of us remember an occasion or two when we thanked Heaven we had recourse to it.

Dental Health

Did it occur to most of us when we planned an austere life that dental health was unrelated to exercise, sunshine, and fresh air? Of course we hoped that our sugar-free, organic diets, heavy with vegetables and fruits, would keep our mouths in shape. We distrusted dentists almost as much as we distrusted doctors; as far as we could tell, they were in on the medical conspiracy to profit from overcharging us. We had faith that living naturally would preserve our dental health.

In a 1975 *Mother Earth News* article entitled "Pennywise Tooth Cleansers," the author declared that "Procter and Gamble and Lever Brothers—and any other number of other manufacturers—would like us to believe that the only proper way to care for our teeth is with expensive highly flavored toothpastes that come in non-biodegradable, throwaway, zinc-and-lead tubes. T'ain't so!"

The article instructed the reader how to make homemade tooth powder or toothpaste by combining baking soda, salt, glycerin, flavoring, and coloring. Whether the concoction worked as effectively as store-bought toothpaste, I have no way of knowing. But the article reflected our distaste for the established health industry.

One of the popular myths, an ex-homesteader friend recently reminded me, was that honey was always healthful. "Somehow it was believed that you could have all the honey in the world that you wanted," he said. "As long as it wasn't refined sugar, it was okay for your teeth. And of course this isn't true."

Having bought into the honey myth, he soon began to sense that this natural sweetener was not as advantageous to his teeth as he had believed. Because he was isolated in the country and broke too, he postponed seeing a dentist for ten years. Instead, "I just ignored all the signals my mouth was giving me. I was never in pain, thank goodness. But if I hit a sore spot in my mouth while I was chewing, I'd say, 'Oh, it'll go away.'"

Later, when he reestablished himself in civilization, he finally worked up the courage to make a dental appointment and, expecting the worst, was vastly relieved to be told that his teeth needed work but were not beyond repair. "I felt like I had a whole new lease on life. Making that one stop to the dentist did more to me to relieve my tension than anything I could have done, for years. I'm in pretty good shape now. I go to the dentist. I don't fool around with that for two seconds now."

In Troy, local gossip had it that one of the older natives down the road had extracted all her own teeth with pliers. "Can you believe it?" we commented to one another with shudders whenever this particular thread wove its way into the fabric of the day's gossip. It probably didn't occur to us that the poor woman couldn't afford—and never had been able to afford—the luxury of a dentist, and that self-extraction took place by default, not preference. Our reaction of horror also illustrates the difference between most back-to-the-land people and a true country person. We *wanted* to be natural and live naturally, but only to a point. We wanted our teeth.

Rob Morningstar didn't even own a toothbrush in his early years at God's Free Universe Commune in Hawaii. He and his friends subsisted almost entirely from foraged fruits and nuts. Naked, natural, and free, they did not worry about their teeth. Although they lacked protein, they would not fish because "we were all Yogis, and killing anything was bad karma," explains Rob. Periodically the young, single mothers who received food stamps bought grains, legumes, and beans to share with the group, but this was the only protein they ate.

Later their protein-deficient diets caught up with their teeth and bodies. "Many people, like me, didn't own toothbrushes," says Rob. "For years, dental care was minimal, and fruit acids did their thing on people's teeth. Many of the people of our group who were 100 percent fruitarians ended up looking like survivors of Auschwitz, thin as rails with brittle hair and bad teeth."

Although many of the mothers gradually began to add more protein to their children's diets, Rob remembers "some dedicated fruit-folks who kept their kids on a fruit-only diet until the kids were five or six, and those kids always looked so pathetic, thin and small with mousey hair."

Rob is now thankful that his naturally strong teeth were not irreparably damaged during the toothbrushless years.

"Ultimately it was the need for a better, broader diet that caused me to begin to explore the world of working for money, in order to be able to purchase more nutritious food," he adds.

Low-income Rural Choices

We soon learned that "country payments" were largely a myth. During my homesteading years I heard of only one case of a successful country payment—a friend bragged about having compensated a dentist near Portland with a couple of bushels of corn. As a rule, the medical and dental establishment preferred cash. Believe me, I tried.

June Holley is another exception. She managed to exchange ten bags of manure for a root canal. But, she points out, the dentist was a friend of the family, which helped. Bartering worked in other areas of life, yes. We held clothing swaps in Troy, exchanged child care, or traded five chickens for another's goat's milk. But when it came to health services, country payments were largely an idealist's dream.

There were, however, free and sliding-scale health clinics and other government-funded programs that offered options to low-income patients, including hippies. Many counterculture people used them if the ailment justified the long drive and the time taken off from an hourly-wage job, always an important consideration for the working poor. One homesteader describes the mixed feelings he experienced while receiving free medical care from a government-funded program for impoverished people: "I was in there with people who'd been in this rural area for a long, long time, who did not have schooling and did not have the means to have schooling. Basically, you'd feel a couple of things. One, that you were smart and crafty for having gotten around the high-priced medical system. Two, you felt sort of like a sly fox, thinking, 'Here I am with all these people who've never had any educational opportunities, never had any money in their backgrounds, but I'm now taking what the government offers, just as they are,' and try to feel good about that, as if you've gotten away with something. But then you knew that you were probably not getting the best medical care that you could if you were affording your own program or with an insurance company."

Doctor visits in rural areas were nothing to look forward to, free or not. Often you couldn't get an appointment for a month. When you finally did, the wait was excruciating. Sick people from miles around crowded into the waiting room, hacking and expectorating, sniffling and gasping, filling the air with a deadly quagmire of swirling viruses and bacteria. One winter day Kent came down with a violent stomach virus that had him dashing to the hopper every five minutes, for hours. By the next day the symptoms persisted and he had already lost a lot of weight. Feeling miserable, he decided he had no choice but to spend what little money we had for a doctor's visit. A doctor near Bangor took walk-ins. Making several rest stops along the way, Kent drove weakly to the office. The waiting room was packed. Six hours later the doctor finally saw him.

"Jesus," declared Kent that night. "Six hours! I waited and waited, my stomach turning inside out. I almost turned around and came home, but I'd driven twenty-five miles to get there."

"What did he say?" I asked.

"What a quack! He wrote me a prescription for tranquilizers, for Chrissake!"

It wasn't just my perception that the health-care choices were not ideal at the time I lived in Maine. Rural health care has never been able to keep up with its urban counterpart. Problems reported with rural health care in 1978 included a shortage of physicians and delays in emergency treatment. Physicians were in short supply because "health professionals may not want to live and raise a family in an area which lacks social and cultural amenities." A *Time* magazine article in 2001 repeated essentially the same news; not much has changed.

Alternative Home Health Care

In many homesteading situations, if we knew what we were doing, using a little goatweed here or chicory there made much more sense than paying for a doctor and an expensive prescription. When Sandra Sleight-Brannen's ten-month-old son burned his hand on the hot oven door, she applied an herbal salve of honey and comfrey. After a snake "planted its fangs in my left thumb," Ken Davison home-treated the bite. "What can you do if you are poor [and] have no health insurance . . .?" he asked. He hurried home, where his wife applied ice cubes to the wound, and then he made cuts in his thumb, sucked out the venom, spitting it out afterward. After taking two antihistamine pills and applying a poultice made of comfrey leaves, he rested and was fine, save for his black thumb.

Many babies were born on communes and homesteads. In keeping with the rejection of Western medical practices, many back-to-the-land women, disenchanted with doctors and hospitals, chose natural home births at a time when it was still considered radical. If "natural is better" was our mantra, in the case of childbirth we may have had a point. Institutionalized hospital births had devalued this miraculous process, so women like Pam Read Hanna chose alternatives.

"The medical profession was then overwhelmingly male, and doctors' manner toward women was often condescending," notes David Frum. "As memories of dangerous deliveries faded, 'natural,' 'tribal,' 'non-western,' and 'herbal' displaced 'scientific' and 'modern' as the highest accolades of medical praise."

After delivering her own children, Pam became a midwife, attracted to the profession by the lessons she'd learned from her own children's births. She knew how important it was for a woman to feel supported and not become annoyed. Her husband had angered her during the eighteen-hour labor with her first child. "Don't make a woman in labor angry," she advises, "because she'll tighten up all her muscles, which will give her more pain and make it a lot harder."

Over a twenty-year period, Pam delivered forty-three babies and sent another five laboring women to the hospital when she faced medical situations she did not feel qualified to handle. "The scariest delivery I ever did was for this hippie couple," she says. "The baby was born, a boy, and big, but I could tell the minute I touched his flesh that he was all deflated. There was no air in that child's body. I looked at the cord and it was pencil thin and straight. Most cords are all gnarly, but this was really thin and straight. He wasn't getting any air. I'd read up on this, but I'd never experienced it before. Everyone was totally hushed; I think they sensed there was something wrong because he didn't cry. So I picked him up, and I did this accordion technique that I'd read about. I filled my mouth with air. You have to be careful about mouth to mouth with a little infant because you might breathe too much into him and damage his lungs, so you just puff up your own cheeks and blow that much air in. I did that about three times, and I accordion-moved him on his back, and he started wailing. When he was born he was purple, and gradually the color just came into him. Finally, waaahhh! Oh my God! Actually, all this was just seconds, I don't even think it was a minute, but it seemed like an eternity. I was very calm and focused during the delivery. Only after it was I absolutely shaking."

Pam delivered the baby of a friend who had contracted German measles. "You know that disease is bad for pregnancies; I knew that way back then. He came out with a harelip that was pretty startling, though he was healthy enough. The harelip was sewn up. But he was also deaf. So that propelled this couple back into society because that was too much to deal with. He's a young man now, he's got two kids of his own, and he's really doing great."

Sandra Sleight-Brennan delivered both her sons in the cabin on their land in Stewart, Ohio. A midwife attended, and Sandra's husband and good friends supported her. She says, "Having a home delivery was just another way of showing that 'I don't like the way the system works; I want it to work *this* way, and trying to change it to do that. It was a way of pushing at the limits and not accepting convention as God, as the way things have to be, always questioning. And I think that's what we all did." Sandra held her first newborn and thought, "This is just amazing!" She says, "He had this cone head, molded by delivery. That was right about the time when the Cone Heads were popular on *Saturday Night Live*, so the resemblance was startling."

Home births worked well for many women, but it wasn't for everyone. A friend of mine in Maine delivered her second baby at home. She wanted to try it because everyone else was doing it—and even more, she had no insurance and couldn't afford a hospital delivery. I later viewed her series of black-and-white photos taken during labor and delivery: first, she's on the floor mattress gently panting while her husband sits beside her smiling; then, as the series moves on, her face tightens and his smile fades; then she is moaning while he holds her; and at the end, as a huge baby head and neck are being tugged out of her, the camera captures her wide-open, contorted mouth. All went well; she and the baby did fine. But not long after, her husband landed a job in town. With benefits. So when she became pregnant again, she told us she couldn't *wait* to go to the hospital this time and preferably be knocked out cold, or at least have serious numbing drugs.

In most cases, home deliveries were successful, though Timothy Miller observes that "the lack of complete medical facilities at hand undoubtedly cost a few infant lives."

Natural Is Not Always Better

Although natural approaches to health often produced good results at a price we could afford, we were wrong if we assumed that natural was *always* better. For instance, we back-to-the-land people swore by comfrey. The herb was idolized for its innumerable, all-purpose healing properties that the established medical profession was too obtuse to recognize. In a *Mother Earth News* article in May 1974, Nancy Rubel wrote that "we'd heard so much about [comfrey's] virtues—we set aside a small rectangular spot on our acre for a bed of 30 comfrey cuttings." She recommended it as a vegetable because "it's rich in calcium, potassium, phosporus and vitamins A and C. And—since the protein content of those big leaves runs a very high 21 to 33%— you can count on this plant as an alternative to soybeans. . . ." Another of the six good homestead uses of comfrey, she continued, was as a tea. Comfrey tea "will feed your body rather than sloshing the water-soluble vitamins, as regular tea . . . does." She also endorsed it as "a comforting drink," which the children should have too. In a sidebar, "More About Comfrey," the author offered an anecdote entitled "Comfrey as a Healer," describing how comfrey had been used as a postsurgical medicine for her twelve-year-old son who had injured a finger in a machine. He soaked the finger in comfrey, and he "also drank some comfrey tea during this period."

Convinced of comfrey's healing properties, I frequently harvested the leaves that grew on our property, crunched them into the tea strainer, and added boiling water. The greenish liquid, with a tablespoon of honey mixed in, tasted flat to bitter, depending upon the quantity and quality of the leaves, but I forced it down, gulp by gulp, certain that its therapeutic qualities would do their magic.

Warnings have now been issued about comfrey tea. The FDA, the FTC, and reputable sources such as the *New England Journal of Medicine* have taken an official stand against the internal use of comfrey. "One should entirely forgo the internal administration of the drug [comfrey], due to the presence, however small, of pyrrolizidine alkaloids which have hepatotoxic and carcinogenic effects," the 1998 *Physicians' Desk Reference* advises. How quick I was in those days to embrace every pronouncement issued by my back-to-the-land compatriots while rejecting each one issued from the Establishment. Now I feel the truth lies somewhere in between.

Herbs are not necessarily safe, let alone remedial, just because they grow freely in nature. They can be dangerous, if not lethal, if taken in excessive amounts or mixed with the wrong contraindications. Herbs may also "have the potential to be misidentified when collected, mislabeled, contaminated, or adulterated."

Writing in the *Scientific Review of Alternative Medicine*, W. Betz reports, "In 1990–1991, some 100 women were diagnosed with total destruction of their kidneys through irreversible interstitial fibrosis. Their medical conditions were all traced to a group practice of 'alternative' doctors who had prescribed the women medicinal cocktails containing Chinese herbs."

Nature is full of hazardous substances. When Cynthia's boyfriend Ted came down with dysentery from drinking the water of the Eel River, he grasped the truth that natural is not always better. "Our landlady had said that it was clean. And we were stupid enough to believe her. That wasn't too smart. I didn't have any problem. Ted got real sick and it took a while for him to get over that," says Cynthia.

As our ancestors could have told us, many infectious diseases thrive in "natural" water. A homesteader could not assume that the well water, lake water, rivers, or brooks were pristine. Untreated water sometimes carried the bacteria or viruses for cholera, typhoid, hepatitis A, Cryptosporidiosis, giardiasis, or dysentery, a detail we may have overlooked in our enthusiasm for natural substances. Hepatitis spread at Morningstar Ranch in California. Pam Read Hanna, who lived there, remembers bringing jugs of creek water to one of the men who was "heavy into purity and wouldn't drink anything that came from a man-made pipe." Many people contracted hepatitis. Noted Pam in her memoir, "As a community, we got more hip to the need for cleanliness around food, but as more and more people came, it became harder and harder to keep up even minimum standards, so everybody pretty much had to be responsible for himself/herself."

According to Timothy Miller, "poor sanitation facilities [and] dubious water supplies" in many communal farms "contributed to epidemics of hepatitis and other diseases that afflicted dozens, if not hundreds, of communities."

The Bright Side of Kent's Broken Arm

The breeze carried the promise of spring that day in 1979 as the sun shone on the budding trees. Our side yard was strewn with greasy vehicle parts, as usual. Kent, in a smeared white T-shirt and jeans, was kneeling on the ground fidgeting with a used motorcycle, which, if he could get it to run, might actually save us money on car parts. His hands glistened black with oil as he leaned close to the pedal, wrench in hand, removing a spring. Then suddenly—there was a loud snap of some coiled motorcycle part bursting free with a vengeance, and Kent rolled back onto the ground clutching his arm, his face white.

"What happened?" I cried from the front porch.

His eyes closed, he breathed heavily, not answering.

I ran over to him.

Finally, he said softly, between clenched teeth, "I just broke my arm."

But there was a bright side! We now had health insurance, picked up through one or the other of our employers.

I drove him to the Waterville Hospital, by now a familiar trek.

At the hospital reception desk we filled out the forms and settled down for the long wait in green plastic chairs beside a yakking television set. At last the doctor called his name, ordered the x-rays, evaluated the damage, and dispensed the pain meds. A cast was plastered onto his arm. He would be disabled for about a month. He would not be able to lift the car onto blocks to repair malfunctions, or to fell trees or carry hundred-pound sacks of grain or stack heavy logs.

But we had insurance!

I couldn't agree more with Eliot Coleman that insurance companies are profiting from our gambles on whether we'll live or die, stay healthy or become ill. Today I resent paying those premiums as much as I did in the seventies. And in today's dollars they drain an even larger slice from the income. But I've surrendered to it. Because if it's simplicity I want, it's simpler to play along with the system. Many of America's working poor want health insurance and cannot get it or cannot afford it, which is distressing. But to actively snub it on principle because the insurance companies are rich seems like a form of misguided rebellion.

For many of us, our idealistic renunciation of the health care system was tested when reality shoved its way into our lives, shattering the delusion that we were insulated from illness, accidents, chronic conditions, and diseases because we lived wholesomely. We realized that if we wanted to benefit from twentieth-century medicine and technology, we could not spurn it indefinitely and still expect it to catch us in its safety net when trouble arose.

As we grew older and raised children, the lure of a job-with-benefits grew compelling as we faced medical problems that only compounded our precarious financial situations.

❧ *Janice Walker had been enjoying the communal life in Atlanta, but ultimately her need for traditional medical care for her son lured her back into* the mainstream marketplace. Soon after her ultimate street-corner wedding, her marriage dissolved—but then she met her real soulmate. They went home together that night and stayed as a couple for the next few decades until he died two years ago—even though they could not inhabit the same house because of his alcoholism.

When her son was born hearing-impaired, with a cleft palate, she phoned her sister as a go-between, who in turn called their parents. They hadn't even known Janice was pregnant.

"I wouldn't have called them, but my son had a birth defect, and I guess I needed them," she admits. "And my dad, who hadn't spoken to me for years because of my hippie lifestyle, went out and bought a fire truck and all this stuff and brought it to the hospital." The weakened economy and the rising cost of living forced her to move in with her parents. She hated doing this, but "I had a son. I had an obligation. I had a responsibility. He deserved a place to live, he deserved medical care, which began to get harder and harder," she says.

At first the state paid her son's medical bills, but Janice knew she would have to reenter the mainstream to provide the rest. Her son would have twenty-seven operations in the next few years and would have to take medications. No more panhandling or part-time gigs without benefits. "As my salary went up, they kicked me off the free stuff. But job-related insurance didn't pay for it all. There were still gaps, so I needed to make more in order to give him a nice life. As insurance got worse and worse over the years, more and more had to come out of my pocket."

She took a secretarial position at a new company, Family Center, Inc., a subsidiary of A&P, which planned to open a new chain of stores called Family Marts, and for the next ten years she worked her way up to executive-level management. When her boss told her she could forget about getting ahead in the company unless she wore makeup and stockings and painted her fingernails, she decided to comply. At that point she was more than willing to play the corporate game for the sake of her son.

"Okay, this is the costume; I will wear the costume," she concluded.

CHAPTER EIGHT

Relationships—Friends, Lovers, Family, Community

"The highest idealism, it seems, often cannot overcome human pettiness."—Timothy Miller, *The 60's Communes: Hippies and Beyond*

". . . the cabin walls seemed to shrink till you felt like you were in one of those Flash Gordon serials where the walls came together like a vise to squeeze the pulp out of you."—T. C. Boyle, *Drop City*

"If you should happen to hear a glowing report about the perfect community somewhere, one with no rough edges, presume you're not getting the whole story."—Geoph Kozeny, *Communities Magazine*

❦ *Sandy Sanchez, pregnant with her second child, gave birth in the backseat of the car as her husband drove wildly toward the Roanoke, West Virginia, hospital. "If I'd known the birth was going to be so easy, I'd have opted to skip the hospital altogether, but I'd had a blood clot when pregnant with my first child and had spent many weeks hospitalized, so we were being cautious," she explains.*

Sandy had been standing on the hill looking for blueberries when her labor came on, strong and insistent. She had called to her husband, who had helped her into the car. Shortly after, the baby had slid out quickly as she lay panting in the backseat, doing her Lamaze breathing.

"Her father stopped alongside the road to check her out, decided not to cut the cord himself but laid her on my chest and drove like a demon, informing me each time he ran a red light." After the backseat birth, Sandy's husband began to pressure her to move back to civilization. The birthing experience had "freaked him right out of West Virginia."

"The fact is," she continues, "the thought of leaving was so far from my mind that I had been ignoring all his little hints. This event gave him the reason he needed to say in so many very loud and clear words that it was time to go back to civilization. Actually he launched me on a major guilt trip about what our children would be deprived of if we stayed. I did come to the conclusion that such a retreat from modern society was something I might choose for myself after being exposed to modern society, but that it was selfish to make that decision for children who would undoubtedly long for what modern society had to offer, in spite of its pitfalls and dangers."

Sandy had loved living on their picturesque homestead in Appalachia and would have stayed forever. But her husband had never prized it the way she had, never fully embraced the lifestyle, and during the three years they lived there the strain between them mounted.

They both worked hard but worked differently. "I worked slowly," explains Sandy, "savoring the feel of the garden soil, the fragrance of tomato plants, the colors of the forest when we put up our winter firewood in the brisk autumn days, and the quality of the light at different times of day in different times of year. He, on the other hand, always worked hard and fast, insisting on his idea of maximum efficiency—which involved a certain amount of wheel spinning—anxious to finish the task at hand. After a while he learned there was no end to the work, that it was a cycle, but he never learned to enjoy that cycle."

Living on the land, says Sandy, is similar to appreciating fine music. "It is important to pay attention to the beat below and the melody line above, or you will miss the whole point, which is pleasure." She felt that the earth spoke to her; if it was also speaking to her husband, on the other hand, he was not hearing what it was saying: "It froze him in the winter, burned him in the summer, and just plain wore him out over time."

Sandy had achieved harmony with the land, but somewhere along the way she lost that quality with her husband. They barely noticed at first because they spent so little time together. "He had his chores and I had mine, so the only thing we actually did together was gather firewood for the winter in the crisp and exquisite fall days. I walked miles daily, wrote a lot of poetry, and read a lot during the winter when we were often snowed in for weeks at a time. I have no idea what he did because I had stopped paying him any mind. I was married to the land, noticing and recording in poems its every mood and nuance."

Although their differences were set in motion during the years on the land, the conflict overflowed into the years afterward. When they left West Virginia they moved in with Sandy's in-laws while her husband started a business career. Soon they bought a small farm in Maryland, outside of Washington, D.C. But their marriage did not survive the return to civilization, and her husband moved out and settled in the capital. By 1980 a divorce was under way. It was during this process that Sandy learned more than she had ever known about the law, and she was appalled by the systematic abuse of women in the courts.

During these bitter divorce proceedings, Sandy took a beating in court, which inspired her to become a lawyer herself. She wanted to serve as an advocate for women and other silenced peoples who did not know how to work the system. She graduated from the University of Denver Law School and practiced law for twelve years before shifting careers again.

Although he seized most of the money and assets during the 1980 divorce, Sandy says, her husband was not awarded the land in West Virginia. He didn't want it anyway, and she was grateful to have it: "I fought to keep that place because I thought one day I would return. He gave it up easily, worried about his more valuable real estate in D.C.'s Logan Circle area and the business that had become his life. Later he tried to appeal the order that awarded me the land by claiming that I had misled him about its value. This time, stereotypes just happened to work in my favor: I was, as a woman, not supposed to have any business savvy, and he, the male, owner of city real estate, was the one

*who would have known the 'true value' of the land. In fact the 'true value' of
the land was beyond the comprehension of both the judge and my ex."*

A wealthy New York stock trader who purchased the large cattle farm
next to Sandy's land in West Virginia discovered that his water source was on
her property. He made her an offer she couldn't refuse. Although it felt like
"cutting off my legs," she needed the money after the divorce and reluctantly
sold the land. She was paid enough "to enable me to support my children for
a few years and buy a very small house in an old neighborhood where I could
look out and see trees."

Today Sandy is happily remarried, lives in Denver, and has recently retired from her career as a lawyer which she spent helping women and minorities fight the system. Now she substitute teaches in the Adams County
school system and has published two novels, The Nun *and* Stillbird-by-the-
River *and* Mary Queen of Scots. *She still dreams about the homestead in
Appalachia.*

❦ By the 1970s the social rules of the past lay scattered and broken in
the wake of a new American pursuit: individual fulfillment. Because of
its sheer size, the 76-million-strong baby-boom population born between 1945 and 1960 had begun to overturn American culture with its
revolutionary ideas about premarital sex, cohabitation, and the right to
dissolve unsatisfactory relationships. As the boomers reached adulthood and their social attitudes seeped into the mainstream, the importance of pursuing individual gratification, even at the expense of others, became firmly established. American divorce courts reflected this
as spouses filled them by the millions. Between 1965 and 1975 the divorce rate in the United States doubled.

"In an age that emphasized personal happiness and immediate gratification, millions of Americans no longer were willing to sacrifice personal expectations of fulfillment and self-realization in order to maintain
marriages or relationships that failed to meet their demands," observes
William H. Chafe in *Making America*. The historian Eric Foner believes
that the New Left's "growing demand for liberation and personal fulfillment" laid the groundwork for the "me" decade of the 1980s.

Not only was the stigma removed from divorce during the 1970s, but the popular culture and the media had made divorce downright chic, celebrating it as a tool for personal growth as the pendulum swung away from the restrictive social orders of the past. Where married couples had once been admired for sticking it out for a lifetime through good times and bad, in the 1970s "the real heroes were those who chucked their marriages," writes David Frum. The growing divorce rate, furthered by widespread no-fault divorce laws, did not suggest that couples were any unhappier in the twentieth century than they had been before, only that now they cared enough about "the content and quality of family life and marriage to be willing to dissolve an unsatisfactory marriage (and commonly to replace it with a more successful one)," writes the historian Tamara K. Hareven.

Back-to-the-Land Breakups

Given the epidemic divorce rate, breakups between back-to-the-land couples were not surprising, really, merely ironic. We had moved to the land expecting a kinder, gentler place, a nurturing space where we could spend quality time with our partner shelling peas and canning tomatoes. Removed from the fast-paced mainstream, we could slow down, relax, and revive the *joie de vivre* in our marriages. We imagined ourselves as models of sangfroid, sitting on the porch of an evening, he cleaning the chainsaw with a rag, she darning the wool socks, exchanging witticisms as the crickets chirped in the dusk. Going back to the land would help us nurture the love.

Love is what we were all about! Counterculture people were "profoundly dedicated to peace and love" as an ethic. Numerous stories have circulated of communes who opened their arms to defeated young people with no place to go and turned their lives around, or communities of homesteaders who helped their neighbors raise walls and harvest wood. But closer to home, friction often sizzled. Loving humanity was a cinch, but a spouse could be more challenging. I knew a beatific homesteader who thought nothing of lovingly handing a twenty-dollar bill to a broke stranger he'd picked up hitchhiking, and who would then go home and mock and berate his wife for taking a break from the weeding.

Psyched up for joy and peace, we were slapped in the face with nonstop, exhausting manual chores, financial struggles, and a dearth of personal space. The reality of daily life hardly fanned the flames of romance.

Imagine yourself, part of a couple, living in the woods. Say it's been snowing furiously all night, three feet of snow has drifted across the driveway, and the car's battery is dead anyway, so you're snowbound. It's fifteen degrees outside, and the icy drafts are gusting boldly through the house's leaks and cracks. The dirty clothes stink and could walk to a Laundromat themselves, but only the wringer washer stares at you from the shadowy corner of the cabin, its metallic wringers like a twisted mouth, smirking. You wish *he* would do the laundry for once! Why is it always your duty to stand for two hours hand-pouring water into the machine, stuffing the filthy clothes in, and feeding them through the wringer? But of course he's too busy with more vital tasks—chain-sawing the wood or fiddling with the dead car.

Meanwhile he's gazing at you as you stand there in your flannel nightgown and L. L. Bean boots, a crabby expression on your un-made-up face, wondering why *you* can't be more efficient and organized, like Molly down the road, whose glass jars of beans and peaches neatly line the shelves and who *likes* washing clothes with her washboard because it keeps her connected to her spirit. The fire hisses softly as a log crumbles in the woodstove. He's growing bossier all the time, to motivate you to complete your fair share of the work, while you're growing resentful of his bullying.

Meanwhile, as you set up the washer, you're remembering that it was his idea to live this way, and maybe it wasn't such a hot one after all, and he's reflecting on what a shame it is that he doesn't have a partner who is really *into* this, the way he's into it.

With the negative vibes swirling thickly, you roll the wringer out of the corner and set it up near the sink. You hoist the cauldron off the stove and heave the water into the machine. As usual, about a gallon splashes onto the floor. He looks up from his seed catalogue, frowns, and says, "Geesh, can't you pour that without spilling it?"

This comment sparks the urge to kill. In a regular home an irritated partner can walk out, slam the door, and drive into town for a few hours. Here, however, until the snow melts you're securely trapped in the same twenty-by-twenty-foot, one-room area with low ceilings. You can't even retreat into the bathroom, lock the door, and just be alone. The outhouse is fifty feet from the house while your indoor commode, no bigger than an airline bathroom anyway, has a layer of frost lining the inside walls and only a thin curtain separating it from the living area.

Beyond the standard annoyances of daily living, you also have hair-splitting principles to wrangle over. You're living alternatively because you vehemently believe in preserving the environment. Your partner does too, of course. But your heart is set on solar heating while your partner covets wood heat. You quarrel. You want to fertilize the garden with free chicken manure from the local factory, but your partner believes using chicken manure contributes to the exploitation of chickens. You argue. As highly dogmatic people—that's why you both dropped out of society in the first place—you both have numerous personal creeds to defend.

When back-to-the-land relationships dissolved, one partner usually quit the land, often having no other option but to reassimilate into civilization. Expelled from the Good Life, the departing person inevitably met a new partner who more than likely wasn't attracted to backwoods living, so this sealed the end of the back-to-the-land odyssey. Meanwhile the partner who remained on the farm often grew lonely or depressed, or couldn't handle the chores alone, so he or she also moved on. Coming back from the land, you see, was not always totally voluntary.

No one has studied the breakup rate among back-to-the-land people, but I'm willing to bet it surpassed the national divorce rate. Said one homesteader, "Most of the couples I knew who were with us in the

The reality of daily life on the land created tension for many back-to-the-land couples.

countryside, almost all of them broke up. One guy's wife went off to work a part-time job in the city just to raise money. She never came back. He was so heartbroken he torched his own house, barn, and everything he'd been working on the whole time. To me that was probably the most symbolic act that anybody around there could have made at that point, because all the people we knew, for one reason or another, began to tumble out of that situation."

Another person told of a back-to-the-land couple who had owned a place a mile back in the woods. "The wife of the couple was driven nearly nuts by this place. The minutiae of just trying to survive the winter was driving her absolutely bats. The husband didn't mind it; he was working out while she was growing the garden and just going nuts! Finally their relationship was eroded by her frustration and the terrible distance from anything she could regard as normal culture.

She liked growing the garden, but everything else she experienced as a terrible deprivation. He had the car there, and the distances were not walkable. You can't walk ten miles down the road to have tea with somebody who might be compatible! I drove up to see her one day when he was at work. She opened the door just a little crack, as though it might be some stranger who might be going to kill her, and only when she saw who was there did she actually open the door and let me in. It was probably a really good thing she went back to New York City."

Linda Clarke

Linda Clarke and her husband bought their farm in Watkins Glenn, New York, in 1978. Their beautiful cold house sat on a hillside in the midst of thousands of acres of state forest. "You'd drop a washcloth on the bathroom floor in winter, and it would freeze solid in under five minutes," she says.

The well water was badly polluted, they soon discovered. Sewage emptied into the ditch in front of their house and backed up into the shoveled well. A rat infestation threatened the hens.

Linda actually relished the challenge of solving the problems that kept surfacing. Busy all the time, she grew the garden, raised her two children, nine and four, cooked entirely on the woodstove, and cared for the animals. She generated clever ideas for marketing cash crops; for example, she sold winter sucklings for Christmas dinners. "I made these fancy advertisements, hitting for the upscale gourmet market, and I got a damn good price for those piglets," she says proudly. She studied the rat problem and devised an effective system for conditioning rats to feed at poisonous sites, which killed them. She wrote an article about her rat-free farm, which was published in *Countryside Magazine*.

"The farm was a place where I could take all of both my intellectual abilities and my physical abilities and thoroughly challenge them," she says. "I could use my *brain* and my body. That was so important for me as a woman. I was the theorist, the expert on the place. I could study, read books, and learn about better fertilizers. At the same time, using the sheer physical strength required of farm work felt so good. There was so much that I learned that I *could* do."

On the other hand, her spouse, a control freak, "felt continually threatened by my energy and never stopped trying to boss and control most of the details of my life." What's more, she and her husband lacked a shared goal.

"The farm was beautiful, but we had no common goals for managing it, just day after day of petty conflicts over details. I thought the plan was to grow and market pork and eggs and maple syrup, and as soon as possible get the setup for commercial goat cheese production, and of course market vegetables and anything else we could make or grow. We sold bread at a farmers' market but never really figured out the economics. I really don't know what my spouse's goals were for the farm, but they never seemed to match with mine. We never articulated a plan and agreed on it or tried to implement it."

As their quarrels intensified, Linda became miserable, growing "crazier and crazier." By 1981 she was seriously depressed. She detested the thought of bailing out, but she explored the options with a therapist and finally concluded that the only way to regain control of her life and take care of her children was to leave. In 1981 she took her children and left the land, happy to be free of her abusive spouse but also terrified.

"I had two children, four paper bags of clothing, and a hunter pony in my possession."

For years she struggled to keep afloat, between welfare, low-paying jobs, and unemployment. Today she is enrolled in a doctoral program in history, studying women who became nurses in the Civil War. She has a new partner, grandchildren, and peace.

"I *loved* it there!" she says. "I was deeply attached to it. My spirituality is really tied to animals, farm, and earth. I wouldn't have missed the farm years for anything. But it didn't work out, and I had to let it go."

Communal Accord and Differences

In his best-selling novel *Drop City*, T. C. Boyle portrays communes as filthy, fractious, and disorganized. Contrary to popular perception, some communes and land cooperatives succeeded. The key to their survival was clear-cut, internal regulation.

Marlene Heck, for example, lived for a year and a half with the Mulberry Family, an urban cooperative established in the early seventies in Richmond, Virginia. The carefully selected members were expected to cook, clean, contribute money, and serve on committees. As a member of the shopping committee, Marlene was responsible for collecting food money and buying groceries. Home-cooked meals were prepared nightly.

"It was fabulous having a *meal* every night. Some nights it was a big bowl of salad, but other nights you had really good cooks. They were those remarkable people who could look in the refrigerator and take a few beans and a little bit of bread and some salad and cook up a fantastic meal for us."

Mulberry House disbanded peacefully as the members began to pair off, marry, and establish themselves professionally. Marlene, a professor at Dartmouth, realizes she could never live like that now. "I see this in our students every day. You think, 'How could *I* have lived like that? I need more privacy; I need more control, I'm just sick of walking into the kitchen and finding out the peanut butter's been used. *I've* got to make the coffee.' You can do communal living when you're twenty-two, twenty-three, twenty-four, but you get to a point where you think, 'I want something different. It's now time for me to have my *own* kitchen, my *own* yard.' People got to a different stage in their lives and needed different kinds of arrangements, and I think it was mostly a desire to have families, to have privacy, to have one's own place rather than a shared space."

Amiability may have ruled Mulberry House, but the conflict that erupted in many group arrangements is well documented. There is "compelling evidence that the good old days were not as good as portrayed by communitarians, whether in ancient Athens, medieval Europe, or in eighteenth- and nineteenth-century America," observes Edward W. Younkins in *Capitalism and Commerce*. Communes had "a powerful individualistic cast," notes the historian Eric Foner, which may have undermined collective goals.

Robert Houriet, author of *Getting Back Together*, lived on a commune in Vermont in the seventies. One problem that surfaced, he recalls, is that counterculture people, often naive about human nature, trusted others too easily. Then they got burned. "Everybody is good, everybody is a brother; it's lovey-dovey. . . . You think evil doesn't exist, so you go along and—boom! You are swallowed by a shark!" Alarmed by the evil they discovered in fellow members, communards were even more traumatized by the evil they discovered in themselves during prolonged cohabitation. "They saw things in themselves that they couldn't accept," says Houriet, so they left.

Communes collapsed for numerous reasons, including "lack of clear communal goals and structures . . . aggravations of shared space, irritating personal habits, members' overexposure to each other, and members' finding that in many cases they really didn't like each other once they got well acquainted," notes former commune member Matthew Israel. The same controversies faced by married couples increased exponentially in group situations. Timothy Miller confirms that "physical proximity often proved intolerable, and huge numbers of communes did not long endure—indeed often foundering on exasperating interpersonal relationships."

Factions usually developed, impeding the cooperative mission. Ken Davison belonged to a back-to-the-land community in Arkansas that included 150 families at its peak. He remembers when "seeds of dissension started to grow within the community" because "people divided over religion, pacifism versus self-defense, politics—just about anything you can imagine." Individual resentments festered too. He recalls feeling affronted when a neighbor neglected to offer him one of his extra roosters after Ken had given *him* a dismantled log cabin. "He was living in the house that I gave him and helped him set up, and he would not even give me an extra rooster?"

Even one out-of-sync member could easily rattle the serenity of an entire assemblage. A homesteader recalls that "as we started to marry, and as other people came and lived on our land, we just stopped getting along as well, and that made it hard to live all together. One member of the group was more dogmatic than the rest of us about keeping things a certain way. When my first wife joined the group, she became a kind of threat to the big picture there, and that was hard for everybody."

A commune member remembers a child whose antics disrupted the peace: "One of my downside memories of that period of time was a kid named 'Freedom,' who had had way too many uncles. And his mom wouldn't discipline him; if you had a problem with him, you had to discipline him yourself. The kid was a terrorist. He got put in the car for misbehaving one time and ripped out the windshield. If 'Freedom' is still alive and not in jail, that will be hard to believe."

One cooperative farm whose people were bickering too much enlisted the aid of paid consultants who specialized in human dynamics. The series of lectures on the proper process of group interaction inspired members to create rules and bylaws. Morale healed, fostering the farm's golden era, says one member—before new problems surfaced and deflated morale once again.

Inside One Commune

Allan Sirotkin grew up in Detroit and attended the University of Michigan. Active in the Democratic party, he was chosen as a delegate to the state convention in 1968. That tumultuous political year changed his outlook, and from that point on he felt "that working *in* the system wasn't getting it." A business person from early on, Allan opened a food co-op in Ann Arbor, and through it he forged business connections with other co-ops. They rented trucks and drove across the country, looking for organic farmers at a time when organic farming was not yet widely practiced. His interest in healthful food made him think, "Well, geez, I'd like to try to grow my own. Why don't we be the supplier rather than the buyer?" He and a group of friends started looking for land.

Allan followed a friend from the co-op to DeKalb, New York, where they stayed through the summer in "an old building that was barely livable." They discovered a large network of back-to-the-land people in the region: four communes had already been established. Allan joined one and stayed for eight years.

Congeniality prevailed among the seven adults and three kids at Birdsfoot during the early years. Members worked diligently, grew vegetables, and sold them to retail stores. "For me, the early period was the golden age of our commune. I'd say we were purists as communes went at that time. Everybody lived there, and all the money we earned was put into a big pot, and we decided how it should be spent."

The first signs of strife surfaced when members disagreed about work contributions and money-making efforts. Allan continues, "Eventually we had problems with people who didn't want to work. At one point a group of three people out of the seven of us pretty much dropped out of life. There wasn't a lot of incentive for them to go back to work because they got as much as they got anyway. Of course there was a lot of drama between the people who were earning more money and those who didn't want to work. The money earners began to feel like they weren't getting their worth out of the other people. Although there wasn't any conflict for me, it was hard. Time and money are related. If you're putting in all your money, but your time isn't being redeemed in return by unemployed people, hard feelings erupt. As a group we'd say, 'Okay, everybody's got to do, say, four hours of work,' or we tried assigning amounts of rent and requiring everyone to put in x amount of money. But if people didn't do it, there was no way to enforce it."

The gap between the hard workers and the casual workers widened. For example, the cooking was rotated. Each member cooked for the whole group one night a week. A hard worker might arrive in the kitchen early and spend two hours preparing a nourishing dinner for the group, where a casual worker would, as Allan describes it, "run down the hill and spend ten minutes grabbing leftovers, throwing them in the big pan, throwing the pan on the oven, and then throwing the food on the table."

The commune was governed by unanimous consent—on the surface at least. All members had to agree on a decision or else the group couldn't proceed. This rule, Allan now realizes, turned the commune into a permanently hung jury, or a dictatorship with an underground resistance movement. "Unanimous consent is a very interesting governing process," he says. "It empowers people who are very verbal and aggressive, and disempowers people who are very quiet, who don't really say what they want and just let the stronger, louder ones run the show. Quieter people who give in to the group all the time feel fairly resentful. It degrades them to have to go along with the others. It would be much more empowering for them to be able to say, 'Look, I don't agree with this. You guys can do it if you want, but I just don't agree with it,' or 'Look, I understand that the group rules say that six to one passes, and you're going to do this anyway, but I at least got to stand up for what I felt and say *no*.

The arrival of new people also threw them off balance. At first the members were young and single, but one by one they fell in love and wanted to bring new partners to the farm.

Allan says, "You couldn't say no to someone's request to bring a new partner in because you had a lot of respect for this person who had been living on your farm and who was now in love. But the new person didn't quite fit into the group, and that created conflict."

Stage three of the drama occurred when people began having or bringing in more children. The hope of unanimous consent then became even more far-fetched. "Kids are so manipulative at playing one parent off another—let alone seven of them," he said. "They'll say, 'You don't want me to do it! Well, how about *you?*'"

"I can remember having a discussion about whether or not to buy hair conditioner for the daughter of one of the women there," he continues. "In some ways, these discussions were tainted by the rift between people who worked versus people who weren't working. We didn't have the money to buy both the conditioner *and* a part for the tractor. Conditioner seemed relatively a luxury to me. But for a teenage girl it wasn't. I wasn't a parent at the time. I don't know how I would have made that decision now. But I remember that discussion, and now I can really see how difficult it was for parents whose kids wanted this or that to have to deal with seven other adults to get something."

Finally, the stickiest situation the group confronted was property ownership, an issue they had dismissed as trivial in the early years. Allan explains, "The deeds were made in one person's name—because of the feeling, you know, 'We don't care about ownership.' People lived there, but no one owned any of it for a long time. But when things really started getting *bad*, somehow it *mattered* whose name was on the deed. Then suddenly there was discord with the owner when he decided that he wanted just a little more out of the property than originally planned. After a brief period of pandemonium, he ended up selling off a third of the property to someone else, and then we got the deed to it. It was a real learning experience."

Birdsfoot carries on today with a turnover of members and a stronger system of economics and governance. Allan left in 1982 and opened a vegetarian restaurant. He had hoped to run it collectively with several other members of the commune. But trying to launch a restaurant cooperatively proved to be as tricky as governing a commune. In business, decisions could not wait for unanimous consent.

"Making decisions like that as a group was just unbearable," he remembers. So he opened the restaurant independently, with his name on the deed, and sold it in 1995. Today he is the owner and CEO of Green River Chocolates in Hinesburg, Vermont.

Scene from a Marriage in Maine

Moving to the country did not eliminate conflicts with neighbors, any more than it saved us from clashes with spouses and friends. How wonderful if such a place really existed where all human dissension evaporated!

Most back-to-the-land people forged cordial relationships with the locals and never lacked for assistance, support, and kindness. In Troy, our neighbors delivered loads of manure in their trucks and helped us pile it onto our garden. They lent us their tools. They exchanged friendly comments on the weather and the baby poults as we stood in line at the Troy General Store. But, as in all neighborhoods, country or city, there were exceptions.

Our dog Zeke was never a particularly sharp mutt, but maybe we had failed him by not training him properly. We had adopted him from the pound three years before buying the land. He rode in the car with us when we moved to Maine, but upon arrival we didn't pay him much mind except to build him a run in the yard. Keeping the house warm and hauling the water from the well were full-time preoccupations. Zeke frequently broke loose from the run and tore happily through the woods. We tried to confine him to the log cabin, but when anyone pushed open the wide, heavy front door he would streak past and disappear into the trees. On one occasion he hurried up the dirt road and fathered a spring litter of puppies with neighbor Sue's dog. We adopted two, a rust one and a grey one, and named them Chuck and Farley. Then Zeke broke out one day and never returned. Later a rumor drifted back to us that one of our neighbors—who is now a lawyer, so I certainly won't mention his name—had shot him for trespassing.

Chuck and Farley, the puppies, were not allowed to run free, but as they grew, they too learned how to squeeze out the door, especially during the night when I was too groggy to restrain them effectively. Howling to go out, they'd awaken me with their chorus, so I would slip on my Bean boots, descend sleepily from the loft, and carefully push open the cabin door, intending to lead them to the dog run where I could hook them and leave them to do their business. But as soon as I pushed our heavy door outward, the first dog would break my grip and bolt, racing into the woods, followed by the other, whose strong body would knock me to the ground. The next morning they usually reappeared in the yard.

The neighbor who had reportedly killed Zeke informed us one day that Chuck and Farley had been trespassing on his property. Would we prefer that he put them out of their misery with his gun as a favor to us, or would we rather take them into town and have them put down? The dilemma sparked a heated debate between Kent and me.

"No!" I screamed to Kent. "They're our pets, and we don't have to kill them! We'll build a fence or do something."

"We don't have any friggin' money to build a fence."

"You could build something from our own trees."

"Even if we build a fence, they could still break out."

We had a horrible argument, he insisting that we needed to conform to the mind-set of local Maine culture since we were going to live there for the rest of our lives; me crying and telling him I didn't want to be part of that culture if they thought shooting pets was okay. In the end, the dogs were driven into town and euthanized, which I felt then and still feel was wrong. This clash of views over the dogs once again signaled my unsuitability for homesteading and foretold my later decision to leave the marriage and the Good Life.

❧ *John Armstrong enjoyed working alongside his wife Darma on their homestead in Michigan. When she left him, he was devastated. "Then I was alone, and suddenly the place didn't seem so wonderful," he notes in his unpublished essay "The Hard Return."*

Initially John was energized by the challenge of hard labor and the pleasure of having Darma by his side in this picturesque, North Woods setting. He savored their back-to-the-land way of life.

As he describes it, "We worked hard, but we managed to steal bits of time for picnics and long walks in the woods where we sometimes sat quietly next to ponds watching ducks and beavers forage for food. In the spring we enjoyed listening to the yipping of coyotes and the drumming of ruffed grouse as they engaged in their mating rituals. Ravens were ever present and bears continued to roam the property at night, which is why we bought a puppy—a twenty-dollar malamute who quickly grew into a wonderful companion."

They even renovated the sauna that came with the property. "Most of our saunas were taken at night by the soft, flickering flame of a kerosene lantern," remembers John. "Rustic but very romantic."

The first sign of trouble appeared when Darma reduced her help around the homestead. John ignored it at first, thinking she simply needed a rest, but when the situation didn't improve he finally confronted her. Darma told him they were working too hard and not having enough fun—she was tired of working from dawn till dusk.

John was baffled. He felt they had struck a good balance between work and play. And even if the days were sometimes heavy with work, he felt their life was tremendously rewarding. But Darma refused to budge.

"Once it was in the open, it was like a wedge had been driven between us. Instead of talking it through, we drifted apart. We argued. I tried to reignite her original passion for homesteading but failed. Finally I came to the realization that Darma was through. Then, during one of our heated arguments, all my frustration poured out, and I shoved her away from me. That's when she must have accepted the fact that I wasn't yet prepared to give up my dream of homesteading, even at the cost of losing her. Darma called her folks, and a couple of days later her brother came along and took her away."

John was angry, confused, and lonely, but determined to continue homesteading. A month later he went home for a visit. That's when his sister Gail prodded for details about his apparent breakup. She posed the question, "Did you ever consider that Darma might not have what it takes to live on a homestead?"

"She's a farm girl for chrissakes," John replied.

"But she never lived in such a primitive fashion. Homesteading is a different lifestyle. Maybe you expected too much of her."

"Look, things had to get done. There was gardening, trimming, canning, taking care of the chickens, rabbits, the endless job of cutting firewood, and . . ."

"John . . . listen to yourself. You've just described the reason Darma left you. She was simply exhausted by the lifestyle you found so wonderful," Gail said.

"But we agreed in the beginning," John protested.

"Agreed to what?"

"To homestead."

"Fine. But what exactly does it mean to homestead? Did you tell her upfront what was expected? Did you ever consider that she may not have known what she was getting herself into?"

"*Come on, Gail.*"

"*I'm serious. She may have grown up on a farm, but I'll bet she never had to dig in the ground with a shovel, split wood, or haul provisions through the snow on a toboggan.*"

"*But that was part of the magic. We were living a lifestyle that few others could—and were damn happy at it.*"

"*You were happy, but it should be pretty obvious by now that she wasn't.*"

In the end, John knew Gail was right, though he didn't want to believe it. After a few weeks he returned to the homestead and found that the magic had disappeared for him too.

"*I didn't work on the house as much, and I only halfheartedly tended the garden. I gave away the chickens and the rabbits and stopped visiting the neighbors. Instead I spent my time reading and reminiscing about our quiet walks along deserted Lake Superior beaches searching for agates, or the warm summer evenings when we swam naked in the cool, dark waters of our own stream. I remembered skiing along wooded hill trails, some of them cut by deep ravines with frozen waterfalls whose icy forms tumbled down like huge heads of cauliflower. We once skied under moonlight in a grove of hemlocks draped in bales of snow, the moon so bright that we could see the coyote tracks as if it were day. Late-night dinners were eaten by the firelight of our woodstove, and on Thanksgivings we served lake trout, ruffed grouse, snowshoe hare, garden potatoes, applesauce made from our own apples, and blueberry pie made from wild berries we picked.*

John realized Darma wasn't coming back—not to the homestead, not to him. "*Those were the memories, never to be forgotten, that I packed up along with my few belongings. I loaded everything I owned into the pickup and headed downstate, never to return.*"

John eventually sold the property, but he retained an enormous interest in the architecture of Keweenau—the saunas, farmhouses, and mining buildings—an interest that led him back to college. He earned a master's degree in architecture and wrote The Way We Played the Game. *John is now re-married and has a son.*

CHAPTER NINE

Turning Points

"For the most part, massive shifts towards simplicity such as the back-to-the-land movements have had a very short life span. People looking for an overnight conversion are bound to be disappointed and will inevitably backslide to the old way."—David Shi, *In Search of the Simple Life*

"When I saw my truck frozen into the ground, I thought, 'I'm just tired of this.' Tired of everything being a big job"—Jim Carlson, college professor, Georgia

"We starved, but hey, you know? It was fun when I was in my twenties. In my thirties I started thinking about the future and thinking about the kids. In my forties I started thinking about breast exams, pap smears, retirement, and college educations for the kids."—Miriam Ross, operator of an internet business, Arkansas

❦ *February 1978, West Virginia: From a distance he was a small dot moving slowly across the white countryside. John Verlenden slogged through the snow with a knapsack on his back, lifting his L. L. Bean boots with effort as he trekked across the uninhabited field of snow. Sub-zero air struck his reddened cheeks, which were exposed below his cap and above his ice-crusted beard. In particular John, who is now a college professor and au-*

thor, remembers the grey sky. "It was a very low, very gloomy-sort-of-feeling day," he recalls. "And I remember that my mood was just about as grey as the sky." That day, after two and a half years, he was leaving the farm for good.

Officially declared the worst winter of the twentieth century, 1977–1978 was unusually cruel, breaking meteorological records as it assaulted West Virginia with blizzard after blizzard, ice storms, howling winds, and sub-arctic temperatures so drastic that the town plow had remained stuck at the bottom of the hill below John and Debbie's farmhouse, unable to push its way up. They did not receive mail for three weeks. They burned firewood at such a fast rate that the woodpile depleted and John had to wade out into the cold to cut more trees with his chain saw. He would buzz the tree into logs right there in the snow, split them on a stump with a maul and a wedge, and lug them into the house, tossing them into the fire, praying the green wood wouldn't kill it.

"All of a sudden, life in the country stopped being a game and started being survival for real," remembers John. "When I went out every day to cut wood, the snow was almost to my chest. I was frightened. I was often out six hours in a day. I'm talking zero degree weather. We would run out of wood almost by the time the next installment would come in, and I'd have to go out and cut down more trees.

"What scared me," he continues, "was that it's not easy to hold a chain saw for a long period of time. They get heavy, they vibrate, and your fingers get numb. There comes a point where you're holding it but you can't feel it. Anybody who has ever operated a chain saw knows that one of the big dangers is having it slip and fall on you. The snow was so deep that my body effectively disappeared in it while I was doing this cutting, and my feet would be so numb I wasn't sure I could jump out of the way if it hit wrong, took a wrong bite of the tree and kicked back. To boot it all, nobody had ever really taught me how to cut down a tree this way. I had learned it out of those damned pictures in the back of Mother Earth News," he laughs. "You realize at a certain point there's only so much you can learn from pictures. It's really not enough to give a person confidence. You think, 'Okay, well, I was supposed to cut it here and make a V, and then come back and cut it the other way,' and meanwhile this gigantic piece of wood is standing over your head thirty feet tall that's got to be a thousand pounds. You're thinking, 'If I don't cut it right, what's going to happen to me?' I was terrified. I was really getting more and more afraid that every time I went out of the house, my ignorance was going to catch up with me."

Ending up in cold West Virginia had been unpremeditated. Two and a half years earlier, in Memphis, John's 1964 panel truck had sat in the driveway, packed and ready to leave for California the following morning. Then an acquaintance John barely knew stopped by.

"Why go to California?" the friend asked. "I've got a farm in West Virginia, and I've been looking for someone to live on it."

John replied immediately, "Sure, I'll take the place."

Reflecting on the impetuosity of his youth, he remarks, "I'm discouraged when I look back and think I was capable of this kind of rashness at age twenty-seven."

As a budding writer, John had identified with Thoreau. He looked forward to immersing himself in country nature and living a salutary author's life while he wrote. He had not planned on spending so much of his time on laboring jobs, which he disliked. In addition to working out at a sewage treatment plant, as well as taking other jobs, he had been very disciplined about keeping a writing schedule. Every day he would walk to the little outbuilding that he called his writing shack, light the woodstove, heat the water for his instant coffee, and write for several hours. In two and a half years he wrote a dozen short stories which were praised by various editors, though not published at the time. Because he was a writer at heart, he found working at the sewage treatment plant frustrating. "I felt . . . 'short-circuited' would probably be too mild a word," he says. "I felt that things were not going as I had planned them. I didn't know how to make them go."

He adds, "While I was living out in the country, I had a terrible, absolutely terrible but undeniable urge to stop in at many of these little mountain cafés and just sit around drinking coffee and maybe having a stack of pancakes, basically diddling away time reading, thinking, chatting if necessary, and chalking it all up to something that could best be palmed off as literary material. So there was kind of a citygoer in me that never really left. I was basically a person out on a farm not really admitting to myself that I wanted to be in a Starbucks."

Tensions in his marriage had intensified. "We were stuck up there, and we had hardly anybody around us," he remembers. Sometimes, when he felt his irritation growing, he would take his sleeping bag out to his writing shack and sleep on the bare floor.

"I remember my wife and I having a huge shouting match in the middle of the woods," he said. "It wasn't physical, but I had never spoken with such abusive, violent language. It shocked me. And again, it told me that the end was near for this experience. When you see parts of yourself come out that you never knew existed, particularly not very good parts, you begin to wonder if you are leading the right life."

These thoughts flashed through his mind as he hiked across two more frozen fields and came to the edge of the highway, where a Greyhound bus bound for Washington, D.C., drove over the ridge. John waved, the bus pulled over, and he boarded it.

🌱 Americans are "a bundle of contradictions . . . [who] passionately hold conflicting ideals," writes Michael A. Ledeen in his reading of Alexis de Tocqueville's *Democracy in America*. Among the psychological tensions de Tocqueville perceived in Americans was the ongoing tug between morality and materialism, two long-standing themes in United States history.

It is a Catch-22 in a country founded on religious values whose economy has prospered relentlessly: as standards of living continue to rise, Americans wrestle with a sense of guilt about how to live with abundance yet avoid "a path to damnation." The historical paradox noted by nineteenth-century pundits was that "the exemplary life, one marked by hard work and moderate comfort," usually generated additional prosperity and therefore increased the temptation to become materialistic.

Our "internal push and pull between religious belief and material ambition," Ledeen writes, explains why, historically, "from time to time we must undergo a spiritual purge and renewal. . . . We replay this passion play with striking regularity," he says, referring to "several utopian communities of the sort that the hippies of the 1960s knew well."

The dissonance between the virtue of simplicity and the appeal of abundance not only drives the nation but also individuals. "Again and again," writes David Shi, "Americans have espoused the merits of simple living, only to become enmeshed in its opposite. People have found it devilishly hard to limit their desires to their needs so as to devote most of their attention to 'higher' activities. This should not surprise us."

Thus, despite our valiant attempt to disown the wasteful, acquisitive culture in favor of simplicity, the inherent pull toward increased comfort, materialism, and commerce was inevitable. Living close to nature and dealing with the realities of farming, animal husbandry, manual labor, unhappy spouses, low-paying jobs, cash-flow crises, and the like, proved to be overwhelming for most of us. Tolerating the objectionable aspects of civilization was the price we had to pay in order to partake in its benefits of employment opportunities, culture, technology, medicine, and education. Technology and the internet had not yet fully blurred the boundaries between country and urban areas.

Self-sufficiency on the land was to have been our bulwark against the apocalyptic famine, overpopulation, war, and chaos that so many books and pundits had predicted. "In 1970," writes Frederick F. Siegel, "it was predicted that by 1980 'urban dwellers would have to wear gas masks to breathe,' and that by 1985 new scientifically unleashed diseases that people lacked natural antibodies for would inflict the world with a plague of vast proportions." But the world hadn't ended after all. Its opportunities, goods, services, and comforts lay right within our reach.

As Timothy Miller notes, "Those who wanted to continue the life (and were worthy of it) could easily do so. For many, though, it was time to leave." By the beginning of the 1980s, say most observers, the tide had turned. Not every person's timetable was identical, of course, but throughout the eighties a transition took place in the lives of back-to-the-landers. Most of them, such as John, left the land altogether, moving into the mainstream in urban areas, while others remained on the land but eased back into a more traditional agenda, one jettisoned principle at a time, as they modernized the plumbing and heating or grew more amendable to professional opportunities. In a 1983 survey of back-to-the-land people published in a 1986 issue of *Rural Sociology*, Jeffrey Jacob reported "a strong element of a white-collar rural petty bourgeoisie" living rurally, either self-employed as professionals or doing consulting work. "Although these affluent and well-educated back-to-the-landers live in the country-side and hold property, it is quite evident for the most part they are not farmers."

Fatigue

We had grown tired. We now understood why our pioneering ancestors had only lived to be thirty-five or forty. The simple life entailed so much *toil.* Jim Carlson, now a college professor in Georgia, left his property in Arkansas one winter for a few weeks and returned to find the pickup truck frozen solidly into the ground. "When I saw that, I thought, 'I'm just tired of this. Tired of everything being a big job,'" he sighed. "The pipes under the house would freeze. Or, go out to water the horses, right? Well, in the winter that meant taking a big ax or splitting maul, going down to the pond, and breaking a hole in the ice big enough to dip the bucket in, then carrying it back up the hill to give the animals their water. For someone who was used to Florida, it would get pretty cold in Arkansas. It got down to zero, and going out in the morning to feed all the animals was tiring and time-consuming. Between that and things breaking down, it got kind of old."

Linda Tatelbaum and her husband moved to Burketville, Maine, in 1977 and settled on seventy-five acres. Two years later the baby came.

"I change his cloth diapers by flashlight at night; I lug a bushel bas-ket of diapers to the Laundromat every week; I haul water while baby sleeps; I grind grain for his pablum, and cook it on a woodstove. I am exhausted. I want my mother, or canned soup, or baseboard heat. Or do I? At least if I could switch on a light when baby cries at 2 a.m., not fumble with a kerosene lamp while milk leaks down my chest and baby howls. At least if I didn't have to go down to the cellar every time he wants apple juice. At least if I had a drain, so I didn't have to lug water in *and* out. At least if my mother could come and I didn't have to write her a manual for how to boil water on the woodstove for a cup of tea. I'm so tired."

Yes, the novelty of chopping wood, hauling water, and using kerosene lights had worn thin. The sheer physical discomfort alone was enough to change most of our minds, not to mention the complicated nature of things, which could slowly drive a person mad.

In 1981 Ellen Rocco installed plumbing in her farmhouse, though when she and her first husband went back to the land in the St. Lawrence Valley area of upstate New York in 1971 they had planned to live off the grid. "The big thing was to get unplugged from the big Connection," she says. "I hauled water for almost ten years."

Their 120 acres of land included "a shell of a farmhouse" with no insulation or running water. In the early days she worked out as a substitute teacher for a while. "I'd get a phone call from school at quarter to seven or seven and have to be at school at eight. I was a grubby hippie then. Somehow I had to heat water on the woodstove, clean myself up, find some clothes that would look reasonably presentable—I had to do that whole thing in a freezing cold house, in the dark, with no running water," she remembers.

"My brother, who is an astrophysicist and a radical environmentalist, had told me early on, 'If you're going to use paper products, the one paper product you really shouldn't use is paper towels—incredibly wasteful, blah, blah, blah.' I don't even know if that's true, but it was in my head that paper towels were really evil, so I didn't buy them—I used rags and other things. I'd been living up here for about fifteen years and I had never bought a roll of paper towels. The whole time. By the time my son was born, I had running water, but the whole experience was still exhausting. I decided that since I'd been such a good girl and hadn't used paper towels, not only could I now buy paper towels, I could use disposable diapers for a year."

Over the years she has installed not only plumbing but wiring, an oil furnace, insulation, and new walls. "I am not a purist. I'm absolutely not a purist. Of course, this is not like your middle-class suburban home," she points out. "It's an old country house, not a yuppie farmhouse."

Today she manages a public radio network of nineteen stations from Burlington, Vermont, to Jefferson County, New York, and from Glens Falls, New York, to Ottawa.

Insolvency

Not only were we worn out but broke. We needed jobs that paid a living wage, preferably with benefits. It was a no-brainer. As the money dried up, the light began to shift. Idealism didn't pay for the filled cavity or the kids' school clothes. Although members of the Drop City Commune in Trinidad, Colorado, "considered poverty a state of mind," I know I had been unable to reach a state of enrichment while my head spun with worries about how we'd afford a new car battery. As Pat Manuele noted earlier, "Brad was depressed about the hard economic times we had fallen into despite all our efforts."

Pam Read Hanna and her husband, Findley, left Morningstar Commune when their son, Siddhartha, was ready to enter kindergarten. Daughter Psyche was three, and Pam was pregnant with their third child, Sage. They needed conventional jobs to provide for the children's growing needs. Pam, a midwife, had delivered many of the commune babies. She continued midwifery after they left the commune and moved to a place near New Buffalo, New Mexico, but she was too charitable to charge her clients.

"People would give me stuff—a piece of velvet, whatever they had," she says.

Pam remembers telling her children later, "It gets kind of old to be poor when you have kids. If you're childless, it would probably be another thing; you'd probably hang in there a little longer."

Waning Invincibility

We had planned to emulate the hale and hearty Nearings, who were still chopping wood and building stone houses in their senior years. The land and its bounty would provide us with sustenance and shelter in our old age. But as the months and years passed, our invincibility waned, one sore joint at a time (and hadn't the Nearings drawn hoards of disciples who worked free of charge?).

Jane Fishman's turning point came when her feet began to hurt. She had been cooking at a restaurant for three years. Then in her forties, she said to friends, "I've got to get another job where I'm not standing all day."

Before moving to the land, Jane had worked for ten years in Chicago as a speechwriter and then in public relations for the American Hospital Association. Her speeches about "how wonderful the health-care system was" felt meaningless and phony to her. Arkansas's beauty impressed her during a visit, and when she returned to Chicago "the city looked filthy and tawdry, with bus fumes and the like; none of it was really attractive to me anymore."

She moved to Arkansas and bought seventeen acres in Butler Hollow in the Ozark Mountains. A neighbor helped her build a one-room, tin-roofed house out of scrounged materials, installing a wood-burning stove and a sink even though the house had no running water. She cooked on a three-burner gas stove.

"I had to pee in a little bucket, which I would empty outside, and I took showers at friends' houses in town. I lived in my loft upstairs, where it was quiet. And dark. I had a little radio, which I liked at night. Reading was tough because I had kerosene lamps that weren't really bright enough."

Jane had to gun the engine of her '69 Camaro to drive to the top of the road where her house sat.

"I couldn't even see over the top of the car, and when there was no full moon, you had to know on faith that you'd arrived. I had to sell that car quickly and get a truck."

She had lived in her country home for less than a year. "I was there long enough to know that if you didn't have any wood ready for yourself when you came home at night, you would freeze, so I knew enough to get wood prepared, to get kindling, and to get newspaper, so I kind of had that down. I never really had a fire that burned through the night, which is what you would do if you were really good, so I'd have to get up in the morning and do that."

Several heavy snowstorms blew in that winter, so Jane decided to go to Texas where she could live out of her truck, plant trees, and earn some quick money. The week before she was to leave, she heard friends talking about going to Key West for the winter.

"Do you have any more room?" she asked eagerly. In Key West she got a job cooking in a restaurant. Three years later, when her feet began to hurt, a friend asked her, "Why don't you be a newspaper reporter? There's a program at the University of Florida."

"You know, that sounds like a really good idea," she said.

Enrolling in school, she also worked at the Red Lobster, where, at forty-four, she was the only employee who didn't have a credit card. "Everyone at the Red Lobster was majoring in business. When I graduated from the University of Michigan in 1966, everybody had majored in English."

Jane has been writing full-time for the *Savannah Morning News* for fourteen years. She keeps a big garden and bicycles around the city.

"I garden better than I ever have and eat more of my own food than I ever have, so you really don't have to be back-to-the-land to do that," she says. "I think people, at least in the late seventies, wherever they were, grew a little disillusioned with a lot of things in the country, and I'm sure I was in that wave of disillusionment."

She also observed that her friends who remained in the country continuously modernized their properties. "I'd go back to see them, and one time, they had a new redwood deck, and then the next time, they'd redo the whole bathroom in some fancy way, and then they would build a bigger house, so they were still out there, but they had a lot more amenities.

"People change."

Kathy Barrows had established a job, home, and life in Brazil for twenty years, so much had she disliked the U.S. capitalistic system. But when the threat of ex-patriatism loomed, she had to make a decision.

"Brazil is not the kind of country I would want to become old in," she explains. "As people get older, they're caring for their grandchildren and their great grandchildren, and they tend to associate only with their family and older people. Their life becomes much more enclosed. It's not a society where you find elders going to college at age seventy, doing elder hostel, or traveling. I realized that I wanted to come back to the United States, not only for the medical options but to be an active elder and to have those kinds of cultural opportunities that would allow me to have independence and freedom as I got older and not be looked upon as if I were weird."

Like other back-to-the-landers who wanted to live outside the mainstream culture, Kathy had taken the more radical step of leaving the United States in the 1970s. Smitten by Latin culture, she moved to Sergipe, Brazil, and then to Bahia, where she taught English as a second language. Because she was such a rarity—a divorced woman living alone and actually enjoying it—she made the cover of *Veja* magazine. "Years later people would still walk up to me in this city of over two million and ask, 'Aren't you the woman who was on the cover of *Veja*?'"

Somehow the time abroad stretched out to twenty years, and the question of citizenship arose. As much as she detested the materialistic mentality of the United States, the idea of completely severing ties troubled her. She concluded that the United States was a better choice for her mature years. It offered her more opportunities and safety nets. Besides, her eighty-seven-year-old mother who lived alone in the States needed care.

Now in her mid-fifties, Kathy hopes to earn her last three credits to qualify for Social Security and Medicare. "If they exist—which I seriously doubt—but if they do, maybe I'll be covered by Medicare and I'll have a little bit of Social Security payment." Kathy remains torn. She appreciates the windfall income she receives from an inherited real estate property, a positive by-product of a healthy economy. "I have to admit that life in America has its advantages. Here I don't have to worry about a monthly inflation rate of 25 percent or fume as I wait in hour-long lines at one of seventy checkout stands in a so-called hyper-market.

"But I'm back and I've made the decision to be here."

Engaging Our Minds

Desperation for a job or a longing for a warm house may have lured us back into the fold, yes, but it was more than that. We needed mental sustenance as well. Engaging our minds, making social contributions, and gaining better access to education and culture could often best be done within the mainstream. Although some of us found outlets for our talents through direct interaction with the land, many of us could not find intellectual fulfillment without reengaging with established institutions in the capitalistic system. "After all," David Shi writes, "most of the 'high thinking' of this century has been facilitated by prosperity. The expansion of universities, libraries and research centers, the proliferation of learned publications, the democratization of the fine arts, and the ever-widening impact of philanthropic organizations—all of these developments have been supported by the rising pool of national wealth."

His need for "a sense of completion" brought David Starnes to his current profession, a salaried job with benefits. Before getting his graduate degree, he had frequently "tossed my fate to the wind" by quitting jobs he did not like when he tired of them, "without any stepping stones, without any idea of what was coming next."

From 1972 to 1977, David lived in a forty-dollar-a-month farmhouse in Colorado for which, as he states, "I abandoned a responsible job and lifestyle in Washington State for personal freedom on a postage stamp piece of land." He loved his years on the farm. He and his friend heated with wood, used an outhouse, and bathed in a portable tub, hand-filled with water. They raised vegetables in a small garden and kept a horse, chickens, and lots of dogs and cats. Friends regularly filled the house, and "the best times were with other people."

During those years David lived one day at a time financially. He moved to the farm with some savings, but "once that was depleted, I learned to do without—and sometimes was *forced* to do without." He sold eggs and artwork, managed a sandwich shop, worked in a greenhouse, and co-owned a secondhand bookstore, which later folded.

Having no checking or savings account, his cash consisted of "whatever money was in my hands."

"I didn't know what I wanted to do," he says. "I didn't want to be like other people; I didn't want to work in an office; I didn't want to have to wear a suit and tie, yet I didn't want to hang out with counter-culture people either and talk about how bad things were. But I definitely didn't want to work in the mainstream."

In 1979 David left the farm and moved east. He painted houses, did carpentry, worked on public radio. He loved having the freedom to walk away from a job if he grew tired of it. But he says, "I paid for it. Having to borrow money or depend on other people; that was the worst part."

In 1991 David returned to school to complete his undergraduate degree, and by 1999, with a masters degree in hand, he landed a job in academia, where he remains today.

"It may seem strange to say at this stage, but I wanted to feel as though I had done something with my life. I just felt like I had made so many wrong turns and bad choices that I felt like I had to complete something from start to finish for once, without pulling out." David, a talented poet, loves teaching, though he says from time to time he still has to struggle with restlessness.

Don Wirtshafter recognized his talent for public speaking and legal research in 1977 when a strip-mine company threatened to begin operating six miles from his land. Abandoning his quiet life in the log cabin, Don led the local charge against them, researching the laws on strip-mining at the law library.

"We embarrassed them silly!" says Don. "I got to stand up at the public hearing and be the one to speak first against strip-mining. It was the local hippies versus the mine owner, who came with his gold-studded watch, lawyers, engineers, and hydraulicists. We made it the best-watched mine in Ohio for about six months before they shut down."

Fired up by his success, he joined a law firm as a paralegal, and five years later entered law school. Don knew that his days of keeping to himself in his log cabin had come to a close.

David Starnes enjoyed doing manual tasks when he
lived on the farm.

"Becoming a lawyer was the only way I was going to win the environmental legal cases I was already in the middle of."

Michael Doyle left his farm in Waumadee, Wisconsin, to complete
his education. Without a college degree, he couldn't write his own
grants to pursue his passion, history. Known as the "hippie historian"
during his early years at Yaeger Valley Community Farm, he used to interview local farmers for the sheer joy of it. His love for history remained alive even while he farmed his land, worked for the food co-op,
and drove a rural mail route. In 1976 he wrote his first successful grant,
which enabled him to start a historical society in the county seat of
Alma, Wisconsin, and to conduct an intensive survey of its historical
built-environment. With enthusiasm he co-wrote a book that contained the history of the county. Because history was his passion, he
helped organize two other historical societies.

He knew he had a gift for organizing, researching, and raising money, but whenever he had applied for grants, the funding agencies required that a "humanistic scholar" be associated with the proposed project. In other words, Michael couldn't write his grants independently without a college degree.

The last of the original farm members to leave Yaeger Valley Community Farm, he enrolled at the University of Wisconsin at Madison. When he took his first American history courses, he was disturbed at the way recent history was being presented, especially the way the professors covered the counterculture and the back-to-the-land era. He had been there! He had done that! If they couldn't teach it accurately, he decided, he would. When he finished his doctorate, he made American history and the rise of the New Left his area of scholarship. Later he became co-editor of the book *Imagine Nation: The American Counterculture of the 1960s and '70s*.

Figuring It Out

Patricia Foley, who settled in Maine in 1972, observed, "The back-to-the-land people who couldn't do it were the people who didn't know yet what was going to make them happy or what wasn't, young people who hadn't figured out yet what they wanted—they just knew it wasn't back there in civilization. But it also wasn't here on the land either."

Whatever *I* had been seeking was not in the Maine woods after all. As the tribulations accrued and the reality of homesteading revealed itself, I knew I would have to discover what it was that I *did* want and figure out where to find it.

While employed at the Waterville Steak House, I'd often hole up in a corner during breaks, sometimes the only stolen moments in my day, and read Alan Watts or *Les Misérables*. When I graduated to the secretarial position, I always kept a book nearby, discreetly racing through a few pages during slow times. Reading was air to me. If I was not advancing my knowledge, expanding my imagination, or challenging my own views through reading, I felt flat.

One summer, a year before I left, I saw a want ad in the newspaper for a college instructor who would teach writing and literature. My heart pounded. Such a position sounded heavenly. But alas, I did not have a masters degree, only a B.A. in history. I had once scoffed at the notion that anything as silly as a career could define me. On the other hand, maybe it wasn't as much a matter of a career defining me as it was a matter of a career guiding me on a path of discovery within an established body of knowledge.

One cool November night, as the wind blew through the opened screen door of the Reeds' house, the group of regulars milled around the potluck table, scooping up baked beans, salad, banana bread, and cookies onto our paper plates. One of our friends, John, a red-bearded, semi-hippie college professor at the University of Maine, leaned across the plate of cookies and yelled over the buzz of loud conversation, "How would you like to be a graduate teaching assistant?"

He explained that his department at the University of Maine needed a few more GTAs to teach freshman writing in the winter semester, beginning in January. I'd be paid to teach, he said, and would receive free tuition to take graduate courses toward a masters degree. At that moment the world stood still. Holding my drooping paper plate, I smiled broadly with excitement. I couldn't imagine anything I'd like to do more. My blood pumped as I told John I loved the idea.

Returning to school and teaching felt so absolutely right. The very thought of furthering my education immediately assuaged the hunger that had been gnawing at me.

The Volkswagen started, thank God, on the day in January 1979 I drove the thirty miles from Troy to Orono to begin the graduate program. That morning the sun shone in the clear blue sky, and soft white snowdrifts flanked the two-lane road to Orono. From the start I loved my courses in literature and composition theory. I found what I had been craving: formal education. My own random, home-based self-education needed the guidance of educated professors who could give me a more directed tour through the vast and overwhelming universe of knowledge.

That winter and spring of 1979 a budding Maine writer named Stephen King had been hired as a visiting professor in the English Department at the University of Maine at Orono. He had just published his second book, *Salem's Lot*. It was required reading in one of my courses, and later Stephen King visited the class to talk about his writing process.

The log cabin was dark and silent the night I sat up late reading *Salem's Lot* to complete it for the next class. Deeply immersed in the horror novel, I read feverishly. Everyone else slept. The story grew spookier by the minute. As I read on, my hair stood on end. The embers hissed softly in the woodstove, and an occasional chunk of creosote fell down the stovepipe. The nighttime shadows, the creaks of the expanding wood, the zealous mice feet running through the insulation all teased my rising fear, but I couldn't put down the gripping story. I was so creeped out by the time I realized I needed to go downstairs to pee that I could hardly muster the courage to leave the bed. But slowly I got up, boards creaking as I walked, and descended nervously down the ladder from the loft. At the bottom of the ladder, alone in the one big room of the log cabin, my heart thudded as I proceeded ever so slowly toward the dark, narrow hallway that led to the bathroom. I took one or two steps forward, and became suffused with terror. Quickly I turned back, scurried up the ladder to the loft, leaped into bed, and pulled the covers over my head. I suffered until morning light.

I loved graduate school. A sixty-mile round-trip drive to stimulating classes in an academic community sure beat the hell out of the fifty-mile round trip to a steak house in Waterville. All that winter I threw myself enthusiastically into reading the literature and writing the papers. While I had never been disciplined about doing homesteading chores, I now neglected them entirely. These tasks had become obstacles in the path I now sought.

The truth came out, finally: I liked the *idea* of self-sufficiency far better than the real thing. My visions of a vibrant garden, rows of canned beans and jam on the shelf, a neat woodpile of stacked, dried wood, and, best of all, myself serene and content, hand-sewing a shirt

In 1979, when I left, the log cabin still looked rustic and charming, but I had learned by then that life in the woods wasn't for me.

for one of the boys in front of the woodstove were a glossy magazine's vision of a great life, but not mine. Liking the idea was not enough.

Kent, on the other hand, enjoyed the process.

By the time I completed my masters degree, we had separated. In 1981 I left Maine for good and entered a doctoral program in the South.

🌿 *The bus carrying John Verlenden made an emergency stop on the way to Washington to await an ambulance when a young male passenger on board collapsed and died of a heart attack. John's grey mood thickened. He had left the farm in West Virginia only that morning, and the sudden death of a fellow passenger had been unsettling. Later, during the layover in D.C., a man approached and offered him money for sexual favors. As the realities of the larger world closed in, John felt sullied.*

When he arrived at his friends' apartment in New York City, they were complaining that the superintendent wasn't supplying enough heat. "There was more heat in this supposedly underheated New York City apartment than I'd felt in months," says John. "They had these huge gaps where their windows weren't fitting together, so I just stuffed them with old T-shirts. In an hour the temperature rose at least five degrees. It had never occurred to them to do that. So, okay, there is a payoff. The back-to-the-land movement did teach a certain amount of self-sufficiency."

Having honed his manual skills on the farm, John landed a two-month stint as a carpenter remodeling an apartment for a vacationing tenant. One day during lunch break, he clicked on the television. In West Virginia the signal could barely penetrate the mountains, so he hadn't viewed any TV to speak of for two and a half years. That day John sat transfixed. He watched television for the next eighteen hours, clicking the channels back and forth. "It was like a drug," he confesses. "It felt absolutely wonderful. I was just in a state of unusual but effective bliss. I was thirsty; that's what it was. I realized that the isolation I had wanted out in the countryside I had indeed had enough of. I was now terribly thirsty for some culture beyond what had been going on in my own head."

John did construction in New York theaters for about a year. He and his wife started talking again, and when she moved to a city in the Deep South to attend graduate school, John followed. "And of course that opens up another whole new chapter of my life," he says. Today, John, now re-married, is a college professor teaching in Egypt at American University. He is the co-translator, with Ferial Gazoul, of two books from the Arabic, The Quartet of Joy, by Muhammed Afifi Matar, and Rama and the Dragon, by Edwar al-Kharrat. He has also written a book, My Middle Eastern Education, from Terror to Transformation.

CHAPTER TEN

Finding a Niche in the Mainstream

"Most of us have realized as we've aged that the whole idea of escaping from society because we don't like what it's doing is impossible. We're part of a society whether we like it or not, so then the question changes and becomes, how can we make it a little bit more of a better place?"—Sandra Sleight-Brannen

"One's life should be meaningful, productive, and add up to making the world a better place to live in."—Steven Engelhart

"Nobody has to do *everything*. People are constantly saying to me, very aggressively, things like, 'But you don't do what you recommend—look—you're using a typewriter—you're wearing a machine-made tweed.' Etcetera, etcetera. My answer to this sort of thing is that it's no damned business of their [sic] how I live. I can take what I want from the rest of civilization (if I can pay for it) and leave what I don't want. Sally and I don't make any fetish of it."
—John and Sally Seymour, *Farming for Self-Sufficiency*

🌿 *June 1981: The empty apartment smelled of mildew. I stepped inside. The linoleum floor and yellow cinderblock walls received little outside light,* as the only two windows faced off at opposite ends of the rectangular-shaped space. But for $140 a month, what did I want? This gloomy unit was affordable student housing. I had gotten my wish: I was a student again, about to embark on a doctoral program at Louisiana State University in Baton Rouge.

The scent of Lysol hung in the air. The university cleaning staff had no doubt sanitized the place, but years of Southern humidity, lack of sunlight, and inefficient air conditioning had encouraged the rampant multiplication of one-celled organisms in this and all other units of student housing, which had probably been constructed before World War II. The conditions, I soon found out, had certainly encouraged the multiplication of cockroaches.

The two-story complex contained about two hundred look-alike units squared around a grassy courtyard. My apartment sat on a corner facing the wall of a perpendicular unit, a parking lot, and two dumpsters overflowing with trash. Behind a chain-link fence, the railroad tracks ran parallel to the apartment. The view was not inspiring.

Inside, cockroaches inhabited the walls, cupboards, drains, ceilings, and dark corners. They proliferated like crazy in this breeding ground of a student apartment, though it was officially sprayed by the university once a month. If you lived in the South, you had to get used to roaches. Even the high-end, servant-cleaned $400,000 houses always had a few. I learned to open cupboard doors very slowly so that they wouldn't panic and leap out, plopping onto the floor and scurrying for cover. I learned to close my eyes immediately after I'd flipped on the kitchen light at night, so I wouldn't have to watch the flock of them running toward the walls. I put out roach motels, and many checked in. But twice as many others survived in the cupboards and walls. In fact, the motels probably culled the weaker ones from the population, so the stronger ones thrived.

I bought a subscription to the morning newspaper, and for the first two weeks it was stolen every morning. Dutifully I would phone the subscription department, and they would deliver another by noon. I learned that you could never leave items outside in front of your unit. Bikes, barbecues, outdoor tables and chairs would be lifted in a heartbeat if you looked the other way. They had to be brought inside the apartment, crowding it even more. Needless to say, you would never leave your door unlocked.

A laundry room was located in the middle of the unit. No more wringer washing machine! But you had to stay in the shabby room and watch your clothes spin for two hours or someone would clip them. As a transplant from harmless backwoods Maine, I was disconcerted by the high crime level here. You looked over your shoulder. You didn't walk alone. Every day I read two or three newspaper stories reporting fatal arguments involving handguns.

In making this major life change, I had traded an indoor hopper for a flush toilet, a kitchen shower stall for a bathtub and shower, and a wringer washer and clothesline for electric washers and dryers. On the other hand, I was also trading mice for roaches, cold and snow for heat and humidity, and Nor'easters for daily torrential thunderstorms.

But my mission was to earn a doctorate, not to worry about the aesthetics. I hungered after education. I also craved a steady paycheck with benefits. I admired the courageous freelance artists, writers, craftspeople, and entrepreneurs I knew, but the poverty in Maine had spooked any inclinations like that out of me.

In my graduate classes a new community of discourse awaited me. The topics of discussion now centered on the stages of the writing process or on Peter Elbow's theories of student empowerment, not this year's tomato crops or the latest weather patterns. In one of my classes I met a very pleasant, smart woman who had gone back to the land in West Virginia. Burned out from all the problems, she had come south to get a masters degree. Her husband, a writer named John Verlenden, worked on his novel at home, she told me.

The 1980s were hard years. I stayed poor, battled roaches, studied hard, taught hard, and spent time with Derek and Shawn. They say an economic recession hit hard in the early eighties, followed by a mini stock market crash in '87. I never noticed. I was too broke to be affected and too tired from juggling all the work to care. Each semester I taught two first-year writing courses and took three graduate courses. I wanted to do this and saw it as groundwork for the future, but looking back I'm amazed I had the perseverance to stick with it. Well, flashbacks of Waterville Steak House helped.

As a teacher who taught English as a second language as well as regular students, I gained some overdue enlightenment about how the deficiencies of my own country and culture compared to those of other nations. One girl, for example, had escaped from South Vietnam and had arrived in the States as a boat person. She gave an oral presentation to the class about her life in Communist Southeast Asia. A knock had resounded on the door one night, and two uniformed officers had seized her father and dragged him away. She never saw him again. That was common there during the Communist regime, she said. She marveled at how lucky U.S. citizens were. A student from Saudi Arabia raved about the wide-open spaces in the States. You could drive for days and days across open country and never feel crowded, as he had in his homeland. A student from West Africa said the air was so fresh here. In his own land, thick emission pollution from cars, motorcycles, and mopeds filled the air, burning the eyes and choking the lungs. Visitors couldn't drink the water. My students, mostly new arrivals from a range of countries, talked constantly about the freedom, the opportunities, the abundant natural resources, and the standard of living offered by the United States, which were only fantasies in their own nations. As usual, the teacher learned more from the students.

❦ The eighties flew by. The Falklands War lasted two months. Sally Ride soared into space. President Reagan introduced Star Wars. The AIDS virus was discovered. George Bush became president. In the nineties the Gulf War was fought. Bill Clinton defeated Bush. Meanwhile, for the back-to-the-land generation, our youthful pasts receded into personal mythology and sentiment as we raised children and gave marriage or relationships another try.

We also found suitable money-earning niches within the mainstream. We had to. We'd learned all too well that we could not live agreeably without some participation in the economy. The hegemony of capitalism was too great, too beyond our control to topple or ignore. Its presence seeped into almost every aspect of our lives, no matter where or how we chose to live. But in retrospect, would we really have wanted it to disappear? If somehow we had succeeded at converting everyone in the nation to our way of life, our own safety net would have unraveled. It was the presence of the stable mainstream economy around us that

Cynthia Frost, now a university librarian, still feels
close to nature even though she is back in the
mainstream. She keeps a backyard garden and enjoys
the company of pet rabbits.

had enabled us to experiment with its absence. Historically, capitalism
developed because "it championed the individual and encompassed the
idea that people should be free to pursue their own interests. . . ." And
that's exactly what we did. At some level we must have felt safer stripping down to the bare bones knowing the modern consumer world was
around us, just within reach. Did we really want to trade places with
people in Third World countries who lived involuntary back-to-the-land
lives of simplicity, with no escape hatches?

Michael Maniates, a professor of environmental science and co-
editor of *Confronting Consumption*, asks this very question about today's voluntary simplicity movement, new-age version of our back-to-
the-land philosophy. What if, he poses, the whole nation, including

business and industry, *did* decide to downshift according to the guidelines of the voluntary simplicity movement? What if advertising shut down and people *did* stop consuming? What about the large-scale economic ramifications? "The U.S. economy is driven by consumer demand, which the simplicity movement hopes to throttle. Fulfillment of this hope would lead to production cutbacks, plant closings, and job loss. . . ." Similar to our back-to-the-land canon, modern-day calls for simplifying fail to acknowledge the larger political or sociological implications of the movement.

Several decades have passed since most of us came back from the land, so we've had time to figure out what we wanted to do. We've had time to discover the most pleasurable and least painful way to keep afloat financially and to navigate our ways into occupations that gratified us. As creative, compassionate, adventurous, nature-loving, and socially conscious people, we made it a point to find or create vocations that would best serve as outlets for our interests, talents, and causes. Our youthful vow to shun the rigid life of an Organization Man lives on.

For many of us, our livelihoods have grown directly out of our experiences on the land. In 1975 Steven Engelhart, who had lived in a tepee with his brothers in upstate New York, built a stone house on their land. This started him on the path to his career in historic preservation.

"Our stone house was right from *Living the Good Life*. And practically, page by page. It's a beautiful little building—built by people who really didn't know much about working with their hands. But it was such an *intense* experience. We built this small house in four or five months." After completing the house, Steven took a job with a local stonemason who gave him better, hands-on training.

"This really opened up a whole new world for me in terms of economy and opportunity. It got me back into some areas that I had been interested in when I was in school, and I realized there was more." He worked full-time as a stonemason while completing his undergraduate degree in college. He entered a graduate program in historic preservation at the University of Vermont, and earned his degree in 1985.

"For me the graduate experience was a wonderful coming together of so many things, which had, up till then, felt disconnected, as in 'What am I doing?'" he explains. "I'd always had a love of history, so living on the land brought that in. As a stonemason I'd learned to work with my hands, so I understood buildings and knew how to do things, so that entered into it too. Then, because a lot of preservation work is in the nonprofit sector, it also fed my interest since I was raised by my parents to be a do-gooder. Finally, one's life should be meaningful, productive, and add up to making the world a better place to live in. So there was that as well. And it all *fit*."

Now the executive director of the Adirondack Architectural Heritage, an association dedicated to the preservation of the architecture, historic sites, and communities of the Adirondacks, Steven oversees the organization's projects, workshops, and tours of historic architecture. He, his wife, and two sons live in Keeseville, a small old community of two thousand on the Ausable River in upstate New York. Many of the older buildings there have declined, so he and his wife have bought and restored two old houses.

"The years on the land left their legacy," he says. "I look forward to going to work every day, but I'm not obsessed by work either. I'm a very active parent and father; I've structured my time so that when the kids get home from school, I'm home, and it's great. Part of that is having very early on in life set some priorities. Making money was never a priority for me. Making the money you need to live and to enjoy life, yes, but I've always understood that there were more important things."

Bruce Lemire agrees. Family and freedom, not money, are his priorities. After the most brutal winter of his life in Maine, Bruce left his little patch of land on our homestead in Troy, Maine, in 1979, and drove west. Soon married to a traditional-thinking woman, he focused on making money. He was in love, after all, and wanted to please his wife by providing well. He took a professional job as a salesman, but soon he began to loathe it and detested strutting around the city in a three-piece pin-striped suit in order to acquire the nice house and cars he and his wife thought they wanted. He felt hopelessly trapped. Although he tried a few times to branch off into creative enterprises he liked, his wife would pressure him, saying, "This isn't going to work; I want you to go back to a regular job."

When his seventeen-year marriage dissolved three years ago, Bruce moved into the Colorado mountains with his son. His rustic house, with south-facing, angled windows, offers a commanding view. Full immersion in the mainstream was not for him, so he found new ways to work with it, but not entirely in it. Earning his living through creativity and resourcefulness, he now house-sits, pet-sits, does crafts and artwork, and works at construction, which pays well in Colorado.

"Up here in the mountains," he explains, "many construction workers have a college education. It's a way of earning decent money and avoiding stress. You go home, you don't worry about anything. Step into the job, do your job, you're in the mountains."

He loves scavenging treasures from the town dump. Affluent people toss away valuable items, and he recovers leftovers from construction jobs—wood, glass French doors, woodstoves, cars, wheelbarrows, metals, and all the paints he needs for his artwork. Confident that he has the skills and ingenuity to survive whatever turns the economy might take, he feels free.

"There are people up here who wouldn't know how to survive if they didn't have supermarkets, nice clothes, and a maid to clean the house. So I look forward to a depression," he jokes.

His teenage son holds first place in his life. They spend a lot of time together. Bruce has taught him how to do arts and crafts, and together they attend fairs and sell their work and do construction jobs.

"Now, fortunately, I have freedom," says Bruce happily. "Every now and then I look at the ads in the paper and think, 'Oh, God, I could *not* do that stuff!' I've actually gone right back to the way we were in Maine. Moving up here limited the kinds of jobs, but they're more in tune with what I'd like to be doing. I like using my creative self. That's when I feel most fulfilled. But I will always have enough money to support my son. I take what I consider good care of him. But I don't feel like I'm tied into the system as much as I was before.

"The older I get, the more I'm inclined to spend my time doing what I like. This afternoon, for example: my son and I have already decided that we're going to stop working, go down into the valley, do some shopping and hanging out, probably go to Subway and have lunch. But we have the freedom to do that, whereas if I were working till five o'clock at something I didn't like doing, he would be home by himself. He would far prefer having my company."

❦ Many of us turned our social causes into careers.

In the early eighties, June Holley and two friends on her land cooperative brainstormed ways to fight poverty in their area. These creative sessions sparked the founding of ACENETS, an economic development organization in Athens, Ohio, of which June is executive director. ACENETS's mission is to help Appalachian residents raise money to start small businesses.

June and her first husband settled on the land in southwest Pennsylvania in 1972 after reading Thoreau. "There was something about the idea," says June. "It felt like a grand experiment, to see if you could do it. Could you live really, really simply and actually provide for yourself? That was part of the fun. It felt really pure too." They lived in "a totally disgusting shack" on the land and hauled water from a spring half a mile away, but unknown liens complicated matters, so they found another tract of land, this time in West Virginia, where they built a nine-by-twelve-foot house that June describes as "just hysterical."

After their divorce, June joined Currents, a land cooperative in Ohio, where she stayed for eleven years. For two hundred dollars a month she had land, electricity, a gravity-fed water system, and almost unlimited access to the food pantry. The people on the land traded a variety of practical and professional skills with one another.

"I taught one class a quarter at Ohio University, and I earned like four thousand dollars a year. And I just lived on that with my kid. You'd have old cars, and there was somebody there who knew how to fix cars. One of the people was a doctor, so we had a free doctor. She could look at the kids' earaches and prescribe something. There were really fabulous carpenters. Friendship and other people's talents made up for the lack of money. It really was an ideal setup."

The synergy at Currents—plus the available child care—helped June's creative ideas surface. She and her friends began their fight against poverty by helping some women on public assistance begin a home-care business. Gratified by this accomplishment, they applied for and received a grant. ACENETS was founded in 1985 and now employs thirty-five people.

"We do a lot of work helping people set up festivals," says June. "We have the Paw Paw Festival and the Chili Pepper Festival, and now we're having the Jambalaya on the Hocking Freshwater Shrimp Festival. It's about building community, so that theme I've carried over."

ACENETS not only injects money into poorer communities but helps to enhance the citizens' sense of well-being. "When people start a creative business, it just brings out all kinds of things in them," she says.

June left Currents and moved into town eleven years ago to be closer to her work, which she loves. "It felt like it was time," she explains. "I was ready."

Like June, Carlyle Poteat feels lucky to be able to make a social impact by producing documentaries. "I feel extremely fortunate to be in a position now to be able to do something that makes a difference," she says, speaking animatedly about activist projects, which include filming short segments of post-9/11 peace rallies and demonstrations that will be sent to organizations for grassroots activities. A current pet project is a documentary on U.S. involvement in Iraq and the selling of the war, which Carlyle describes as "an exposé of what the Bush administration's real motivations are and how they are selling the war."

Her career in documentary production was initiated by a chance meeting with David Kasper at an art show. Kasper, a founder of the Empowerment Project in Chapel Hill, North Carolina, invited her to stop by their office. When she learned what they were doing, she was excited about the projects. "It was something I felt drawn toward and wanted to pursue. I became an intern who just got more and more involved, then became an employee, and now I'm part of the core staff of five."

Carlyle went to the land in 1974. She and her husband bought forty-seven acres near Chapel Hill, North Carolina, and built a thousand-square-foot log cabin. As a nature lover, she rejected mainstream culture and preferred outdoor work.

"I wanted to unhook myself from all these things the culture was saying we needed to have. Taking the time to connect with the natural world was much more sustaining than some of the things we were supposed to think we needed."

The community of back-to-the-land people helped one another cut firewood, harvest food, can and freeze, and quilt. With the support of the group, Carlyle lived frugally and worked out only when necessary. "I fasted regularly, I ran every day, I did Yoga, I wrote in my journal; it was a whole lifestyle that was really about connecting with the land and getting to know myself, in a way," she remembers.

She kept in touch with other back-to-the-land artists over the years. Ten years ago she entered a graduate program at the University of Tennessee and earned a masters degree in printmaking. A neighbor who worked in television production proposed that she learn Painter, a software program that simulates natural media. This aroused her interest in combining computer use with printmaking.

"I agreed to work with him on it, and that got me into the whole realm of video and television, that sort of world," says Carlyle.

Like the people described above, John Matz, owner and operator of Sunflower Glass Works, earns his living doing what he loves. After moving to a land cooperative with several other families in 1976, he continued to stay with his job at the welfare department for a year while he constructed his mortgage-free house.

"The day that I put in the windows on my house, I gave them my notice. I had a thousand dollars in the bank. I had all the money in the world. I was ready to retire."

His group had brainstormed ways to generate cash crops from the land. Selling sunflowers was one proposal. Raising and selling chickens was another. John, however, was fascinated by stained glass.

A friend said to him, "Look, I don't want to make toys for *rich* people."

John replied, "All I want to do is have an opportunity to make a living and do something I like."

After retiring from the welfare department, he enrolled in an eight-week night class in stained glass at Ohio University. He cut the last four weeks because "I figured I knew it all." He erected a two-foot-wide table in an old four-by-eight-foot horse stall in the community barn. This functioned as his studio.

"I was working in the winter and the wind was whistling in," he remembers. "I put plastic over the boards. That's where I started doing glass. I just started doing it, and I just got better and better at it. I learned as I went."

John now runs a successful business doing small glasswork pieces and larger residential commissions. He also teaches. When a fire burned down the barn that housed his studio in 1996, he could afford to take a year off with no income in order to regroup.

He no longer fears mistakes. He had been neurotic about constructing the perfect house and had made expensive balsa models before building. But through his art he found that "the best way I've ever learned is by making mistakes. Remember how I built my house and all? That I was pretty crazy and that I was a perfectionist? But doing stained glass is where I learned that perfection is not mine to have. I figured out that when one makes a mistake, that's the universe's way of telling you that you weren't supposed to do it that way anyway. That maybe there's another way."

Rob Morningstar feels blessed to have combined his love for nature with a paying occupation. In 1973 he left Hawaii after God's Free Universe disbanded in 1973 and traveled for a few years, working his way through Mexico, Guatemala, Texas, and California. "Upon my return to Kona," says Robert, "I began to apply my horticultural experience, gained as a nurseryman in Santa Barbara, to coffee farming and growing all sorts of fruits here in Hawaii."

On a trip to Thailand he met his second wife and learned more about Thai customs. His exposure to Buddhism in Thailand reignited his earlier commitment to the religion, for he and the other members of the commune had all been spiritualists. God's Free Universe commune had been filled with what he calls "God-interested" people who practiced all forms of Yoga and who "chanted and prayed constantly, and loved living life in the grace of our various views of the Creator," says Rob. Recommitting to Buddhism brought him added peace and fulfillment.

Over the years he worked his way up to be property manager of a seven-acre botanical garden and working fruit and coffee farm in Kona. He and his wife Awy hold a deed of life estate on the property, which means they have the right to live there free until whichever of them passes away last.

"We owe no rent, and thus we can be very flexible in how we manage our combined incomes. It's a sweet deal!" says Rob, who describes himself today as "a settled down farmer-hippie who farms coffee and fruits."

He treasures his intimate association with the land, just as he did in the old days when he lived at God's Free Universe commune, foraging for food and watching the glorious sunsets over the ocean. Now his own boss, he earns money producing useful, humanitarian food products.

His spirituality remains as vital now as in the communal days, but he has modified his previous beliefs about "the dearly held principles of nonownership." Now the signs posted along the perimeters of his land say clearly, "Keep Out! No Trespassing!"

"I believe I am a steward of this land. What I do with it while it is under my care and stewardship is my life's lasting legacy," he explains. "It is my duty to protect it and try to see that all is well.

"Many people seem to have lost that respect for the land and also those of us that make our livelihood by it. So when it became a choice to abandon duty or enforce the fulfillment of responsibility, I chose the latter. For those who respect what we are doing, we welcome them; those who disdain and just seek to get whatever they can for themselves at whatever price to others, better to stay away from me."

🌱 After speaking out against a strip-mining company, Don Wirtshafter entered law school at the age of thirty-two, commuting to Case Western Reserve University School of Law in Cleveland and finishing in two years and three months. He practiced law for five years. Battling environmentally irresponsible mega-giants became discouraging, however, as the local Chamber of Commerce pegged him as an enemy of business growth. In 1990 he set out to prove to them that he was not an enemy of growth, that he could run a business that did not harm the environment. He became one of the first modern entrepreneurs of industrial hemp.

To make a statement, he co-wrote *The Hemp Seeds Cookbook* with Carol Miller, opened a business called the Ohio Hempery, Inc., and began producing a line of hemp products, including bookmarks, lip balm, salve, twine, and cloth. He expanded into the hemp foods business.

"We started the hemp foods sector, and we are still the leader in it. Andrew Weil's early endorsement of the Hempery's products really helped get the unfamiliar food accepted by the natural foods community." Next he manufactured Wirtshafter's Hempen Ale, which grew quite popular.

Don shut down the Ohio branch of the Ohio Hempery in 2000 and now fills hemp food orders through a Canada branch. His big break came recently. He helped an American invest in the development of medical cannabis in the Netherlands, an operation which was then licensed to a British company. As a result, Don became one of the incorporators of the 300-million-pound G.W. Pharmaceuticals, for which he now works as a consultant. The company plans to place a new cannabis prescription on the market, with many more on the way.

Although he still owns his land, he no longer lives on it because he needs to live closer to town. His latent flair for law and business could not help but catapult him back into the mainstream.

As Don and the other members of his land cooperative grow more mature and are working full-time, "We're more often hiring people to do needed jobs at the farm rather than splitting the work or finding volunteers. So we've evolved that way."

❧ Creative people abound among the back-to-the-land population. Vicky Hayes, a fiction writer, poet, and song writer, and her husband Clarence, a craftsperson, potter, and carpenter, have always put their art first, even when they had to work out. Over the years they have held a variety of odd jobs, occasionally with benefits, but their artistic interests have always remained at the forefront of their lives. They have made sure of that.

In 1974 they joined an artistic community of young back-to-the-land people who lived and worked around Berea College in Kentucky. In the early days they moved into and renovated old houses, raised gardens and animals, and followed their artistic passions. They cooked on a wood cookstove, cut their wood, carried water, and fixed their own cars. Living cheaply outside the system freed them to concentrate on their art without the bother of all the trappings.

"I've had jobs, but they were not long-term jobs. I couldn't tolerate being removed from my work as a writer. It was kind of like being dead," explains Vicky. "I've always been at the poverty level from most people's point of view. Having money would be nice. But I suppose I never wanted it badly enough to make the sacrifice for it. I'm probably more driven by my writing than anything else."

With the life she's chosen, she has had time to reflect. "I've not had a frantic life. I don't own a watch. I've had more time to think about spiritual things and about who I am as a person. I think probably the slower pace has helped our marriage. We both like solitude, we both like natural beauty, and we're not mentally in the rat race though we've *participated* in it many times."

Three years ago she returned to school to finish her undergraduate degree and begin a masters degree in anthropology. She will probably teach. The exposure to literature will inform her fiction writing, she believes; and she can prepare for a stable career in academia, a profession which will allow time to write and travel during summers.

"As I get older, I see I'm not quite as invincible any more. It takes so much more now to survive. I felt like it was time for me to get a stable career. I have every plan of having that stability in the next few years."

❦ It would be hard to miss the fact that many back-to-the-landers have moved into academia, including me. My old wish came true. Years after

reading that Maine want ad for an instructor—and bristling with envy—
I finished graduate school and became qualified for such a position. Land-
ing a tenure-track job, I earned tenure in due time and discovered a glut
of former back-to-the-land people in my profession. They're drawn to
schools for the same reasons I am. They enjoy intelligent conversation,
they want to keep learning, to be intellectually stimulated, to help others,
and to contribute to society. And I won't lie: the long vacations—between intensive periods of very hard work, mind you—are ideal for ex-
counterculturalists who also want balance in their lives.

The media stereotypes former hippies as "high-powered lawyers and
investment bankers and big-time capitalists," says researcher Timothy
Miller, but the people he interviewed for his research were "overwhelmingly *not* that." "They moved into mainstream life in the sense
that they had gotten jobs and had quit living in really marginal conditions, but they tended to become teachers, nurses, and social workers
rather than corporate executives."

"None of us has gone on to what we would think of as 'selling out,'"
agrees Marlene Heck, a professor at Dartmouth. "Now, instead of working for someone in a barber shop, we own the barber shop. Instead of
being a dancer in a ballet troupe, we are now the director of the ballet
troupe. We own our own businesses, such as graphic design or landscape architecture. None of us has gone to work for Goldman-Sachs. I
see our students go out, and in their first year at J. P. Morgan they make
twice as much money as I do. I'm educating people. This is important;
passing along knowledge to the next generation is *important*. But I'm
sure not in it for the money."

🌱 *"In a lot of ways, I like being part of the mainstream," says Jodi Mitchell.
"Sometimes I have regrets, still, of not having bought more into the mainstream. I go back and forth." A former member of Wheeler's Ranch Commune in California and later of a back-to-the-land community in West Virginia, Jodi is now a librarian at Santa Rosa Library in California. In her
youth the thought of working closely with "very upper-middle-class white,
rather conservative" people might have seemed unthinkable, but "You know,"*

says Jodi, "I like the people. They're devoted to their families; their kids are happy. They have the suburban homes that all look alike, they go on vacations—but they seem happy! And they're nice people."

She continues, "I'm torn. I sometimes think, 'Well, did I do the right thing?' I could have bought into a more traditional life, married someone, owned a nice home. I made it a lot harder for myself with the path I chose. It was a more difficult road." As a teenage runaway she lived on the streets of Berkeley in the late 1960s before settling onto Wheeler's Ranch, a well-known commune in northern California. She left in the early seventies and moved to West Virginia where "flocks of hippies were moving because the land was cheap." For several years in West Virginia, Jodi felt somewhat removed from what she calls the "real" world as she became immersed in the back-to-the-land fellowship, participating in the food co-ops, the barn-raisings and house-buildings and all-night work parties. She loved those years, but at the same time she recognized a growing confusion. "I was torn between my desire to be in the mainstream and not knowing how to get back to it," she says, "and my not wanting to be disloyal to my anti-establishment and hippie roots either."

Always politically conscious, she wanted to work for less fortunate people, especially after her experience with local people and poverty in West Virginia. When she moved back to California, and after her first "real" job as a baker in a health food store, she worked her way into a position in the school system with special-needs children, and later forged a career as a librarian. When two jobs opened at the Berkeley Public Library, Jodi, who had always loved libraries and was an avid user, was one of the two people, out of two hundred applicants, who was hired. The job, she says, "turned my life around. People were very kind to me. They took a lot of time training me and working the circulation desk. I was afraid of it because I didn't have a lot of self-esteem. I continued with libraries from there. Any promotion I could get that didn't require a degree, I applied for and got. A lot of it was for my son's sake, so I could get him through high school and get him on into his life.

"I remained politically active. I was involved with the farm workers and supported them. Just in principle, I still don't eat grapes. I drink grape juice occasionally, but I haven't eaten grapes in however long."

Her different jobs always contributed to the well-being of individuals and society. One of her biggest career triumphs was launching a successful outreach program for Hispanic migrant workers in Siler City, North Carolina, during time she spent in that part of the country. As the branch librarian there, Jodi arranged for a health department van to carry books, audio and videotapes, and movies to a segment of the Latino population that was not being served. "I am proud of all that; I rolled up my sleeves and decided there was a need, and it had to be filled. It caused me a lot of grief, personally, but the program was successful."

Jodi says she could not again live as rustically as she did on the commune in northern California or on the farm in West Virginia, but she knows those experiences were invaluable. "I like my hot running water now. I like some of the comforts. And as I get older, I'm sure I'm going to like them even more. I'm having to let go of some of my old ideas. But I was adventuresome and wanted experiences, and I wanted to continue to grow. In many ways I learned a lot that changed my life and how I looked at things."

CHAPTER ELEVEN

Lessons and Legacies

"Industrial society turned out to be a lot more resilient than people like myself had assumed back in '71 or '72. Industrial society not only was not falling apart, it was strengthening in a lot of ways. Subsistence living was very, very difficult. At some point people looked around and saw that other people were out there having more fun."—Copthorne Macdonald, who wrote the "New Directions Radio" column in *Mother Earth News* from 1973 to 1983

"They were good, rich years. Absolutely no regrets. The world is, of course, changing all the time, but one of the things I see in young people these days is this incredible pressure to figure out early what they want to do and who they're going to be. What they don't realize is that that takes exploration. And that takes time."—Steven Engelhart

"A lot of the back-to-the-land people in our area really remained activist at heart. One became a county commissioner, one went back to law school, one is now a planner for the EPA district office in Chicago, and her husband does economic development for minorities up there."—Sandra Sleight-Brannen

🌻 *Seattle, Washington: When Pat Manuele was diagnosed with non-Hodgkins lymphoma in the fall of 1995, she relied on her inner strength* to get through the rounds of chemotherapy. During recovery she thought about the years on the land, which helped her through the roughest periods.

When she was first diagnosed, she told her oncologist about an incident she remembered during her back-to-the-land years at Spring Gap Orchard from 1972 to 1974. She, her boyfriend Brad, and their two friends had worn bandanas over their noses as they cleaned out twenty open or broken bags of pesticides lying along the wall of the shed barn, bags that were left over from the days when the orchard had been a large-scale commercial business. After disposing of the bags by wrapping them in plastic sheeting and sealing them into an old shower stall, Pat and her friends felt achy and ill for two days. Years later, after her diagnosis and six-month course of chemotherapy, Pat did some research and found that DDT, aldrins, Malathion, Parathion, Sevin, and herbicides 2,4-D and 2,4,5-T had been used at Spring Gap Orchard for years before her arrival.

"All these substances are known carcinogens," she says. In her research she also discovered that several studies linked exposure to pesticides and herbicides with increasing rates of non-Hodgkins lymphoma. A recent study, published in Lymphoma Today, suggested higher rates of non-Hodgkins lymphoma in agricultural workers and people who worked with pesticides. Ironically, writes Pat in Eat a Peach, "Our well water [at Spring Gap] came from an area that drained a significant portion of upper orchard and the garden space. The exposure that I had was probably magnified by the extent to which we lived off the land and by a multimedia effect, consuming groundwater, fruits, and vegetables as well as birds, reptiles, and mammals who may have concentrated the residues. A cocktail of chemicals, which through their interaction potentially increased the exposure risk, very likely contaminated the drinking water. The long latency period correlates to known carcinogens acquired through low-dose exposures, fifteen or more years."

Pat, who has been a registered dietitian for twenty years, has worked as a nutritionist with the King County Public Health Department in Seattle for fifteen years. When she left Spring Gap Orchard in 1974, she worked in a Buffalo restaurant, baking sixty loaves of whole wheat bread every week. Local speaking engagements followed as churches invited her to speak about voluntary simplicity and nutrition. In the late seventies she moved to the West

*Coast, graduated from two more schools, and in 1981 married her current
husband. They recently celebrated their twenty-second anniversary. As for
her career, the foundation was really laid during the years at Spring Gap,
where she learned about the earth's seasonal cycles, nutrition, and the critical role of the health of the land. Poverty taught her to budget carefully and
eat nutritiously, knowledge that she now passes on to low-income families.
Today Pat's prognosis is excellent, but to reach that point she has had to undergo rounds of chemotherapy, radiation, and a bone marrow transplant
which left her "deathly sick" and required "another six months of slow recovery." Then, in 2002, she received another diagnosis, this time Hodgkins lymphoma, for which she had to undergo another six months of chemotherapy.
Pneumonia followed.*

*Through all this she gained "time to sit still on the couch during the Seat-
tle winter, to stare out the windows, at the rain, the sleet, the infrequent
snow," and to bask in the memories of her days at Spring Gap Orchard.
"When a place is loved, it is a permanent mark on your memory, a tattoo. I
can walk along that stretch of dirt road, through the openings in the trees,
down the incline into the hollow where I spot the log cabin again. I can adorn
it with any season I wish: the redbuds, the peach or apple blossoms, the trees
leafed or not, the snow. I've opened a sluice gate, and memories come flood-
ing through once again.*

"These unforgettable years formed the essence of my life."

❧ As the back-to-the-land generation moves toward retirement age
(at least as measured by Social Security charts), they appear to be doing so with all the energy and optimism they carried with them to the
land—and brought back. Throughout most of human history until the
last millennium, the average life span was about eighteen years. At the
turn of the twentieth century it averaged in the thirties. "Not surprisingly, our forebears didn't sit around and wonder what they were going
to do in retirement. No one contemplated lifelong learning at seventy-
five," writes Ken Dychtwald in *Age Power*.

"The big boomer generation that was in its teens and twenties
in the 1960s was not destined to disappear when it ceased to be a

'youthful opposition,'" writes Theodore Roszak in *Longevity Revolution*. "Never before have people approaching their senior years enjoyed the advantage of so much education and travel. Nor have they ever bulked so large in the popular culture of the nation. They are avidly pursued for university coursework and museum shows, they are the most reliable season-ticket audience for the opera and symphony, they are a highly prized market for book clubs and the lecture circuit. . . . Never before has an older generation been conversant with so many ideas and dissenting values. These are, after all, people who, in their teens and twenties, lived through a time of principle protest that seemed determined to subject every orthodoxy, every institution, every received idea in our society to critical inquiry."

Not only will most of us have some postretirement years to enjoy, we will be more comfortable than our parents were. Although several scholars and many media pundits have predicted that boomers will be worse off than their parents, a scholarly analysis in *Population and Development Review* concludes the opposite: they will be better off. This is partly due to "decisions about family circumstances that differed sharply from those of their parents," such as having fewer or no children, earning dual household incomes as women moved into the workplace, or never marrying. In addition, contrary to popular perception boosted by the media, boomers have saved money at only a slightly lower rate than their parents, and the addition of employer pension plans gives boomers even a "slight increase" over their parents' savings rates. "On average, the boomers have improved their economic status substantially over that of their parents, despite less favorable market conditions. Their economic status in retirement is also likely to be better," according to researchers.

Yet as we get older and anticipate the future, we still love to look back. Every back-to-the-land person I interviewed for this book was delighted to talk about it and had a storehouse of happy recollections. Let's face it, we all miss it. Those were the invigorating days of our young adulthood, when anything seemed possible.

Looking Back

Keddy Ann Outlaw, now a university librarian in Houston, often reminisces about her days at Big Dog. "I miss sitting around a campfire with my friends," she writes. "I miss the way we used to sing and play guitars together. 'Will the circle be unbroken? By and by, Lord, by and by . . .' I miss being an active observer of the moon, noticing its signs and changes nightly. I miss wearing my steel-toed work boots with a long skirt and a tie-dyed top I sewed myself. I miss chopping wood. I loved chopping kindling on a wood block outside the back door in the woodshed I built out of old barn boards. The sound of it comes back to me now in satisfying chunks and whacks. I felt linked to generations of pioneers. I felt that by chopping wood and carrying water I was on a sacred path. I remember the rainbow circle I painted on the wood floor in front of my cookstove in the farmhouse. It felt like a magic circle of protection. It felt like where I was meant to be. We all want to be in charge of our lives. Those back-to-the-land days are a vividly colorful part of my past. When you create a life where the environment around you is largely self-created, you feel so strong, so connected, so authentic."

Her back-to-the-land days began in 1972 when she and six artistic friends bought fifty acres of forest in upstate New York near Canton. They pitched their tepees and got to work building an outhouse, cutting logs for the cabin, and planting the garden. They named the place Big Dog.

"Think of the age we were when we went back to the land," reminisces Keddy. "We were in our early twenties. We had never owned any kind of home before. Suddenly we were the keepers of a kingdom. The freedom was heady. The roots went deep immediately, if that is possible. Perhaps we were desperately in need of somewhere to root, as well as an authentic way of life."

A year after moving to Big Dog, Keddy married a guy from a nearby commune and they moved to a farm where Keddy learned to cook on a woodstove, harvest maple syrup, and put by food. She also built a studio where she could develop her arts and crafts when she wasn't working out at a health food store or a school library.

But, as Keddy puts it, life became "complicated." Her marriage dissolved. A sad winter alone on the farm convinced her she couldn't keep up with the place by herself, so she moved into town and struggled with depression during the transitional year in which she tried to fashion a new life. "My spirit was broken; in many ways I felt like a failure. Looking back, I see I had hit bottom and didn't know the way out yet. For a while I had to go on welfare. When I became suicidal, I saw a therapist. She was very kind and nurturing. A prescription for anti-depressants helped."

Life slowly improved as she met new people in town. She got a CETA job in a day-care center and signed up for a pottery class. "My life took on a new dignity. I finally felt capable of leading a life of my own and being responsible for myself. Then I took the plunge and applied to graduate school."

Enrolling at the State University of New York at Albany, she earned her masters degree in library science in 1979. She took a job in Texas, where she lives today.

"Over twenty years later I am still with the same library system as a branch librarian. I own my own home and lead a busy, creative life. I had envisioned a life of deepening commitment to the land," she explains. "I had meant to put down deep roots. I had hoped to live 'on the land' forever. In fact, sometimes I feel a roiling, unfinished desire to go back to the land again, and do it right this time, with more money under my belt, in a more hospitable climate somewhere."

The days at Big Dog were invaluable to Keddy. "How safe and protected I felt! The safety came both from the 'tribe' gathered near me and from the sheer acreage of the place. The right to do with it what we pleased was, come to think of it, an American core value. There are sacred boundaries even in suburbia. Now my ordinary home on 7,150 square feet of land is my sacred haven. What I do within the walls of my home is my business. Though the connection I feel is not as primal as what I felt for the rocky, hilly acreage of Big Dog, it is still sacred. It is still a blessing."

The time at Big Dog allowed Keddy a valuable transition between undergraduate college and a career track. At Big Dog, just as in college, like-minded artists and friends surrounded her. "I loved feeling that my fellow communers were family. I was rich in sisters and brothers. From them I learned how to play guitar, do carpentry, and make bread. If we didn't know how to do something, we would figure it out together. In the 'real world' I would be alone. On Big Dog I was never alone unless I really wanted to be."

While there she learned farm-related survival skills and the art of surviving. "It was good to go down to almost nothing," she points out. "Even if that meant I had to eat beans and potatoes for weeks straight, I was ready for the challenge. Food in supermarkets looked so plastic. I wanted the real thing—the tangy goat's milk, the succulent wild blackberries, the homemade pizza with wild morels I made for more than one vegetarian Thanksgiving feast. Food, shelter, and fuel became literally everything. I couldn't take them for granted any more after living on the land. (I still don't, and find it a miracle I can afford to own a three-bedroom house.) Now, yes—my food does largely come from the grocery store, but I appreciate all the effort behind it and try to buy organic when I can."

Her appreciation for a balanced life also originated at Big Dog and continues today. At the farm she learned to flow with the agricultural cycle, working nonstop during the growing season, then mellowing out over the winters "to concentrate on favorite activities, be what they may—pottery, writing, or weaving. I loved the winter's rich, deep silence and promise. Now I find myself dreaming of early retirement (which is soon, as I write), when I hope to become a true 'Renaissance' woman and indulge all my interests. I feel I will have paid my dues with years of public library service. Perhaps after retirement I will find time for more gardening, artwork, writing, and reading. Perhaps then I will learn to oil paint and play the piano. The same things I wanted to do with all my time when I went back to the land are still with me."

As we reflect on our back-to-the-land experiences, we realize how much grit we gained. Sandra Sleight-Brannen and her husband bought thirty-five acres near Stewart, Ohio, in 1976, and over the years, while raising two sons, they transformed their living situation from a plumbing-free eight-by-twelve-foot cabin (which a friend dubbed "a closet in the woods") to a modernized stone house with passive solar heating, running water, electricity, and a flush toilet. In the beginning they planned to be self-sufficient, raising their food and a few chickens and goats. "We thought we probably wouldn't need to bring in a whole lot of income to live that kind of a life. It would be relatively peaceful and stress-free. Well," she laughs, "you know how those things go."

When the children were young, her husband worked out while Sandra made grapevine wreaths and sold them. But they learned, as all of us did, that they needed more money. Because Sandra had a background in public relations, she was able to work from her home as the public relations director for a local company, and later she began to work out and become more involved in her career as a media specialist. In addition to teaching telecommunications at Ohio State University, she's won seventeen national and international awards for the radio features and long documentaries she's produced. "One of the things we gave up is growing very much of our own food. In terms of bringing in money, it made a lot more sense for us to go to jobs than to try to do things here."

Completing their stone house took almost a decade. In the beginning, everything they had planned took longer than they expected. There were always setbacks, such as drilling a well at the top of the ridge near the house but not hitting water, and having to drill another at the bottom of the hill and pumping the water up. "We have enough infrastructure for a small subdivision, just in terms of getting our water to the house," says Sandra, who hauled water for many years and did her laundry at a laundromat.

"We thought we had our little plan mapped out—we'll do the house, then we'll do that, but everything probably took five times longer than we ever thought it would, you know?"

Eventually the plans and the adjustments to the plans fell into place. The experience was empowering. "You have to, number one, know how to rely on yourself," says Sandra, "and you learn a lot of skills, both physically—such as how to build things and work with the land—and also intellectually, such as learning how to work within whatever little government structure there is in rural communities to try to get things done. I think that doing this empowered people to an extent that they felt they could make changes in other areas as well."

The Values

Not only did we come back from the land as stronger people but as people with character. The values from the old days remain firm. June Spencer, for example, is fiscally conservative and socially conscious. When she interviewed for her current university position as a professor, she wore a dress from a thrift store, just on principle. Her principles also bring her to a laundromat, for she prefers not to own a washing machine or dryer. She chooses good-weather days for wash duty so she can avoid using a dryer and can hang the wet clothes out to dry. In addition, she won't use credit cards, never eats at fast-food restaurants, and recycles everything. In her house, only ceiling fans relieve the heat from Southern summers.

"Only within the last few years have I shopped at huge stores like Wal-Mart instead of at thrift shops. It was even difficult to buy a new dress for my son's wedding," she says.

Her social consciousness remains in high gear. Because her Honduran husband owns a family farm in his home country, the couple has toyed for several years with the idea of starting a mission for street kids, offering them jobs for pay on their farm in return for the boys' promise to go to school. In the near future, after her retirement from the university, June believes she and her husband will return to Honduras. With her back-to-the-land experience, she and her husband can teach classes in agriculture as well as English and computer use. "Of one thing I am sure, people are more important than things, and I long for deeper personal relationships."

She cultivated her appreciation for Third World culture during her seventies vagabond days in Mexico, and for her the spell has not been broken. Over the years, since coming back from the land, she traveled between the States and Central American countries. "I still have a hard time staying in one place, and I find that material possessions are often a burden."

In 1987, after accepting Christ into her life, she met her husband, who was then struggling to learn English. He said in broken English, "I want to learn English so I can come to America and be a crop duster." June, at first skeptical, is immensely proud of how hard he has worked, not only to learn the language but to earn a living.

When Hurricane Mitch struck Central America in 1998, June launched the Honduran Relief Effort, raised twelve thousand dollars from her college campus, and sent sixty boxes of food and clothing. Soon after, she received a Rotary University Teaching Grant, enabling her to return for six months to give English as a First Language teacher-training workshops in seven cities around the country. Her purpose was to demonstrate the most effective teaching methods to English teachers at the National Teaching University and help them improve their own English at the same time. Living in Latino culture again, so similar to the way she lived in the seventies (except for the internet cafés now), inspired the idea of making it permanent, which she and her husband will soon do when they start the mission.

🌱 As well as being thrifty and compassionate, we still try to live healthfully, eating well and exercising, and have a high regard for nature and the outdoors. Thomas Kidder, now a video producer and writer for a medical center, does a lot of backpacking, canoeing, and cross-country skiing, "probably more now than I did then."

He adds, "Somehow I think of it as all connected. My love for the outdoors and nature has only grown. I look back at the time on the farm as being the springboard for it, or part of the continuum. We lived close to a river and spent a lot of time exploring it, and walking in the cottonwoods, and swimming down there." Tom also likes the feeling of handling and burning his own wood, and still enjoys having a garden.

Nor have we given up our original principles about doing meaning-ful rather than profitable work. We can look back with pride at our varying occupations because we chose occupations that meant some-thing, not what society expected of us—money was seldom a consider-ation. David Manning had a momentary crisis of confidence in the early nineties. He was invited by his alma mater to be a panelist at a confer-ence on career choices for students. The invitation caused him to re-flect—what would he tell the students? He had gone out of his way to avoid a traditional career. He and his wife had traveled. They had moved "up and down the coast in a beat-up old Chevy station wagon loaded down with the twin albatrosses of a large collection of theatrical junk and a hefty box of manuscripts."

When the invitation arrived, David had little income and a resumé with diverse freelance credits in broadcast media. He had always felt that "someday—some vague time or place in the future—it would all add up. Then the letter arrived. And there was 'someday' staring me right in my forty-two-year-old face, and the sum of the whole didn't even equal, much less exceed, the sum of the parts. . . . For this I had given up having kids, a home, a car, a viable job, a low cholesterol count, new clothes, decent medical insurance, a retirement plan, peace of mind, or any of the other mysterious things that people consider part of a normal life. Meanwhile the next generation had stepped into the void and was making a lot of money. Personally I felt like an exile, iso-lated in a dark shadow between ideal and reality."

Momentarily down, he nevertheless attended the conference. Meeting the young students, however, he saw that they clearly lacked the passion for creativity and purpose that his own generation had held. "My fellow panelists and I spent most of the session trying to get the students to think less about their cold corporate preconceptions and more about developing a sense of purpose and satisfaction."

David felt renewed, his pride restored. He returned home feeling that the experience had "opened new perspectives on my own profes-sional life and, at the same time, made me think that maybe I'd learned something from my work after all."

We still value community, as we did in the early days. Michael Doyle stays in touch with the four families who lived with him at Yaeger Valley Community Farm from 1975 to 1985. Because they remain his oldest and dearest friends, they've talked about forming a similar farm when they retire. As baby boomers grow older, retirement communities for greying hippies have sprung up across the country, he says, as a more appealing alternative to nursing homes or assisted living.

"We recognize there is strength in community. Just as there was a great deal of appeal to us when we were in our teens and twenties and early thirties, I see that there may be times in our lives when we will again look to a communitarian model as ideal. When you look at nursing homes, they're fundamentally depressing."

Members of the Mulberry Family in Richmond, Virginia, communicate through a newsletter and meet for an annual get-together on the outer banks of North Carolina. Although the Mulberry House itself was sold in the mid-eighties, Marlene Heck, a former member, predicts, "There's going to be a desire to live with other people again," so they may use some of the invested money to purchase another house. "After people have had their marriages or their relationships, their children have grown, or their companions have died, maybe we'll come back together as seniors who've lived a full life and now want to live in a group and not maintain our own households, and not be left alone."

Phil Morningstar maintains friendships with the former members of the communes where he lived. As a troubled teenager from an abusive home, he found love and acceptance among the people there and has never forgotten the positive impact it made on his life. "When I meet these old Morningstar people, we just click right away. The light that we had illuminates again."

While most of our back-to-the-land groups went separate ways and remain linked by technology or occasional reunions, some back-to-the-landers who stayed on the land are still linked by close proximity and frequent contact.

Ellen Rocco is part of a close-knit group of women friends who have lived together in the St. Lawrence Valley for thirty years. When one of them was in the final months of her life last year, as she battled breast cancer, the group of women friends stayed at her bedside day and night to care for her and relieve her husband. A couple of weeks before she died, the friend broached the subject to Ellen of how they would handle her body after death.

"It used to be the task of women to prepare the body," says Ellen. "And I asked my friend if she would like us, a few of her closest friends, to take care of her body. She wanted that. The night she died, her husband knew who to call. The five of us had gotten some herbs, and we made it up as we went along because this was a new part of life to deal with. We washed her, we anointed her, we wrapped her, we sang and prayed in our fashion, and it was a transforming experience. Just like the first time someone said, 'No, I'm not going to the hospital to give birth to a baby.'"

Her friend wanted to be cremated but also buried in the community cemetery. "This spring," says Ellen, "we're going to bury her ashes and build a burial garden in this little cemetery, where anyone of us who wants to be buried there will be buried. We're going to plant cool flowers because she was a big gardener and all, and do some kind of nifty thing, maybe build some arches—you know, make it a neat place."

Pat Foley and her husband also enjoy a bond with the other back-to-the-land people in their area who managed to stay. In the early years Pat observed many would-be back-to-the-landers arrive, buy land, attempt farming, and then get divorced and/or return to the cities. She and her husband have held out, she says, because they're both so independent and self-entertaining. In their home they had, at last count, five thousand books and many musical instruments and art supplies.

Recently Pat attended "the wedding of all weddings" in her area. The daughter of one of her back-to-the-land friends was married at a fiddle-playing wedding held in a gorgeous garden. Older hippies from miles around, whom Pat hadn't seen for twenty-five years, arrived with potluck meals, just like in the old days. Fiddle and guitar music filled the air as guests square-danced.

"I thought it was kind of a golden moment. This wedding had that elegiac sort of quality. Time changes us all in twenty-five years, but the community of hippies looked exactly the same, except they were greyer now. But the pony tails and dungarees were still there. There was no real dress code at the wedding. It was just charming. The embodiment of the dream. People had come from miles around to see the wedding and contribute to it. Invitations went out and nobody would have missed it. It was one of the loveliest moments I've spent up here, actually. In a lot of ways, kind of a fulfillment, because setting out, none of us knew how this was going to work out. None of us had enough sense to think we ought to worry about it."

A month later a tragedy occurred. Another couple's teenage daughter died in a car accident, bringing the same community of people together to mourn. The couple who had just hosted the wedding held the gathering for the bereaved parents.

"A potluck memorial service," observes Pat. "There were hundreds of people there, about the same crowd that had showed up at the wedding. They sang songs and ate food and chatted among themselves, and it took most of the burden off the parents, who came down only briefly to greet everyone and then went back to the house. The rest of us just hung around for a while. I think the gathering genuinely solaced the parents. I think they hadn't realized how many people would turn up. It kept them from feeling totally isolated at an awful moment, to realize there was a huge community of friends drawn from a wide geographic area, quite aware of what had happened and willing to be leaned on."

❦ As we recall our back-to-the-land experiences, we become more aware of the passage of time. "We're now the age our parents were when we dropped out," Kent observed recently.

In the early summer of 2002 I revisited Troy. Kent still lives at Middle Earth Homestead in the same log cabin we built in the seventies—though I doubt if he and his wife still call it a homestead anymore. I was visiting Maine to see my son Shawn, who had bought a portion of Kent's land and was building his own house. My oldest son Derek, a computer database manager in a large city, left Troy after college. But Shawn had always dreamed of buying some land and building his own low-cost house in the woods.

I arrived at the Portland, Maine, airport on a messy, wet afternoon with my teenage son from my current marriage. Cold raindrops penetrated our sweatshirts as we wheeled the luggage across the street to the Hertz terminal. In the rental car I fumbled with the gadgets on the front panel, looking for the right buttons for the wipers, headlights, and heater with one hand as I maneuvered the car awkwardly out of the airport. Following the signs for Route 95, wipers swishing, I drove north. We arrived in Unity by late afternoon and checked into the Copper Heron Bed and Breakfast.

The birds woke me at 4:30 a.m.—hundreds of them perched on tree branches outside the bedroom window, singing their hearts out loudly and sweetly. For half an hour they sang vibrantly as a mixed chorus. Later the day dawned sunny and cool, and we drove to Troy. I knew my way as though I had lived there yesterday. Nothing had changed, I observed, as we drove north up Route 202, bumping over the railroad tracks, going past Ron and Eileen Reed's house and attached barn. ("See that house, Paul? When Derek and Shawn were little boys, we used to go over there a lot.") Vibrant green fields testified to Maine's healthy rainfall. Blue and green hills lined the horizons. The cracked, potholed roads hadn't changed. We passed Troy General Store with its set of gas pumps and colorful beer and Lotto ads. At the intersection by the Fernalds' house, I turned right and descended onto Bagley Hill Road. A red fox trotting down the middle of the road quickly darted into the woods. About three-quarters of the way up the hill, at the weathered grey barn, I turned right onto Whitaker Road, the dirt road that led to the driveway of Middle Earth Homestead. Ken and Wendy's log cabin peeked sadly through the trees from the clearing. After their divorce, Wendy moved to New Jersey, remarried, and was widowed. She married again and then died a few years ago. Ken, meanwhile, remarried, divorced, and moved. I pulled in front of Shawn's 3.1 acres of property—the same land where fellow homesteader Bruce Lemire used to live—picked up Shawn, and we drove all day, talking, making the circuit from Troy to Acadia National Park down to Belfast, and Camden, and back. Shawn shared his frustration about the Troy Planning Board, which had decided he could not finish building his house until he jumped through a series of expensive and contradictory bureaucratic hoops. How different from our day when the construction bureaucracy was minimal. In fact, soon after my visit, Shawn left Maine and moved to the city with us. He was sick of it all, tired of wrangling with the Troy Town Council, tired of the isolation, the long winters, the long drives to low-paying jobs. I told him I understood completely.

The next night Kent and Lorren invited us for dinner. Kent now works as a marine survey inspector and Lorren is a hospital administrator. Kent has constructed additions to the log cabin, put in an above-ground pool in the backyard, and added plumbing inside. Lorren has created a beautiful, well-landscaped yard, deep green from all the rain. We ate a tasty dinner and chatted about local friends I had known. Some have divorced, some have died, some have left, and some remain in the same houses on the same land. Just like any population of small-town people anywhere.

Six months later, as I began writing this book, I asked Kent if he wanted to have a voice, and he replied,

"So here we are, almost thirty years later, and you know, life is pretty damn good! We're living where we want to be, we managed to raise four wonderful kids we are proud to call our children. Sure, the area we live in is still economically depressed, but crime is almost unknown here. We have a boat on the ocean, just a short distance away. There are the woods at our back door for walking and skiing and harvesting firewood. The mountains are only an hour away. We have wonderful neighbors and friends. We have good jobs. Our lives are meaningful. And somehow it all makes sense. We are where we should be, where we want to be. How we got here, I'm not quite sure. But I do know that if we hadn't moved here to go back to the land, my life would not be as complete as it is today."

He continues, "From my vantage point, the events surrounding our decision to move back to the land are somewhat clouded. But then, as

I approach sixty years of age, everything is a bit more cloudy! I'd love to be able to say that it all turned out as hoped and planned, but of course, life seldom works out that way. The wheels soon fell off the original plan we were riding on, fueled by a divorce, which was fueled by a lack of money, which was fueled by a rather horrible economy, which could be partly blamed on the place we chose to go homesteading . . . Maine!

"I've learned all types of necessary skills—plumbing, electrical wiring, carpentry, auto mechanics. These skills were developed through necessity. Try finding a plumber in a town of eight hundred people, or even within thirty miles of us. All our neighbors do their own plumbing as well, so there is a support system. This is true for virtually every need that may arise.

"Recently I read that the Nearings, though they made some major sacrifices to 'live the good life,' also were not quite what they would have had us believe they were. Apparently there was a tidy sum of inherited wealth that allowed them to live off the land. Most of us who tried our hands at homesteading soon bailed out of that plan and moved on. We were caught in a sort of time warp—we stayed here and found ways to make our lives make sense. Living off the land while working on the job, if you will.

"Did that decision to go back to the land, made back in 1975, have any relevance? Certainly it affected every member of our family one way or another. Was it the right thing to do? Who knows? How can you divine what the alternative path might have yielded? The fact is, it was the path I chose, and it was the best path for me.

"Would I do it again? In a heartbeat!"

❦ *January 2004, Savannah, Georgia: Would I do it again? Heck, no! The experience was enriching, challenging, life-altering, and exhilarating, but once was enough. How would I pay for my fast modem if I were still shlepping trays at the Waterville Steak House?*

Besides, my current husband of nineteen years would have none of that. He just isn't one of us. He's warm and funny and I love him, but underneath, he's a real straight arrow, the type who always knew what he wanted to do when he grew up, and did it.

I never left the South. After moving here in 1981, it was a revelation to this lifelong Northerner to discover that one's life did not have to be ruled by cold, snow, and the constant anticipation of winter. In the North, bracing for every long, cold winter became part of your biorhythm; as soon as the leaves fell, you'd automatically put snow tires on the car, get out the chains, replace its battery, stock up on wood or oil for heat, unpack the boots, gloves, and hats, and store bottled water in case of frozen pipes.

That ever-present sense of apprehension lifted when I moved to Louisiana in '81. That first winter in Baton Rouge, when the temperature plummeted to all of thirty degrees Fahrenheit on a bad day, that old car engine still sprang to life, every time—music to my ears. No more snow tires and chains, either; regular tires could be used all year. The underside of my car had never known such pampering. For the first time, no rock salt lay in wait on the roads to eat away at its metal.

That first winter I felt blissfully naked without Bean boots or any boots at all, nor thick gloves, nor a wool hat, nor a coat. On Christmas Day the grass was green and the birds still sang. I felt like a character in Disney's Song of the South. *Derek, Shawn, and I ran around the grassy courtyard throwing the football, and we took a walk to a lake and fed the ducks. Gentle green winters worked for me. Oh, once every five to ten years it spits a half an inch of snow, but then the authorities get hysterical and shut down the schools, banks, and government offices.*

I learned all this during my first winter here, and I was sold on the region. Northern friends and family always said, "Winter just wouldn't seem right without snow." Incredibly, I adjusted just fine.

No, I would not go back to the land again, whether in the North or the South, in a cold or a warm climate. I like the vitality of urban areas more than the isolation of country areas. My love for nature is as strong as ever, but I don't have to hole up in the woods or mountains to gaze in wonder at vegetation, flowers, birds, animals, and natural processes taking place all around me. I have the privilege right here in a subdivision in a city.

I step into my backyard and look gratefully at the small fish pond my husband built. I watch the colorful koi glide through the water. The twenty-four-inch fish is orange and black; the three smaller ones are yellow and black, or-

ange and white, and grey. Hundreds of minnows also inhabit the water, fighting over every stray fish pellet. The pond is a small universe, a nucleus that draws an assortment of living things to it, varied creatures in different seasons. Tiny spiders live in the reeds, and at night they climb out and build gorgeous, shimmering webs whose strands stretch from the pond's fountain to the edge of the house roof, down to the rose bush, and over to the lemon tree. During the day I can see them with their thin, arched legs, camouflaged in the plants, moving silently along their own silky strands. Birds swoop down for a quick feather-splashing bath. Butterflies and dragonflies flutter among the tall reeds. Chameleons and lizards dart up the side of the house beside the pond. Squirrels climb the fence and scurry across our yard, looking nervously both ways, then bend over guiltily for a quick drink of water. Our cat walks outside to lie in the sun, sprawls across the patio, stretches, stares lazily at the koi, but is never interested enough to bother them. Observing fish, they say, is tranquilizing. Even the cat agrees.

At night the full moon reflects in the pond like a golden coin. I step outside and hear loud squeaky "awks!" and splashes as titanic frogs on the bank dive loudly back in the water.

Natural beauty surrounds me daily because I'm open to it and look for it. Now, instead of walking beneath tall pines, I walk beneath sprawling live oaks with Spanish moss. The spring air brings scents of azaleas and dogwoods instead of fresh grass and wildflowers. On my walks near the wetlands, I see herons, egrets, storks, and pelicans in abundance, birds I never saw in Maine. Eagles with wide, flapping wingspans swoop down low, sailing past the windshield as I drive through rural areas; hawks and buzzards circle overhead.

Those of us who went to the land and came back learned that we don't have to live in rural Oregon or Wisconsin to see nature. We can do that in most places. We can eat sensibly and exercise. We can work at a rewarding job, earn an income, and still live thriftily if we like. We can live in a suburban area, keep the air conditioner off, hang clothes on a line, and devote ourselves to family, friends, and community. We can create a balanced life to do what pleases us most. Living in an urban area doesn't preclude the possibility of reaching this goal, just as living in the country doesn't guarantee it either.

Would I do it again? Well . . . let me amend that. Only if I had a substantial nest-egg (did I say that out loud?), a new SUV and large automatic washer, could build a house large enough to provide personal space *between family members, could install fast-modem technology to order books from Amazon, and could go, every so often, on a trip. But to afford all that, I've got to keep working. Here. In the city. And there lies the eternal paradox.*

Notes

CHAPTER ONE: THE LURE OF BACK TO THE LAND

page

3 "I felt the simple life calling me": Keddy Ann Outlaw, "Chopping Wood, Carrying Water, Moving On," unpublished essay.

3 "One night in New York City": Sandy Sanchez, "Remembering West Virginia," unpublished essay.

4 Linda Clarke remembers her journey to the country: personal interview.

5 We constituted "a major sector of the population," according to the historian Eric Foner: Eric Foner, *The Story of American Freedom* (New York, 1998), 288.

5 Researcher and author Timothy Miller placed the number of commune dwellers: Timothy Miller, *The 60s Communes: Hippies and Beyond* (Syracuse, N.Y., 1999), xix–xx.

5 Jeffrey Jacob, also a researcher and author, reported in *New Pioneers*: Jeffrey Jacob, *New Pioneers* (University Park, Pa., 1997), 3.

5 A study by the Stanford Research Institute estimated: David Shi, *The Simple Life: Plain Living and High Thinking in American Culture* (New York, 1985), 268.

5 America, with its assurance of the Dream fulfilled, has always been particularly fertile ground: Elizabeth Gilbert, *The Last American Man* (New York, 2002), 86.

6 The irony was apparently lost on us that "the world created by [our] elders": Foner, *Story of American Freedom*, 293.

6 . . . had allowed us the luxury of experimenting with alternative ways of living, as the writer David Shi points out: Shi, *The Simple Life*, 254.

6 John Verlenden, now a college professor, recalls an awkward moment: personal interview.

6 One back-to-the-land memoir offers a ubiquitous profile: Bradford and Vena Angier, *Wilderness Wife* (Radnor, Pa., 1976), 3.

6 We often attributed this inner discontent to the state of the world at the time: I doubt if we were aware that the human race (or at least the segment of it that has had the time and money to explore the issue) has felt chronically out of sorts about the quality of life since the beginning of time. In 1902, for example, Charles Wagner declared in his book *The Simple Life*, "Nothing is simple any longer. . . .

From the cradle to the grave, in his needs as in his pleasures, in his conception of the world and of himself, the man of modern times struggles through a maze of endless complication. . . . With our own hands we have added to existence a train of hardships, and lopped off many a gratification" (New York, 1902), 3.

7   For most back-to-the-land people, dogma played an even stronger role: While most of us were dismayed with the government over the Vietnam War, Watergate, and other misdeeds, the vast majority of us who went back to the land were not associated with any of the well-known anti-government extremist groups who withdrew into the woods to stockpile weapons, form militia, and overthrow the government. Back-to-the-land people, quite the contrary, were peace lovers, nature lovers, and pacifists.

7   Michael Doyle, a back-to-the-lander who is now a college professor, recalls: personal interview.

7   As David Frum notes, "The crucial decade for": David Frum, *How We Got Here: The 70s, the Decade That Brought You Modern Life* (New York, 2000), 159, 160.

7   A 1973 study traced the number of times the media reported certain events: G. Ray Funkhouser, "The Issues of the Sixties: An Exploratory Study in the Dynamics of Public Opinion," *Public Opinion Quarterly,* vol. 37, no. 1 (Spring 1973), 62–75.

7   For example, between 1964 and 1970: ibid., 72.

8   "Before World War II," reflects Frum: Frum, *How We Got Here,* 125.

9   In contrast, writes Amy Saltzman: Amy Saltzman, *Downshifting* (New York, 1991), 57.

9   "Back in my college days," recalls David Manning: David Manning, "An Expert Witness on Career Choice" in *Anna's House: The Journal of Everyday Life* (1992 edition), 43.

9   Former homesteader Sandy Sanchez and her husband were living in New York City: Sanchez, "Remembering West Virginia."

9   The land, notes Robert Houriet: Robert Houriet, *Getting Back Together* (New York, 1971), xiii.

10   Simon Shaw, series producer of the popular documentary *Frontier House,* confesses: Simon Shaw, *Frontier House* (New York, 2002), iv.

10   David Starnes, now a college instructor, feels: personal interview.

10   David's friend Tom had grown up in Montana: Thomas Kidder, personal interview.

11   . . . other songs by Denver: John Denver, "To the Wild Country", 1977.

11   Billy Joel's "Movin' Out": 1977.

11   Kain observed that middle-class people: Maurice Grenville Kains, *Five Acres and Independence* (New York, 1935), 5.

12   Carolyn and Ed Robinson, *Have-More Plan* (Pownal, Vt., 1973), 3.

12   They noted that people who stayed in the city: John and Sally Seymour, *Farming for Self-Sufficiency: Independence on a 5-Acre Farm* (New York, 1976), 10.

12   . . . as Paul Goodman stated in the Introduction: Helen and Scott Nearing, *Living the Good Life* (New York, 1970), ix.

12   A *Glamour* magazine article: Article by Dorothy Gallagher, exact date of publication unknown. This article was given to me by a colleague who saves old *Glamour* magazines. She said it was published sometime between January 1971 and June 1972. Thanks to Karen Pittman.

14 *Mother* influenced John Armstrong to go homesteading: John Armstrong, "The Hard Return," unpublished essay.

14 Cyndy Irvine, who was living in Austin, Texas: Cyndy Irvine, "Remembering New Mexico," unpublished essay.

16 Allan Sirotkin, now the owner and CEO of Green River Chocolates: personal interview.

16 Patricia Foley arrived in Alexander, Maine: personal interview.

16 Phil Morningstar joined Morningstar Commune: personal interview.

16 Tomas Diaz was welcomed: personal interview.

19 *Mother* offered countless opportunities: Following is one of thousands of ads that appeared in *Mother* during the height of the back-to-the-land movement: "We—a young, mellow couple—have strong naturalist and spiritual needs which prompt us to seek an environment in which we would have an integrated contact with nature and can explore and harmonize our relationship to the cosmos. Some of our activities include gardening, vegetarian cooking (one of us is an experienced cook), music, backpacking, cross-country skiing and textile crafts. If you're involved in or aware of any communities, groups or alternative institutions with whom we could share some of our interests and skills, please let us know. We prefer the Northwest or New England." *Mother Earth News*, May 1974, 102.

CHAPTER TWO: EARLY DAYS IN A TECHNOLOGY-FREE ZONE

23 Primitive became chic: Alston Chase, *Harvard and the Unabomber: The Education of an American Terrorist* (New York, 2003), 331.

23 "[They had] . . . this dream of starting over": T. C. Boyle, *Drop City* (New York, 2003), 176–177.

25 Our "pioneer willingness" to live with "pioneer self-reliance and a diversification of skills": Benjamin D. Zablocki and Rosabeth Moss Kanter, "The Differentiation of Life-Styles," *Annual Review of Sociology*, vol. 2 (1976), 291.

25 . . . invokes images of "an agrarian utopia": John A. Murray, *Mythmakers of the West: Shaping America's Imagination* (Flagstaff, Ariz., 2001), 8.

26 The Western has been a focal point: ibid., 54–56.

26 "It was in the Western landscapes": ibid., 56.

27 The spread of business and industry: Richard Tucker, "Environmentally Damaging Consumption: The Impact of American Markets on Tropical Ecosystems in the Twentieth Century. *Confronting Consumption*, eds. Thomas Pincen, Michael Maniates, and Ken Conca (Cambridge, Mass. 2002), 180, 181.

27 . . . nourishing what the environmental historian Richard Tucker refers to as: Ibid., 180, 181.

28 Americans have a "long history": Gary Cross, *An All-Consuming Century: Why Commercialism Won in Modern America* (New York, 2000), 111.

28 "The gospel of the simple life": ibid., 119.

29 "All of those chores that our parents": Irvine, "Remembering New Mexico."

29 In her book *Where We Stand: Class Matters*, bell hooks speaks: bell hooks, *Where We Stand: Class Matters* (New York, 2000), 11.

29 But, like Henry David Thoreau: Henry David Thoreau, "Why I Went to the Woods," *Fifty Great Essays*, ed. Robert Diyanni (New York, 2002), 347.

29 "The silence on our land": Irvine, "Remembering New Mexico."

31 John Armstrong had grown up in a middle-class family: Armstrong, "The Hard Return."

41 "I remember one year, we caught five hundred trout": Stacia Dunnam, personal interview.

43 Sandy Sanchez loved the baths: Sanchez, "Remembering West Virginia."

46 "I absolutely loved this period of my life": internet, from Tomas's website, http://www.laurelrose.com.

47 One writer for an alternative magazine: Katie Johnson, "Dining on Daylilies," *Farmstead Magazine*, no. 17 (Spring 1978), 63.

48 Keddy Ann Outlaw . . . who homesteaded at the foothills of the Adirondacks in New York State: Outlaw, "Chopping Wood, Carrying Water, and Moving On."

48 John Armstrong particularly remembers: Armstrong, "The Hard Return."

CHAPTER THREE: THE HEIGHT OF HAPPINESS

52 "I learned a lot that changed my life": Jodi Mitchell, personal interview.

52 "If somebody was putting on a roof": Bruce Lemire, personal interview.

52 Each summer morning as the sun ascended: Steven Engelhart, personal interview.

54 Timothy Miller observed: Miller, *The 60s Communes*, 233–234.

54 Jeffrey Jacob, who researched back-to-the-land people: Jacob, *New Pioneers*, xv.

55 "Community is and must be a deeply felt experience": Robert Booth Fowler, *The Dance with Community* (Lawrence, Kans., 1991), 4.

55 We had what Paul C. Light refers to: Paul C. Light, *Baby Boomers* (New York, 1988), 121.

55 Having grown up in a time of great economic growth: ibid., 112.

55 "Someone caught in a depression thinks about jobs and income": ibid, 112.

56 Robert Houriet, author of *Getting Back Together*: "Getting Back Together: An Interview with Robert Houriet." (2) Internet: Twelve Tribes: The Commonwealth of Israel. http://www.twelvetribes.com/publications/getting_back.htm.

60 . . . two slippery snow-suited thirty-pound Weebles: A popular child's toy in the 1970s, Weebles were egg-shaped wooden "people" with round smiling faces that stood upright as unsteadily as eggs might. The advertisement's theme song was "Weebles wobble but they won't fall down!"

61 I began to write regularly for him. Having these old articles, from which I've occasionally quoted in this book, has been wonderful in supplementing my memories of the years in Maine.

63 When John Matz, now the owner of Sunflower Glass Studio: personal interview.

64 . . . we attended the first Maine Organic Farmers and Gardeners Association's agricultural fair: In the fall of 2003, MOFGA celebrated its twenty-seventh annual Common Ground Country Fair. Its mission today is the same: to celebrate rural life and encourage sustainable living. About sixty thousand people attended. I feel honored to have attended that first fair.

69 Valerie Summer belonged to a group: personal interview.

72 Gordy Stewart, who is tall, remembers "many things to hit your head on": Gordy "Stewart" (pseudonym at his request), personal interview.

73 Originally from Miami, Janice Walker: personal interview.

75 Naked, her breast milk spurting, Pam Read: Pam Read Hanna, personal interview.

77 Cynthia Frost laughs at the memory: personal interview.

77 In 1971 she and her partner Ted: "Ted" is a pseudonym for Cynthia's boyfriend at the time.

79 Rob Morningstar was seventeen: "Rob Morningstar" (pseudonym at his request), personal interview.

CHAPTER FOUR: GETTING CLOSE TO NATURE AND NATURAL PROCESSES

83 "Three winters spent upon an isolated farm": Upton Sinclair, *The Autobiography of Upton Sinclair* (New York, 1962), 127.

83 "A plow had been purchased": Albert Shaw, *Icaria: A Chapter in the History of Communism* (New York, 1884) 29–37, 47–52, quoted in Robert S. Fogarty, *American Utopianism* (Itasca, Ill., 1972), 90.

83 In Arkansas, at about the same time Kent and I were admiring: "Jim Carlson" (pseudonym at his request), personal interview.

85 Before World War II, 30 percent of Americans still lived on farms: "The History of Municipal Solid," Tennessee Solid Waste. Internet: http://eerc/ra.utk/ tnswep/worksheet_Mc.htm.

85 ... 1930 and 1954, 1.8 million farms disappeared: Dale E. Hathaway, "Migration from Agriculture: The Historical Record and Its Meaning," *American Economic Review*, vol. 50, no. 2, Papers and Proceedings of the Seventy-second Annual Meeting of the American Economic Association (May 1960), 386.

85 ... the expansion of the consumer culture had lured many middle-class American families: Foner, *Story of American Freedom*, 264.

85 When the first English colonists arrived in the New World: Clark Griffith, "Frost and the American View of Nature," *American Quarterly*, vol. 20, no. 1 (Spring 1968), 21–37.

85 They had no choice but to be "scrutinizing events in Nature": ibid., 23.

86 Nature was credited with being a teacher "sent by God": ibid., 24.

86 Later, during the American Romantic literary movement: ibid., 25.

86 This was reinforced by Thoreau's *Walden*: Richard White. "Discovering Nature in North America," *Journal of American History*, vol. 79, no.3, Discovering America: A Special Issue (December 1992), 875.

86 As "the rattle of iron wheels on cobblestone streets or soft-coal smog": Peter J. Schmidt, *Back to Nature* (Baltimore, 1990), 3.

86 ... more middle-class people "longed for contact": ibid., 4.

86 In early America the agrarian myth . . .: Richard S. Kirkendall, "The Agricultural Colleges: Between Tradition and Modernization," *Agricultural History*, vol. 60, no. 2 (Spring 1986), 1.

87 By the mid-nineteenth century, the rise of the middle-class: Michael Newbury. "Healthful Employment: Hawthorne, Thoreau and Middle-Class Fitness," *American Quarterly*, vol. 47, no. 4 (December 1995), 684–685.

87   . . . access "the ideological virtues of the independent farmers . . .": Ibid., 688.

87   . . . and, "to the playtime repertory of earlier years": Myron A. Marty, *Daily Life in the United States, 1960–1990: Decades of Discord* (Westport, Conn., 1997), 8.

87   "Today we're living in Alberta": Sharon Wooley, *Mother Earth News,* May 1974, 79.

88   The relationship with nature "remind[s] us daily of the chain of life": Ma-Na-Har Cooperative Community, 1971. Quoted in Fogarty, *American Utopianism,* 173.

88   Bill Pearlman, a poet who lived on a commune in New Mexico: Bill Pearlman, "Warped Reveries," unpublished essay.

89   June Holley, now the executive director of ACENETS in Ohio: personal interview.

90   "Gone is the romance those movies": Shaw, *Frontier House,* vii.

90   No wonder five million of the seven million: John Martin Campbell, *Magnificent Failure* (Stanford, 2002), 29.

90   . . . failed homesteaders were "citified dreamers": ibid., 29.

91   "A wild southwestern prairie in the flowery months": Shaw, 47–52, quoted in Fogarty, *American Utopianism,* 91.

91   At Slaughterhouse Creek commune: Marty Rush, "The Naked and the Dead: Daily Life at the Slaughterhouse Commune," *Colorado Central Magazine* (May 1995), 24. Internet: http://www.cozine.com/archive/cc1995/00150244.htm.

98   "Issues of shoddy construction and overoptimistic designs": Carol Steinfield and Claire Anderson, "Water-wise Toilets," *Mother Earth News,* May 21, 2003, 1–2. Internet: http://www.motherearthnews.com/192/home192_toilets.htm.

99   Peter Matson had read *Walden Pond:* Peter H. Matson, *A Place in the Country,* (New York, 1977), 87, 88.

100 Jane Kirkpatrick observes that: Jane Kirkpatrick, *Homestead* (Bend, Ore., 1991, 2000), 143.

100 "With turkey basters": ibid., 145.

102 "Little did I know how much milk": "Lucy Joseph" (pseudonym requested), personal interview.

103 When Jane Musser's goat gave birth: Jane Musser, "Hawthorne Homestead Revisited," *Mother Earth News,* January 1975, 47.

106 Some good friends of ours in Troy raised turkeys: Margery and Jack Wilson, "Talking Turkey," *Farmstead Magazine,* no. 15 (1977), 42.

106 A *Mother Earth News* article describes the process: *Mother Earth News,* March 1975, 47–48.

107 There the authors write, "Unfortunately, these people": Seymour, *Farming for Self-Sufficiency,* 243–244.

107 Miriam Ross, her husband, and three children: personal interview.

107 Gail Adams and her family: personal interview.

107 In the Ozarks, Jane Fishman: personal interview.

108 Don Wirtshafter remembers: personal interview.

108 Pierce Walker, a real farmer from Indiana: Studs Terkel, *Working* (New York, 1972), 4.

108 Pat Manuele and her boyfriend Brad: Patricia Manuele, *Eat a Peach,* unpublished manuscript.

CHAPTER FIVE: NOT-SO-GENTEEL POVERTY

110 "The poverty portrayed by left-wing intellectuals": Dorothy Allison, "A Question of Class," in *Literature and Society*, 3rd edition, eds. Pamela J. Annas and Robert C. Rosen (Upper Saddle River, N.J., 2000), 885.

110 "I had given up having kids, a home, a car": Manning, "An Expert Witness on Career Choice," 43.

110 After the hailstorm: Manuele, *Eat a Peach*.

112 As the U.S. Office of Management and Budget reported: U.S. Office of Management and Budget, 1983, 30–31, quoted in Peter Gottschalk and Sheldon Danziger, "A Framework for Evaluating the Effects of Economic Growth and Transfers on Poverty," *American Economic Review*, vol. 75, no. 1 (March 1985), 153.

112 Between 1967 and 1973, according to a report in the *American Economic Review*: Jeffrey G. Williamson, "'Strategic' Wage Goods, Prices, and Inequality," *American Economic Review*, vol. 67, no. 2 (March 1977), 34.

112 Besides, price increases in just a few areas of the economy: Barry P. Bosworth, "Nonmonetary Aspects of Inflation," *Journal of Money, Credit and Banking*, vol, 12, no. 3 (August 1980), 529.

113 Two issues of *Mother* in 1973 and 1974 included the articles: *Mother Earth News*, no. 23 (1973) and no. 27 (1974).

113 In 1950, for example, a man earning a working class wage: Frum, *How We Got Here*, 331.

113 . . . capitalism was nothing but a system designed to create: "Capital Comforts," *Canada and the World Backgrounder*, vol. 68, no. 6 (May 2003), 4.

113 But, explains Copthorne Macdonald: personal interview.

114 In *The Nature of Economies*: Jane Jacobs, *The Nature of Economies* (New York, 2000), 46.

115 Timothy Miller recognizes this "confusion": Timothy Miller, *The Hippies and American Values* (Knoxville, Tenn., 1991), 111.

115 While renouncing wealth: ibid., 112.

115 "While we speak about luxuries and necessities": Thomas Hine, *I Want That! How We All Became Shoppers* (New York, 2002), 15, 16–17.

115 . . . Michael Maniates thoroughly analyzes: Michael Maniates, "In Search of Consumptive Resistance: The Voluntary Simplicity Movement," *Confronting Consumption*, eds. Thomas Princen, Michael Maniates, and Ken Conca (Cambridge, Mass., 2002), 199–235.

115 "If everyone else is wearing an expensive suit": Ibid., 204–205.

116 "Often," says Hine: Hine, *I Want That!*, 15.

116 Frank Levering and Wanda Urbanska recognized this tension: Frank Levering and Wanda Urbanska, *Simple Living: One Couple's Search for a Better Life*, (Winston-Salem, NC, 2003), 118–119.

116 "Sooner or later, we are going to have to acknowledge": James Twitchell, *Lead Us into Temptation: The Triumph of American Materialism* (New York, 1999), 19.

118 "In her essay . . . she writes": Allison, "A Question of Class," 885.

118 Thoreau, in fact, is described: 1995 Grolier Multimedia Encyclopedia, 1.

119   . . . according to Timothy Miller, "either blue-sky romanticism": Miller, *The Hippies and American Values*, 112.

119   . . . our desire to "redeem [our] souls" : Paul Berman, "The Moral History of the Baby Boom Generation," *Working with Ideas*, ed. Donna Dunbar-Odom (New York, 2001), 201.

120   Barbara Ehrenreich, *Nickel and Dimed: On (Not) Getting By in America* (New York, 2001), 6.

120   Jeffrey Jacob's research: Jacob, *New Pioneers*, 53.

122   "The stress points of a life off the land": ibid., 77.

123   They "felt as free . . .": Nearing, *Living the Good Life*, 147, 145.

123   According to Vivien Ellen Rose's well-researched doctoral dissertation: Vivien Ellen Rose, "Homesteading as Social Protest: Gender and Continuity in the Back-to-the-Land Movement in the United States, 1890–1980" (Ph.D. dissertation, State University of New York at Binghamton, 1997), 287–288.

129   Gail and her husband, Larry: "Larry" is a pseudonym.

132   Their oldest daughter, Christina Adams, personal interview.

135   Chaim I. Waxman writes: Chaim I. Waxman, *The Stigma of Poverty* (New York, 1977) , 81.

CHAPTER 6: GENERATING CASH FLOW

136   "The pressures of moving back and forth": Jacob, *New Pioneers*, 103.

139   In a 1979 article, Daniel Yankelovich referred to us : Daniel Yankelovich, "Work, Values, and the New Breed," in *Work in America: The Decade Ahead*, eds. Clark Kerr and Jerome M. Rosow (New York, 1979), 3–26.

139   "In many surveys conducted in the 1950s": ibid., 22.

139   "In the New Breed," continues Yankelovich: ibid., 12.

139   In the 1970s, agrees Amitai Etzioni: Amitai Etzioni, "Work in the American Future," in *Work in America: The Decade Ahead*, 30.

140   Robert Acuna, a real outdoor laborer: Terkel, *Working*, 10, 12.

141   "I'd rather somebody picked up a crowbar": Tennessee Williams, *The Glass Menagerie*, in *Literature: An Introduction to Reading and Writing*, 2nd edition, eds. Edgar V. Roberts and Henry E. Jacobs (Engelwood Cliffs, N.J., 1989), 1529.

146   Carlyle Poteat, a video producer, remembers: personal interview.

148   "I liked the camaraderie of hotel life," she notes: Kathie Weir, "Coming Out on the Other Side," unpublished essay.

150   Yaakov Oved observes: Yaakov Oved: *Two Hundred Years of American Communes* (New Brunswick, N.J., 1988).

150   "Without a minimum of approval": Henry Near, "Communes and Kibbutzim: Past, Present and Future?" A review essay, *"Studies in Comparative International Development,"* vol. 28, no. 4 (Winter 1994), 73.

151   Jeffrey Jacob also recognizes this dilemma: Jacob, *New Pioneers*, 47.

CHAPTER SEVEN: STAYING HEALTHY, AND PAYING FOR IT

154   Hospital costs had risen dramatically: Godfrey Hodgson, "The Politics of American Health Care: What Is It Costing You?," *Atlantic Monthly*, October 1973, 56. Internet: http://www.theatlantic.com/politics/healthca/hodson.htm.

154   ... by the 1970s, a stay in the hospital: Michael Crichton, "The High Cost of Cure," *Atlantic Monthly*, March 1970, 16. Internet: http://www.theatlantic.com/unbound/flashbks/health/crichton.htm.

155   Medicare and Medicaid, enacted in the sixties: Godfrey Hodgson, "The Politics of American Health Care: What Is It Costing You?" 60.

155   Although general inflation had contributed: ibid., 58.

155   "Both you and your overworked doctor will be better off": *Mother Earth News*, March 1975, 69.

157   Coleman said, "Look in any city and pick out the biggest": *Berkshire Sampler*, December 19, 1976, 5.

157   ... he was already on the lecture circuit: Rose, "Homesteading as Social Protest," 293.

160   "Occupational injuries and accidents": Fred Harris, "America's Rural Health Crisis," *Congressional Record*, 117, part 16, June 22, 1971, 21228–21230, quoted in Roger Feldman, David Deitz, and Edward Brooks, "The Financial Viability of Rural Primary Health Care Centers," *American Journal of Public Health*, vol. 68, no. 10 (October 1978), 981.

160   "the open country with its natural surroundings": Norma Cobb and Charles W. Sasser, *Arctic Homestead: The True Story of One Family's Survival and Courage in the Alaskan Wilds* (New York, 2000), 228.

161   But when "the bullet ripped into": Ibid., 47.

161   "Doctors said they would arrange payment": ibid., 50.

161   Several years later, when her husband injured his eye: ibid., 231.

162   "Gone is the driven, nervous man I was once married to": Sallyann J. Murphey, *Bean Blossom Dreams: A City Family's Search for the Simple Life* (New York, 1994), 15–16.

162   But farm life did not thwart Greg's later illness: ibid., 218.

162   She said, "You think about a woman's options in 1883": Shaw, *Frontier House*, 171.

163   In a 1975 *Mother Earth News* article: Thomas W. King, "Pennywise Tooth Cleansers," *Mother Earth News*, February 1975.

166   Physicians were in short supply because: Feldman, Deitz, and Brooks, "The Financial Viability of Rural Primary Health Care Centers," 981.

166   *Time* magazine article in 2001: Jessica Reaves, "Rural Health: Fresh Air and Really Bad Care," *Time*, September 10, 2001. Internet: http://www.time.com/time/health/article/0,8599,174445,00.html.

166   When Sandra Sleight-Brannen's ten-month-old son burned his hand: personal interview.

166   After a snake "planted its fangs in my left thumb": Ken Davison, "Snakebite: When There Is No Health Insurance." Internet: http://www.homestead.org/snkebite.htm.

167   "The medical profession was then overwhelmingly male": Frum, *How We Got Here*, 127, 128–129.

169   In most cases, home deliveries were successful: Miller, *The 60s Communes*, 187.

169   In a *Mother Earth News* article: Nancy Rubel, *Mother Earth News*, May 1974, 54.

170   He soaked the finger in comfrey: ibid., 57.

170   "One should entirely forgo the internal administration of the drug [comfrey]": *Physicians' Desk Reference* (Montvale, N.J., 1998), 1164.

170 Herbs may also "have the potential to be misidentified": "Anticholinergic Poisoning Associated with an Herbal Tea," *Morbidity and Mortality Weekly Report*, vol. 44, no. 11 (March 24, 1995), 195.

170 Writing in the *Scientific Review of Alternative Medicine*: W. Betz, "Epidemic of Renal Failure Due to Herbs," *Scientific Review of Alternative Medicine*, no. 2 (1998), 12–13, quoted in "Unconventional Therapies, Herbal Remedies," BC Cancer Agency Care and Research, February, 2000. Internet: http://www.bccancer.bc.ca/PPI/UnconventionalTherapies/Comfrey.htm.

171 Untreated water sometimes carried the bacteria or viruses: "Disease and Their Pathogens." Internet: http://www.mwra.state.ma.us.

171 Pam Read Hanna, who lived there, remembers bringing jugs: Internet: Pam's Chronicles I, posted on http://www.diggers.org.

171 According to Timothy Miller, "poor sanitation facilities": Miller, *The 60s Communes*, 200.

172 I couldn't agree more with Eliot Coleman: Today Eliot Coleman still lives on his beautiful homestead in Maine and has earned an international reputation as an author and lecturer. Over the years he may have modified his position on insurance.

CHAPTER EIGHT: RELATIONSHIPS—FRIENDS, LOVERS, FAMILY, COMMUNITY

174 "The highest idealism, it seems": Miller, *The 60s Communes*, 226.

174 ". . . the cabin walls seemed to shrink": T. C. Boyle, *Drop City*, 198.

174 "If you should happen to hear a glowing report": Geoph Kozensky, "In Community, Intentionally," *Communities Directory* (Rutledge, Mo., 2000), 21.

174 Sandy Sanchez, pregnant with her second child: Sanchez, "Remembering West Virginia."

177 . . . the importance of pursuing individual gratification: Marty, *Daily Life in the United States, 1960–1990*, 183.

177 Between 1965 and 1975 the divorce rate in the United States doubled: Frum, *How We Got Here*, 80.

177 "In an age that emphasized personal happiness": William H. Chafe, "Women and American Society," in *Making America: The Society and Culture of the United States*, ed. Luther S. Luedtke (Chapel Hill, 1992), 335.

177 The historian Eric Foner believes: Eric Foner, *Story of American Freedom*, 305.

178 ". . . the real heroes were those who chucked their marriages": Frum, *How We Got Here*, 74.

178 . . . only that they now cared enough about "the content and quality of family life": Tamara K. Hareven, "Continuity and Change in American Family Life," in Luedtke, *Making America*, 324.

178 Counterculture people were "profoundly dedicated to peace and love" as an ethic: Miller, *The Hippies and American Values*, 106.

184 Marlene Heck, for example, lived for a year and a half with the Mulberry Family: personal interview.

184 There is "compelling evidence that the good old days were not as good": Edward W. Younkins, *Capitalism and Commerce: Conceptual Foundations of Free Enterprise* (Lanham, Md., 2002), 209.

185 Communes had "a powerful individualistic cast": Foner, *Story of American Freedom*, 294.

185 Robert Houriet, author of *Getting Back Together*, lived on a commune: "Getting Back Together," 6.

185 . . . including "lack of clear communal goals": Matthew Israel, "Two Communal Houses and Why (I Think) They Failed," *Journal of Behavioral Technology*, vol. I (Summer 1971), 7–17, quoted in Miller, *The 60s Communes*, 181.

185 Timothy Miller confirms, that "physical proximity often proved intolerable": Miller, *The 60s Communes*, 180.

185 Ken Davison belonged to a back-to-the-land community in Arkansas: Ken Davison, "The Rise and Fall of a (Ozarks) Community: Some Things to Consider Before Getting Involved" (July 10, 1997): http://www.homestead.org/risefall.htm.

191 John Armstrong enjoyed working alongside his wife: Armstrong, "The Hard Return."

CHAPTER NINE: TURNING POINTS

194 "For the most part, massive shifts towards simplicity": David Shi, *In Search of the Simple Life* (Layton, Utah, 1986), 229.

197 Americans are "a bundle of contradictions": Michael A. Ledeen, *Tocqueville on American Character* (New York, 2000), 83.

197 Alexis de Tocqueville, *Democracy in America*, first published 1835.

197 . . . how to live with abundance yet avoid "a path to damnation": Daniel Horowitz, "Consumption and Its Discontents: Simon N. Patten, Thorstein Veblen, and George Gunton," *Journal of American History*, vol. 67, no. 2 (September 1980), 302.

197 Our " internal push and pull": Ledeen, *Tocqueville on American Character*, 82.

197 ". . . from time to time we must undergo a spiritual purge": ibid., 74.

198 "Again and again": Shi, *The Simple Life*, 277.

198 "In 1970": Frederick F. Siegel, *Troubled Journey: From Pearl Harbor to Ronald Reagan* (New York, 1984), 215.

198 As Timothy Miller notes, "Those who wanted to continue": Miller, *The 60s Communes*, 227.

199 In a 1983 survey of back-to-the-land people: Jeffrey C. Jacob and Merlin B. Brinkerhoff, "Alternative Technology: A Survey from the Back-to-the-Land Movement," *Rural Sociology*, vol. 51, no. 1 (1986), 48.

199 Linda Tatelbaum and her husband moved to Burketville, Maine: Linda Tatelbaum, *Carrying Water as a Way of Life: A Homesteader's History* (Appleton, Me., 1997), 2–3.

200 1981, Ellen Rocco installed plumbing: personal interview.

201 Members of the Drop City Commune in Trinidad: Miller, *The 60s Communes*, 34.

203 Kathy Barrows had established a job, home, and life in Brazil: personal interview.

204 "Years later, people would still walk up to me in this city": Kathy Barrows, unpublished essay.

205 "After all," David Shi writes: Shi, *The Simple Life*, 279.

208 Later he became co-editor of the book *Imagine Nation: The American Counterculture of the 1960s and '70s* (New York, 2002).

210 My visions of a vibrant garden: Even today, magazines still try to sell the idea of a serene country life as the answer to life's problems. Not long ago *Essence* magazine presented a piece on a modern back-to-the-land couple who moved to the country and simplified their lives, adding great joy. Actually, when you read the fine print, you see that they had moved from Detroit to a rural community in Georgia and lived in a $265,000 house.

CHAPTER TEN: FINDING A NICHE IN THE MAINSTREAM

213 "Nobody has to do everything": Seymour, *Farming for Self-Sufficiency,* 243.
217 Historically, capitalism developed because "it championed the individual": "Capital Comforts," *Canada and the World Backgrounder,* vol. 68, issue 6 (May 2003), 5.
217 Michael Maniates, a professor of environmental science: Michael Maniates, "In Search of Consumptive Resistance: The Voluntary Simplicity Movement," in *Confronting Consumption,* 233.
226 Vicky Hayes, a fiction writer: personal interview.
228 The media stereotypes former hippies as "high-powered lawyers and investment bankers and big-time capitalists": Timothy Miller, personal interview.

CHAPTER ELEVEN: LESSONS AND LEGACIES

231 When Pat Manuele was diagnosed with non-Hodgkins lymphoma: Manuele, *Eat a Peach.*
232 A recent study, published in *Lymphoma Today:* vol. 1, no. 3 (Fall 2002), 6–8.
233 Throughout most of human history until the last millennium: Ken Dychtwald in *Age Power: How the 21st century Will Be Ruled by the New Old* (New York, 2000), 1, 2.
233 "The big boomer generation that was in its teens and twenties": Theodore Roszak, *Longevity Revolution: As Boomers Become Elders* (Albany, Calif., 2001), 27.
234 "Never before have people approaching their senior years": ibid., 24, 25.
234 Although several scholars and many media pundits: Richard A. Easterlin, Christine M. Schaeffer, and Diane J. Macunovich, "Will the Baby Boomers Be Less Well Off Than Their Parents? Income, Wealth, and Family Circumstances Over the Life Cycle in the United States," *Population and Development Review,* vol. 19, no. 3 (September 1993), 497–522.
234 This is partly due to: ibid., 507.
235 Keddy Ann Outlaw, now a university librarian in Houston: Outlaw, "Chopping Wood, Carrying Water, and Moving On."
239 June Spencer . . . is fiscally conservative: June Spencer, "Back from the Land— But Not Quite," unpublished essay.
241 David Manning had a momentary crisis of confidence: Manning, "An Expert Witness on Career Choice," 41.
241 They had moved "up and down the coast": ibid., 42.
241 When the invitation arrived, David had little income: ibid., 43.
246 "So here we are, almost thirty years later": Kent Thurston, e-mail message to author, September 17, 2003.

Selected Bibliography

This bibliography lists only a few of the works cited in the foregoing pages, the ones most directly relevant to the back-to-the-land movement.

Allison, Dorothy. "A Question of Class," In *Literature and Society*, 3rd Edition, Eds. Pamela J. Annas and Robert C. Rosen. Upper Saddle River, NJ: Prentice Hall, 2000.

Angier, Bradford and Vena Angier. *Wilderness Wife*. Radnor, PA: Chilton Book Co., 1976.

Berman, Paul."The Moral History of the Baby Boom Generation," In *Working With Ideas*, Ed. Donna Dunbar-Odom. New York: Houghton-Mifflin, 2001.

Braunstein, Peter and Michael William Doyle. *Imagine Nation: The American Counterculture of the 1960's and '70's*. New York: Routledge, 2002.

Campbell, John Martin. *Magnificent Failure*. Stanford University Press, 2002.

"Capital Comforts." *Canada and the World Backgrounder*, vol. 68, issue 6 (May, 2003): 4–10.

Chafe, William H. "Women and American Society." *Making America*. Luther S. Luedtke, Ed. Chapel Hill: The University of North Carolina Press, 1992: 327–340.

Cobb, Norma and Charles W. Sasser, *Arctic Homestead: The True Story of One Family's Survival and Courage in the Alaskan Wilds*. New York: St. Martin's Press, 2000.

Communities Directory. Rutledge, Missouri: Fellowship for Intentional Community, 2000.

Coyote, Peter. *Sleeping Where I Fall: A Chronicle*. Counterpoint Press, 1998.

Cross, Gary. *An All-Consuming Century: Why Commercialism Won in Modern America*. New York: Columbia University Press, 2000.

Davison, Ken. "The Rise and Fall of a (Ozarks) Community: Some Things to Consider Before Getting Involved" (July 10, 1997): http://www/homestead .org/risefall.htm.

———. "Snakebite: When There is No Health Insurance" (July, 1998). http://www.homestead.org/snkebite.htm.

Etzioni, Amitai. "Work in the American Future." In *Work in America: The Decade Ahead*. Eds. Clark Kerr and Jerome M. Rosow. New York: Van Nostrand Reinhold Co., 1979: 27–34.

Ferguson, John. *Utopias of the Classical World*. Ithaca, NY: Cornell University Press, 1975.

Fogarty, Robert S. *American Utopianism*. Itasca, IL: F.E. Peacock Publishers, 1972.

Foner, Eric. *The Story of American Freedom*. New York: W.W. Norton & Co., 1998.

Frum, David. *How We Got Here. The '70's. The Decade That Brought You Modern Life*. New York: Basic Books, 2000.

Fussell, Paul. *A Guide Through the American Status System*. New York: Touchstone Books, 1992.

Gilbert, Elizabeth Gilbert. *The Last American Man*. New York: Penguin Books, 2002.

Haines, John. *The Stars, the Snow, the Fire*. St. Paul, MN: Graywolf Press, 1977.

Hareven, Tamara K. "Continuity and Change in American Family Life." In *Making America: The Society and Culture of the United States*. Ed. Luther S. Luedtke. Chapel Hill: The University of North Carolina Press, 1992: 308–326.

Hine, Thomas. *I Want That! How We All Became Shoppers*. New York: HarperCollins, 2002.

hooks, bell. *Where We Stand: Class Matters*. New York: Routledge Press, 2000.

Houriet, Robert. *Getting Back Together*. New York: Coward, McCann and Georghegan, 1971.

Israel, Matthew. "Two Communal Houses and Why (I Think) They Failed" *Journal of Behavioral Technology* I (Summer 1971): 7–17.

Jacob, Jeffrey. *New Pioneers*. University of Pennsylvania Press, 1997.

Jacob, Jeffrey C. and Merlin B. Brinkerhoff. "Alternative Technology: A Survey from the Back-to-the-Land Movement." *Rural Sociology*. Vol. 51, No. 1 (1986): 43–59.

Jacobs, Jane. *The Nature of Economies*. New York: Modern Library, 2000.

Kains, Maurice Grenvile. *Five Acres and Independence*. New York: Greenberg, 1935.

Kinkade, Kathleen. *A Walden Two Experiment: The First Five Years of Twin Oaks Community*. New York: William Morrow & Co., 1973.

Kirkpatrick, Jane. *Homestead*. Bend, OR: Maverick Distributors, 1991.

Levering, Frank and Wanda Urbanska. *Simple Living: One Couple's Search for a Better Life*. John F. Blair Pub., 2003.

Light, Paul C. *Baby Boomers*. New York: W.W. Norton, 1988.

McCrum, Mark and Matthew Sturgis. *1900 House*. London: Channel 4 Books, 1999.

Maniates, Michael. "In Search of Consumptive Resistance: The Voluntary Simplicity Movement." In *Confronting Consumption*. Eds. Thomas Princen,

Michael Maniates, and Ken Conca. Cambridge, MA: MIT Press, 2002: 199–235.

Marty, Myron A. *Daily Life in the United States, 1960–1990: Decades of Discord.* Westport, CT: Greenwood Press, 1997.

Matson, Peter H. *A Place in the Country.* New York: Harcourt Brace, 1977.

Miller, Timothy Miller. *The 60s Communes: Hippies and Beyond.* Syracuse, NY: Syracuse University Press, 1999.

———. *The Hippies and American Values.* University of Tennessee Press, 1991.

Murphey, Sallyann J. *Bean Blossom Dreams: A City Family's Search for the Simple Life.* New York: Hearst Books, 1994.

Murray, John A. *Mythmakers of the West: Shaping America's Imagination.* Flagstaff, AZ: Northland Publishing, 2001.

Nearing, Helen and Scott. *Living the Good Life.* New York: Schocken Books, 1970.

Oved, Yaakov. *Two Hundred Years of American Communes.* New Brunswick U.S.A. and Oxford U.K.: Transaction Press, 1988.

Pierce, Linda Breen. *Choosing Simplicity: Real People Finding Peace and Fulfillment in a Complex World.* Gallagher Press, 2000.

Princen, Thomas, Michael Maniates, and Ken Conca. *Confronting Consumption,* Cambridge, MA: The MIT Press, 2002.

Robinson, Carolyn and Ed. *Have-More Plan.* Storey Books, 1973.

Rose, Vivien Ellen. "Homesteading as Social Protest: Gender and Continuity in the Back-to-the-Land Movement in the United States, 1890–1980." (Ph.D. diss., Binghamton University, State University of New York, 1997.

Roszak, Theodore. *Longevity Revolution: As Boomers Become Elders.* Berkeley Hills Books, 2001.

Rush, Marty. "The Naked and the Dead: Daily Life at the Slaughterhouse Commune." *Colorado Central Magazine* (May 1995): 24. http://www.cozine.com/archive/cc1995/00150244.htm, July 31, 2003.

Saltzman. Amy. *Downshifting.* New York: HarperCollins, 1991.

Schmidt, Peter J. *Back to Nature.* Baltimore: John Hopkins University Press, 1990.

Seymour, John and Sally. *Farming for Self-Sufficiency: Independence on a 5-Acre Farm.* New York: Schocken Books, 1976.

Shaw, Simon. *Frontier House.* New York: Pocket Star, 2002.

Shi, David. *The Simple Life: Plain Living and High Thinking in American Culture.* New York: Oxford University Press, 1985.

Smith, Annick. *Homestead.* Minneapolis, MN: Milkweed Editions, 1995.

Tatelbaum, Linda. *Carrying Water as a Way of Life: A Homesteader's History.* Appleton, ME: About Time Press, 1997.

Thoreau, Henry David. "Why I Went to the Woods." In *Fifty Great Essays.* Ed. Robert Diyanni. New York: Longman, 2002.

Twitchell, James. *Lead Us into Temptation: the Triumph of American Materialism.* Columbia University Press, 1999.

Yankelovich, Daniel. "Work, Values, and the New Breed." In *Work in America: The Decade Ahead*. Eds. Clark Kerr and Jerome M. Rosow. New York: Van Nostrand Reinhold Co., 1979: 3–26.

Younkins, Edward W. *Capitalism and Commerce: Conceptual Foundations of Free Enterprise*. Lanham, MD: Lexington Books, 2002.

Zablocki, Benjamin D. and Rosabeth Moss Kanter. "The Differentiation of Life-Styles." *Annual Review of Sociology*, Vol. 2 (1976): 269–298.

Index

Foner, Eric, 5, 177, 185
Food: canning, 124; Common Ground
Country Fair, 64–65; expense of,
132–133, 164; gathering, 32, 43, 47,
48, 80, 164, 237; preparing, 45–47;
raising, 33, 42, 44–45, 46–47, 78,
80–82, 84, 102–109. See also Gardens;
Livestock.
Fowler, Robert Booth, 55
Frontier House, 10, 90, 162
Frost, Cynthia, 77–79, 79, 153, 170, 217
Frum, David, 7, 167, 178
Fuel supply for woodstoves, 31–33,
94–96, 95, 195–196

Gardens, 48, 84, 107–109; actuality of
work, 65, 175; fair exhibitions, 65. See
also Food.
Georgia, back-to-the-land movement,
73–74, 172–173
Gilbert, Elizabeth, 5–6
Goats, 42, 78–79, 81, 102–103
God's Free Universe Commune, 79–80,
164
Government of communes, 188–189
Government programs, 121
Grooming, 116

Hair cutting businesses, 145–146
Hanna, Findley, 75
Hanna, Pam Read, 153–154, 167–168,
171, 201
Hareven, Tamara K., 178
Harrington, Michael, 118
Have-More Plan (Robinson and
Robinson), 12
Hawaii, back-to-the-land movement,
79–80, 164
Hayes, Vicky, 226–227
Health care, 153–173; accidents, 19–20,
59–60, 100–102, 126, 158–162,
166–167; alternative care, 155–156,
163, 166–171; barter, 165–166; births,
71, 153–154, 167–169, 173, 174–175;
conventional medicine, 156–162,
165–166; dental health, 162–164;
infections, 170–171; insurance,
156–160, 172–173; mythology,
154–160, 162; rural health care
deficits, 159–160. See also Death.
Health concerns, as a motivation, 8–9

Heating. See Cold; Water; Woodstoves
Heck, Marlene, 184, 228, 242
Hemp businesses, 226
Hine, Thomas, 115–116
History, careers in, 183, 207–208,
218–219
Hodgson, Godfrey, 155
Holley, June, 89, 165, 221–222
Home improvements, 50–51, 100–102,
199, 200–201
Homesteading (historical): hardships of,
90; Montana, 10–11, 162. See also
Pioneers.
Honey, healthfulness of, 163
Hooks, bell, 29
Horses, 199
Horticulture careers, 224–225
Houriet, Robert, 9, 56, 185
Hudson, Kathleen, 65–66

I Want That! How We All Became
Shoppers (Hine), 115–116
Icaria Community, 83, 91
Illness from back-to-the-land experience,
170–171, 232. See also Accidents;
Health care.
Income, 120, 136–152, 249–250;
attitudes about, 219–220; businesses,
70, 72–73, 76–77, 120, 123–124,
140–141, 145–146, 149–150,
182–183, 186–189, 205–206; cash
crops, 107–111, 116, 120, 186–189;
government programs, 121; myths of,
112–113; unemployment, 137. See also
Careers; Expenses; Jobs.
Inflation, 112–113, 155
Insurance (health), 156–160, 172–173
Irvine, Cyndy, 14–16, 23, 29–30
Israel, Matthew, 185

Jacob, Jeffrey, 5, 54, 120, 122, 151, 199
Jacobs, Jane, 114
Jobs, 111, 122, 137–152, 164; discomforts,
140–143, 146, 148, 150–152, 208;
editorial, 150; farm work, 147;
hardships of, 140–141; medical
problems leading to, 168, 172–173;
resort jobs, 148; restaurant work,
141–143, 146, 148–149, 202, 203;
secretarial, 148–149; social life and,
139–140. See also Businesses; Careers.

A NOTE ON THE AUTHOR

Eleanor Agnew teaches writing and linguistics at Georgia Southern University in Statesboro, Georgia. Born in Platts-burgh, New York, she studied at the University of Vermont, the University of Maine at Orono, and Louisiana State University, where she received a Ph.D. She has also written *My Mama's Waltz* (1998). She lives in Savannah Georgia.